THE LONG TABLE

THE LONG TABLE

FROM THE AUSTRALIAN OUTBACK
TO THE HOUSE OF LORDS

THE AUTOBIOGRAPHY OF
BARONESS GARDNER OF PARKES

TRIXIE GARDNER
with a foreword by Baroness Boothroyd OM

COUPER STREET BOOKS

Couper Street Books is a publishing brand involved in the professional
production and publication management of books. All rights in and
responsibilities for the contents remain with the author.

001

Copyright © Trixie Gardner, 2019

The moral right of the author has been asserted in accordance
with the Copyright, Designs and Patents Act 1988.

Every effort has been made to trace copyright holders and to obtain their
permission for the use of copyrighted material. Any omissions or inaccuracies in
the form of credits are unintentional and corrections
may be made to future printings.

All rights reserved.

No part of this publication may be reproduced, stored in a retrieval system, or
transmitted in any form or by any means, electronic, mechanical, photocopying,
recording or otherwise, except as permitted by the UK Copyright, Designs and
Patents Act 1988 without the prior permission in writing of the author, nor be
otherwise circulated in any form or binding of cover other than that in which it
is published and without a similar condition including this condition being
imposed on the subsequent purchaser.

Designations used by companies to distinguish their products are often claimed
as trademarks. All brand names and product names used in this book are trade
names, service marks, trademarks or registered trademarks of their respective
owners. Neither the publishing brand nor the author is professionally associated
with any product or vendor mentioned in this book.

Front cover photo courtesy of Peter Willis:
The McGirr family and friends, 1936.
Back row: unidentified woman, unidentified man, Greg McGirr.
Middle row: Gregory, Nonna, Raymond, Gwen. In front: Trixie.

Cover design: Couper Street Books
Typeset by Couper Street Type Co.

First published worldwide in 2019

A CIP catalogue record for this book is available from the British Library

ISBN (HB) 978-1-9993477-2-7
ISBN (TPB) 978-1-9993477-7-2
ISBN (ebook) 978-1-9993477-0-3

www.couperstreetbooks.co.uk

For Kevin

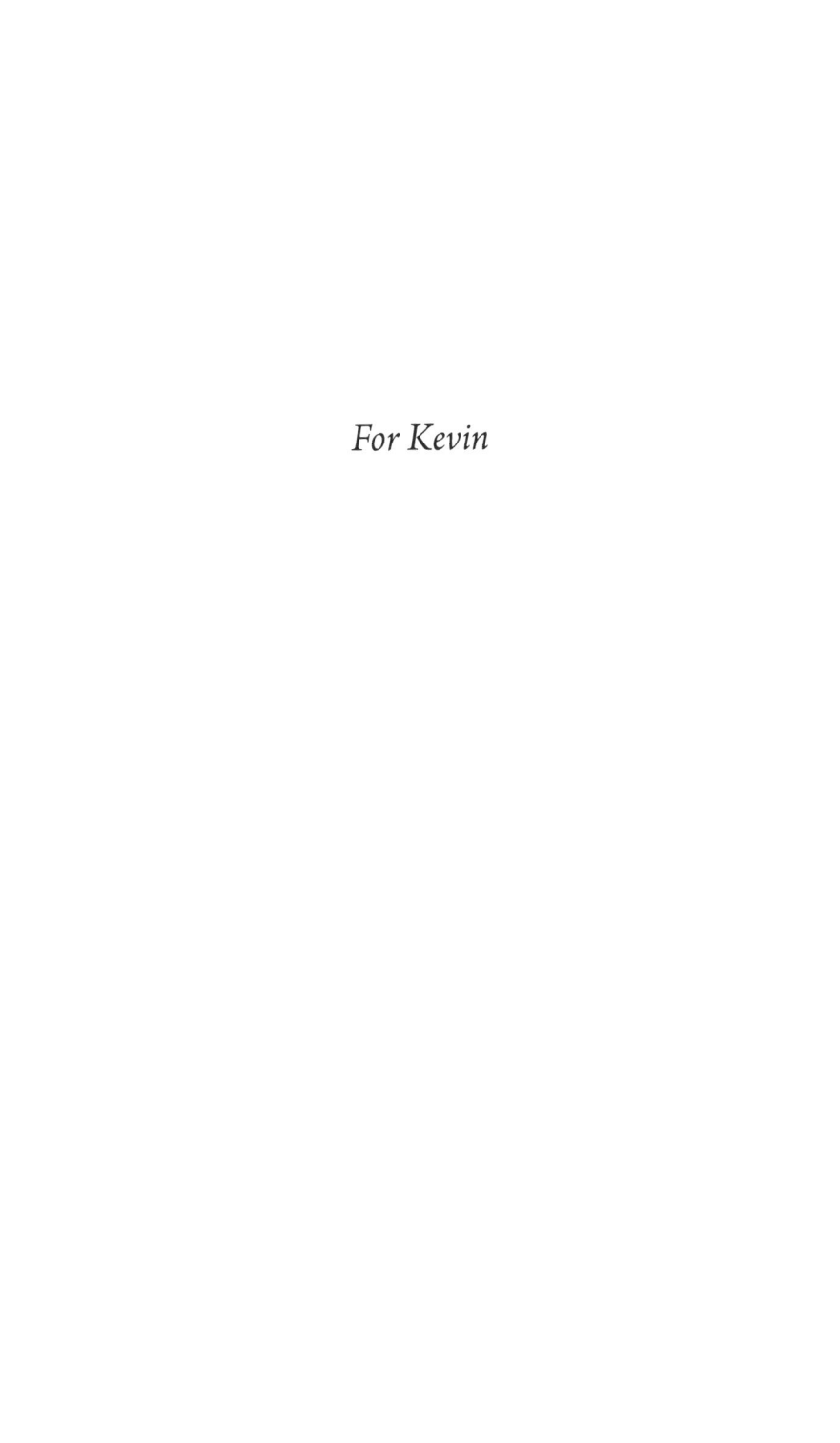

Preface

Writing an autobiography wasn't on my "to do" list. I haven't lived my life with the notion that I was someone important or special whose experiences are worthy of recording, but I do feel extraordinarily fortunate to have led an interesting and fulfilling life. As I approached my 91st birthday, my daughters finally persuaded me that there was value in writing down an account of my meandering journey through the world before my memory completely fails. Speaking of which, I take full responsibility for any omissions or inaccuracies. The marbles are mostly there but they are rusty and unreliable at times. The family tease me by saying I have a "kangaroo brain" because I will be telling one story and then jump to another when I suddenly remember something more interesting, and then do the same two minutes later. Luckily I have had a good team of people helping me get my memories into some sort of readily digestible order for this book. But if I do meander it is only because I find people endlessly fascinating, and I derive such joy in reminiscing. I hope readers find something amongst this collection of anecdotes to interest and entertain, and perhaps move them.

Baroness Gardner of Parkes
February 2019

Acknowledgements

I am grateful to the many people who contributed to helping me produce this book. My daughters – Sarah, Rachel and Joanna – have provided invaluable support as well as vital memory jogging! Family members in Australia, especially Greg Bateman, Mary Fitzpatrick, Beatrice Gray, Greg McGirr, Peter Willis and Catherine Worsnop, have kindly offered their time and essential input, as have the people of Parkes and Dubbo, in particular Roseanne Jones and Serena Murray. I thank Couper Street Books, Dan Prescott and Claire Wingfield for their expertise. For plugging many factual gaps in my memory, I am indebted to the kind people who work in the House of Lords Library, the IPU and the many other organisations I have been involved with. I am deeply grateful to Susannah Saary for crafting my stories into a compelling book, and I give special thanks to my dear friend, Betty Boothroyd, for contributing a generous and entertaining foreword.

Contents

Foreword by Baroness Boothroyd, OM	xiii
Prologue: Speaking Strine	1
PART ONE: AUSTRALIA	5
Chapter One: Greg and Rachel	7
Chapter Two: The Eighth Child	17
Chapter Three: A Birthday in Paris, 1937	23
Chapter Four: War on the Horizon	29
Chapter Five: University Careers: a Family Tradition	42
Chapter Six: A Woman Goes Walkabout	52
PART TWO: LONDON	65
Chapter Seven: Aussie Dentists in London	67
Chapter Eight: An Unexpected Proposal	71
Chapter Nine: "A Good Grip on This Earth"	74
Chapter Ten: A Very Parisian Wedding	78
Chapter Eleven: A New Family	85
Chapter Twelve: The Demon Dentists of Old Street?	98
PART THREE: WESTMINSTER	119
Chapter Thirteen: A Frying Pan for Labour	121
Chapter Fourteen: The Road to Westminster	126
Chapter Fifteen: The GLC	131
Chapter Sixteen: Blackburn, 1970	141
Chapter Seventeen: Cornwall, 1974	149

Chapter Eighteen: Europe or Home? ... 157
Chapter Nineteen: "This One Looks Important" ... 161
Chapter Twenty: House of Lords, 1981 ... 168
Chapter Twenty-One: On Westminster Bridge ... 173
Chapter Twenty-Two: Gardner's Question Time ... 180
   Can I retain my Australian citizenship? ... 182
   Can we guarantee free NHS dental check-ups for all? ... 186
   Can we get better education for all? ... 191
   Can we ensure private landlords are regulated? ... 193
   Can we limit the height that people can grow their hedges? ... 196
   Can we make our roads safer for everyone? ... 198
Chapter Twenty-Three: The Long Table ... 200
Chapter Twenty-Four: United Nations, IPU Visits and Plan International ... 212
Chapter Twenty-Five: Being Conservative ... 225
Chapter Twenty-Six: Being Australian ... 238

PART FOUR: FAMILY AND FUTURE ... 255

Chapter Twenty-Seven: Kevin Gardner, 1930–2007 ... 257
Chapter Twenty-Eight: So Many McGirrs ... 282
Chapter Twenty-Nine: The Next Generation ... 294
Chapter Thirty: Surviving! ... 310

Epilogue: Keep Going ... 327
Postscript ... 333
Appendix: *Curriculum Vitae* ... 335

Foreword

by Baroness Boothroyd OM

I was delighted to be invited to write a foreword for the – may I say, long awaited – autobiography of my dear friend, Trixie Gardner. Although we are members of different political parties, we are contemporaries. We hail from an era when women really had to fight to be heard. And although our parties may fundamentally disagree on the best way to resolve the multitude of issues that politicians are responsible for dealing with, Trixie and I remain united in one overriding belief: that, as Members of the House of Lords, it is our duty to help safeguard and improve the lives of the British people.

I first became aware of Trixie when I heard that she had been selected to fight Barbara Castle, for Barbara's long-held seat in Blackburn, in the 1970 General Election. I remember thinking that this would be quite the baptism of fire! Barbara had held the seat since 1945, for 25 years, and she was a senior Cabinet Minister in Harold Wilson's Government. I could only have admiration for another woman who was going to take on that fight!

By that time, I had fought for a seat in Parliament in two elections but had yet to win. I knew, all too well, what Trixie was in for. Although I would never have wished for a member of my own party to lose their seat, I hoped Trixie would give Barbara a decent fight. She did. Although Barbara held onto her seat, Trixie significantly reduced her majority.

At my fifth election encounter, I was successful in being elected as MP for West Bromwich in the 1973 by-election, just before Trixie fought her second General Election in Cornwall, in 1974, in an attempt to take the seat from the Liberal Party. She was again unsuccessful, but I admired her tenacity.

What Trixie and I both came up against, through the 1960s and 1970s, was more sexism than you could shake a stick at. The first question that any journalist would ask us was along the lines of "What will voters think of a woman candidate?" There was not the faintest hint of interest in our policies. They were only interested in the novelty (to them) of us being female. In the press, they commented on our hair, our figures and our fashion choices, and speculated about who would be doing the washing up at home in our absence!

Well, for Trixie, as for myself, the attitude of the press was all water off a duck's back. We had bigger fish to fry. Our gender had absolutely nothing to do with our political causes. It was a tough climb up the political ladder for women, but there was much work to be done and we were determined women. Most women are colourful, strong candidates – a fact ignored by the media, but it applied both to Trixie and to me.

Trixie was a fearless force in local government in London, both on Westminster City Council and as a Member of the Greater London Council, and was deserving of the life peerage she was offered in 1981. I knew she would bring a huge amount of knowledge and experience with her, and would make valuable contributions to debate in the Upper House of the UK Parliament. At the time, I had no idea that I would one day be joining her in that red-carpeted side of the Palace of Westminster!

I have always marvelled at how Trixie fits in everything she does. In the early 1980s, in particular, she was flying between the House of Lords, GLC meetings, and various commitments in her roles as UK delegate to the UN Commission on the Status of Women and British Chair of the European Union of Women. And with a husband and three young children to boot! The Gardners were a real family affair. Trixie's husband, Kevin, was her backbone, and involved in politics himself, serving as a Councillor on Westminster City Council and Lord Mayor. Their three bright and charming daughters are a credit to them; as children they were always buzzing around at events, socialising with adults and making intelligent conversation; as adults they have all been successful in their chosen fields. I remember Kevin being a down-to-earth and kind man, with a wonderfully dry wit. He was taken from them far too soon, in 2007, and I know Trixie misses him terribly.

Trixie herself is a credit to her own parents. Her father was a huge figure in state politics in New South Wales in the first half of the twentieth century, and Trixie's mother was a celebrated champion of increasing opportunities for women to receive a university education, and a tireless campaigner for the Bush Nursing Association. It is sad they did not survive to see Trixie's contribution to British politics. They would have been tremendously proud of her.

Trixie has a permanent "perch" on the second bench in the Chamber, right behind the Chief Whip. You truly cannot miss her or her Aussie twang, regularly asking one of her famously direct questions, drawing on her years of experience; she captures the respect of the House. Trixie is one of those people who you feel is truly interested in the answer when she asks, personally, "How are you?" She takes the time to stop and ask, and she takes the time to listen. She takes an interest in everyone, from her fellow peers to the catering staff; she knows all their personal stories. And there is nothing Trixie delights in more than having a laugh at herself; sharing a story about some funny mishap she's made. With her distinctive accent and no-nonsense Australian approach, she is a joy to be around.

I have always felt I had much in common with Trixie. While we sit on opposite sides of the Chamber, we are both united in our loyalty to the people we represent, dedicated to the causes we fight for, and determined to leave the world a better place than we found it. We are both realists, looking for practical solutions to problems, and unwilling to give up until we've found them.

Life in politics is full of ups and downs. As a woman you have even more challenges than your male colleagues because your first battle is the fight to be heard and respected, before you've even started to make your point. Sad to say this is almost as true today as it was when Trixie and I started out. But I'm pleased to say that there are more female faces in Parliament, and I hope we see their number grow.

I value Trixie's friendship enormously, and I respect her as a colleague. She is a great parliamentarian. This is an opinion I know I share with many who know her and have worked with her. She is a treasured member of the House of Lords, and as the eldest active member of both Houses, she is revered throughout Westminster. She is just shy of 92 years young at time of writing, and I'm always thrilled to see her, still going strong.

I congratulate Trixie warmly on the publication of her life story. I am proud to be her friend.

Baroness Boothroyd OM
May 2019

Prologue

Speaking Strine

Shortly after making my inaugural speech to the UN Commission on the Status of Women in New York, for which I was the UK representative from 1982–1988, I was handed a note that read, "We congratulate the UK on their contribution and we particularly appreciated the accent in which it was delivered."

While to my relations and most of the Australian population I have a definite "Pommy" accent, the rest of the world cannot help but recognize my distinctive Australian twang.

However, I think my way of speaking goes beyond my accent. In Australia we are famed for being plain speakers. We tend to speak our minds and we don't mince our words. When I appeared in the House of Lords, in 1981, and started asking pertinent questions that didn't beat around the bush but drove straight to the point and demanded answers, I certainly ruffled some feathers; as I had been doing for many years in local government, as a member of both Westminster City Council and the Greater London Council (GLC). But you only get things in government by pushing your point, and people in my constituencies have repeatedly told me, over the years, that they voted for me because I didn't just talk a good talk… I actually "got things done". Well, I didn't get into politics for any other reason than to help people, to give a voice to people who didn't have the ability to speak up for themselves.

At the time of writing, I've been a member of the House of Lords for almost 38 years. In that time I've seen six prime ministers in office. The Conservative and first female Prime Minister, Margaret Thatcher (who had initiated the nomination that led to my Introduction in 1981) until she resigned in 1990; John Major, who won the Conservative Party leadership election after Thatcher resigned and was in power until 1997; Tony Blair, the first Labour Prime Minister for over 18 years, who served from 1997 until he resigned in 2007; Gordon Brown, who succeeded Tony Blair and led the Labour Government until 2010; David Cameron, who won the General Election for the Conservative Party in 2010 and remained in power until he resigned following the Brexit referendum in 2016; and finally, Theresa May, who took power in 2016 and is in office at time of writing (early 2019).

While the party in government (whether it leads by a majority or not) and the name of the prime minister may change, the needs of people, and the issues they face, do not. The issues I have fought the hardest for include the provisions for public health care, the basic living standards that I believe people have a right to enjoy in their own homes, and the safety of road users. I have won battles and I have lost battles, but the war rages on. Until every member of society has access to adequate shelter, nourishment and health care, those of us with a voice in Parliament should not rest.

In December 2009, during a debate on citizenship and the administration of processing people's "right of abode" documents, I made some points about the relationship between Australia and the United Kingdom as members of the Commonwealth of Nations. "I think of the Commonwealth as a family united by the English language," I said. "Although some people here think I talk Strine rather than English."

"Strine" is a term coined in the 1960s to describe the colloquial strain of English used by most Australians. The term originally referred specifically to the habit Australians have of running words together and shortening them wherever possible. For example you might say to your co-workers on a Friday afternoon, "avagoodweegend" and "enjoy yer barbie" in reference to a barbecue. We will do anything to shorten words, usually with an "oh" or ee" sound at the end. Presents are "pressies", relatives are "rellies" and "arvo" is the afternoon. We swim in "cossies" and drive "utes" (utility vehicles or pickup trucks), and if you are "crook" you are feeling under the weather as opposed to being a criminal! The term

"Strine" generally refers to all Australian slang, such as using the term "fair dinkum" for something being true and fair.

I grew up in a very large family and if you didn't use your voice, you wouldn't have got very far. My father was a politician, my mother was an activist, and we were raised to believe that we had a duty to speak up about what we believed in.

Thanks to my upbringing, I have never been afraid to voice my opinions and concerns. I hope I have been as avid a listener, too, because you learn far more when you listen, than you do when you speak. In our extensive debates in the House of Lords, it is important to do both. We have a duty to the British people to revise the legislation that will affect their lives and counsel the elected members of the House of Commons. I try to do that in plain language, in the Australian way!

The United Kingdom, Australia, and all other countries that are members of the Commonwealth, the European Union, and indeed the United Nations, speak a whole range of languages. But it doesn't matter which words we choose, we should all be singing from the same hymn sheet. We must stay united in our efforts to combat suffering and inequality, and strive for international peace. That continued effort is what has always made me proud of being an Australian citizen, a UK resident and a member of the British Parliament.

PART ONE

Australia

1

Greg and Rachel

On 18 May 1921 in Sydney, Australia, the first ever State Minister of Health and Motherhood, announced that the New South Wales Parliamentary Labour Party had approved his draft Bill providing "endowment for motherhood". The scheme would provide a pension for widowed mothers and an allowance for every child under 18. The Bill was designed to ensure that "children actually receive benefit and thus tend to build up a healthy and strong Australian community".

This Bill was the first of its kind in the world.

The man who introduced it was my father.

John Joseph Gregory McGirr (always known as Greg) was born in October 1879 in central New South Wales in a town that had taken its name from the man known as the "Father of the Federation", Sir Henry Parkes. Parkes is a New South Wales mining town around 350km west of Sydney, separated from the coastal areas by the Blue Mountains. Until 1873, the settlement had been known as "Currajong" and then "Bushman's". It was renamed Parkes in 1873 after a visit from Sir Henry Parkes and, having grown significantly during the gold rush of the 1870s, was officially given the status of a "town" in 1885.

The McGirr family had originally settled in the place that became Parkes because it was at the end of the line for the *bullock* train. (I stress this because when I made the reference in my speech on social mobility that I gave in October 2017, Hansard – the verbatim record of all proceedings in both Houses of Parliament – initially incorrectly recorded the words as the *bullet* train, and I had to point out that the high-speed Japanese locomotive, colloquially known as a "bullet train", had not been invented in the mid-nineteenth century!) A "bullock train" is a line of cattle. Before the roads and railways were built, teams of farmers drove their cattle between the mines and different settlements as a way of transporting goods.

Cattle settled in Parkes long before people did. Many men had tried to get across the Blue Mountains by going through the valleys, but no one had ever succeeded. Eventually a few of them braved the more treacherous but direct route over the ridges of the mountains and made it across. When they got to the other side they found plenty of wonderful healthy cattle already there; they had found their way to the good grazing land on the other side of the mountains by themselves. A settlement soon grew and flourished.

My paternal grandfather, John Patrick McGirr, arrived in New South Wales sometime in the mid-nineteenth century. He was the second member of his family who ended up emigrating to Australia. His brother had set sail from their native Ireland to become a schoolteacher some years earlier. Settling in Parkes, by that time known as "Bushman's" after the Bushman lead mine, John McGirr earned his living as a dairy farmer. He married another Irish immigrant, Mary O'Sullivan, and they made a fine contribution to the growing population of Australia, producing seven children in total. The family lived in "Tara Villa" in Parkes.

My father, Greg – the McGirrs' second-born son – also seemed destined for a life of farming until a lucky break befell him. A wealthy family in the area had paid for a place for their son at the prestigious St. Stanislaus' College, a Catholic boarding school in Bathurst (around 150km east of Parkes), but the boy refused to go. The family approached my grandparents to offer the place to their eldest son, Patrick.

Ironically, the McGirr family had founded this very school. Friar James McGirr was its first President. But fees were high and places were coveted, and nepotism presumably frowned upon.

My uncle Pat's response to this kind offer, which came at a time when he must have been in his teens, was to say it was too late for him to make best use of the opportunity and that his brother Greg would stand to benefit more from taking up the place. He even offered to do Greg's milk round (which would mean doing a double shift) when my grandfather said he couldn't spare his second son from those duties.

Greg McGirr certainly did benefit from the opportunity, completing his education at St. Stanislaus' College and going on to study Pharmacy at the University of Sydney. Nevertheless, there was some adjusting to be done when Greg first attended his new school as he came from a very different background from the other boys.

Every boy intending to go to St. Stanislaus' was sent a uniform and clothes list. On this list was an item no one in my father's family – or even in the whole of Parkes – had ever heard of: "pyjamas". He wasn't the only one for whom pyjamas were a new concept; one boy even turned up to school *wearing* his pyjamas (reportedly not realizing that they were nightwear), complementing his outfit with a top hat! Having failed to purchase any pyjamas himself, my father arrived at school with his regular nightshirt and would wait until lights out every night before putting it on, for fear of being ridiculed. The boys at this school took no prisoners and were rather eccentric and unpredictable. One nervous young priest arrived from Ireland fearful of the stories he'd heard about what "wild colonials" the Australians were. Not wanting to disappoint him, my father's more rambunctious classmates would tie the poor priest up and dance around him singing the famous song, "Wild Colonial Boy" about a ruthless Irish–Australian outlaw from the early nineteenth century.

In 1904, Greg McGirr was in the first ever year of students to graduate in Pharmacy from the University of Sydney.

The owner of a chemist shop on Pitt Street in Sydney, who was keen to inform customers that they had a qualified pharmacist on the premises, offered my father a job. This man had originally hoped that the "qualified pharmacist" on the premises would be his own son but the boy had failed to graduate so my father got the job. That first shop was the start of a huge chain of chemists; my father helped turn Washington H. Soul Pattinson into one of Australia's most successful companies!

*

Dad's real "lucky break" was, thanks to his Pharmacy degree, developing a poison for rabbits. In Australia, at that time, rabbits were a real problem. One rabbit could eat as much grass as an entire sheep and the place was almost overrun by them. Rabbits had to be culled or farmers would lose too much of their stock as there would be no grazing land left for them. Historically, they'd used a phosphorus poison, an effective way of killing rabbits but, being highly flammable, also a very effective way of starting bush fires! Dad developed an alternative from an alkaloid poison called "strychnine" that didn't ignite. He managed to get a patent for "McGirr's Rabbo Poison", which he sold for £100 in 1906. People said he could have got far more for it if he'd held onto it for longer, but Dad always defended his decision, saying if he hadn't sold it he wouldn't have earned anything from it at all, because he didn't have the money to mass produce it himself. He took the money and used it to invest in his own business, often saying, "I made my fortune from that £100."

My father opened his own chemist shop in Parkes and went on to establish several more. One was in Kings Cross. A man used to come into the shop and tell Greg, "What you do when you have a corner site like this is you curve the window a bit. You lose a bit of space but you get more frontage." Greg thought that sounded rather silly and took no notice of him at first. However, he later tried the idea in a chemist shop he opened in Parkes and found it worked; it seemed the man knew what he was talking about. And it was hardly surprising, then, that my father later realized that this man was none other than Mark Foy, who became one of Australia's most successful entrepreneurs. For many years it was said that Mark Foy was the only man in Australia who could write you a cheque for a million dollars that would actually clear at the bank.

Building on his success with chemist shops, my father later decided to start investing in pubs. Pubs – some of which also offered temporary sleeping quarters for tradesmen passing through country towns – were a good business in Australia at that time because, while a law had been passed in 1916 banning the sale of alcohol after 6pm in the evening, you could carry on drinking whatever you'd bought before 6pm, so sales would go through the roof as this deadline approached. That last-minute rush to the bar became known as the "6 o'clock swill" because it was reminiscent of watching pigs around a feeding trough, with men (at this time women were banned from drinking in public bars) bumping into each other and spilling drinks. The men would buy as many beers as they could afford and carry, line them up and drink until the last drop was gone.

A "binge-drinking" culture remained long after the 6pm restriction was lifted in 1967, and became a real problem in Australia. Recent campaigns to make people aware of the problems of excessive drinking have been a long time coming. In March 2008, the Australian Government announced that they were allocating $53.5 million to their "National Binge Drinking Strategy" to address the binge-drinking culture amongst young Australians. There are widespread campaigns such as "Drinkwise Australia" and "Think Again", and authorities are very strict about drink driving, sometimes setting up checkpoints (known as "booze buses") to catch offenders.

In 1906, the year he sold his rabbit poison, Greg McGirr also made his first attempt at entering politics. He ran in the third-ever Federal elections (the Australian Federation having been founded in 1901), supported by the Australian Labour Party (as it was then known, only officially changing its name to the American spelling of "labor" and becoming the "Australian Labor Party" in 1918). They were keen to get professionals into power and they liked the fact that my father had a university degree. He was 27 when he ran for office. He ran as one of three Labour Party candidates vying for a seat as a senator for New South Wales in the Federal Parliament, but none of them got elected. Four years later, rather than run for the Federal Parliament again, he tried his luck at the State level, for a seat in the new NSW Legislative Assembly (the lower house of the Parliament of New South Wales), going up against a sitting Liberal member.

Again he was unsuccessful.

My father finally found his seat (as the Member for Yass) in the NSW Parliament thanks to a by-election in 1913, the year before he got married. He was re-elected to this seat three times. In 1920, boundary changes forced him to fight for the Cootamundra seat, which he won.

Keen to get his younger brother, James, into the NSW Parliament, Greg McGirr resigned his seat in 1922, forcing a by-election. The law at the time stated that applications for the seat had to be entered before midnight on the same day that the MP resigned. Always the canny businessman, Greg resigned at one minute to midnight so that James could be the only one to put in his application. James was duly elected uncontested! Greg successfully won the Cumberland seat in west Sydney and thus the two brothers served as MPs together for a few years, and James went on to become Premier of New South Wales for the ALP from 1947–1952. Their eldest brother, Patrick, also had a long career in politics. He served as the ALP MP for Macquarie from 1917 to 1920 and the following year found a seat on the Legislative Council (the elected upper house) of the NSW Parliament, which he held until 1955, just two years before he died.

The three McGirr brothers were something of a political dynasty in New South Wales.

My father made a significant contribution to Australian politics in the state of New South Wales during his time in office. He was party whip for a year in 1916–1917 and became the very first Minister for Public Health and Motherhood in 1920, which was when he started campaigning for child welfare payments. Press cuttings from the time showed that his right-wing rivals tried to mock him for this, calling him "Mother McGirr" but my father was very proud of his work to help start state child-support payments in Australia and many women's organisations gave him their grateful support.

Greg McGirr also found himself in disputes with his own party, over the direction the Labour Party was going. He had briefly become the Deputy Leader of the party in 1921, but clashed with the Premier, James Dooley, who was a huge political rival of his. When Dooley was expelled from the party in 1923, the Executive of the Labour Party of NSW made my father the acting leader, and thus for a few months Greg McGirr was the Premier (the Head of State Government) of New South Wales. But the Federal Executive intervened and appointed another member as interim leader before the famous Jack Lang (known as "The Big Fella") took over. Jack Lang and my father were long-time rivals, and this was obviously the last straw for him. My father resigned from the party in 1923 and tried to establish a new party, the "Young Australia Party", which he funded himself. When he was unsuccessful as a candidate for his new Young Australia Party and lost his seat in the 1925 election, he left politics to focus on his business pursuits and rapidly expanding family.

Rachel Rittenburg Miller was born in November 1887 in Maitland, New South Wales. Her parents were Mary Anne Elizabeth Burke, who was descended from Irish immigrants, and John Jacob Mueller who was born in Prussia in 1847 and emigrated to Australia because he was an expert cattle handler. We assume that he changed his name from Mueller to Miller to make it sound less Jewish, as many Jews felt the need to do in those days to avoid persecution, however there are family members who insist there is no proof that John Jacob Mueller was even born a Jew. My mother's birth certificate apparently did not specify any religion, which was fairly unusual in those days.

My maternal grandparents, John and Mary (the same first names as my father's parents – not exactly uncommon names but still a funny coincidence) had three children. My mother's two older brothers, Charles and Percy, both tragically died in 1890 when they were aged 7 and 5 respectively. They had attended a birthday party and every child who had been at the party died shortly after contracting diphtheria from an infected birthday cake. Fortunately, my 3-year-old mother hadn't attended the party or I would never have existed.

In January 1899, when my mother was only 11 years old, tragedy struck again and her father died. I can't imagine how my poor grandmother got through this; she had already had her fair share of grief in life, having lost her mother at a young age, leaving her to raise her younger siblings herself. Luckily, a family friend – a jeweller (who was most certainly Jewish) called Mr Hermes – offered to marry my grandma and raise my mother as his own daughter. They moved to Queensland to live with him and that's where my mother completed her high-school education.

As a stepfather, Mr Hermes must have been a comforting and stabilising presence for my grieving mother. We have records of her attending a convent school in Charters Tower, Queensland as "Rachel Hermes" in 1904, and later as "Rachel R Miller-Hermes" at her "Grammar School". There are records of her excelling in piano, and in 1906 she passed the matriculation exam for the University of Sydney at St Scholastica's College in Glebe Point, which is a western suburb of Sydney.

We are not sure exactly when, but at some point between 1907 and 1909, my mother began studying at the University of Sydney. There, she became good friends with an older girl called Mary – "Minnie" to her friends – McGirr, who introduced Rachel Rittenburg Miller-Hermes to her brother, Greg McGirr.

We believe Greg and Rachel got engaged very soon after meeting in Sydney but for some reason my mother broke it off and returned to Queensland in 1912, to work as a schoolteacher at the newly established Charters Towers High School. She was reputedly the first female teacher in Queensland to have attended university; indeed, she was one of the very first women in Australia ever to study at a university (even so, women were not actually awarded an official degree like their male counterparts!).

There has always been family speculation that Grandma Hermes did not approve of the idea of her daughter becoming a Catholic in order to marry Greg McGirr, and it's no secret that Grandma and my father were not the best of friends. However, Greg had his heart set on marrying my mother and travelled to Queensland to win her back, which he did (from a dentist she had become engaged to in the intervening period!).

Greg and Rachel were married in November 1914 at St. Stephens Roman Catholic Cathedral in Brisbane. My mother was 27 and my father was 35. They moved back to North Sydney where they lived first in Miller Street, until 1918, and then in a house they named "*Sunshine*" on Alfred Street.

By the end of 1923, just five years later, Greg and Rachel had produced five children and had a sixth on the way. Their first son, Jack, was born in September 1915 and their eldest daughter, Beatrice (always known as

Muffie), was born in December 1916. They then had three more girls: Gwen was born in May 1918, Patty in November 1919 and Clarinda in December 1920.

When my mother was around six months pregnant with her sixth child (my brother, Raymond, who was eventually born in April 1924), tragedy struck. In January 1924, three-year-old Clarinda died on the operating table during a routine procedure to remove her tonsils. The whole family was distraught and my father was apoplectic. The official cause of death was recorded as complications from the tonsillitis but my father was adamant that Clarinda had died as a result of medical negligence. In the end, I believe the official death certificate stated "diphtheria", which was a common cause of childhood illness at the time. In those days there were a lot of deadly diseases around and people didn't really know much about what was going on. They just had to trust the doctors who, half the time, were as much in the dark. Nothing was ever proved, but I imagine it was a very subdued household that Raymond was born into three months later.

When you consider the timing of all this – it was in May 1925, only a year or so after he'd lost his little girl, that my father failed to keep his seat in Parliament after switching parties to run as a candidate for his self-funded Young Australia Party – it's no surprise that, after their seventh child (and third son), Gregory, was born in August 1925, my parents decided to leave Sydney and relocate the family to Parkes.

My father already had business interests in his birthplace, Parkes, and had been buying properties throughout New South Wales – mostly pubs and hotels – so it was a central place from which to travel out to see his various tenants.

My parents bought a large house that they called "*Sunrise*" and my father had a big ballroom added as an extension to it. (The house and ballroom still stand today.)

If they thought they might escape the traumatic memory of what had happened to Clarinda in Parkes, my parents were mistaken. There were references to "Clarinda" everywhere. The first wife of Sir Henry Parkes was called "Clarinda" and he had also named a daughter after her. One of the main streets in Parkes was (and still is) called "Clarinda Street". It is fitting that my parents decided to commemorate their daughter in Parkes and donated a beautiful stone fountain to the town. They buried Clarinda in the local cemetery next to Greg's parents and erected identical stone angels on her tombstone and on top of the fountain.

My father also later donated the high altar and reredos (a decorative screen placed behind the altar) to the new Catholic Church, marking this with a plaque that reads *"…donated by Gregory McGirr in memory of his parents, John and Mary McGirr and his daughter Clarinda."*

2

The Eighth Child

In July 1927, with the family all settled in their new house, *Sunrise*, in Parkes, my mother gave birth to her eighth child and fifth daughter. She was determined to name this new baby after herself. Although her name was Rachel, her nickname had always been "Trixie" (short for Beatrice, the name that was almost given to her and that she'd given to her own first-born girl), so I was christened Rachel Trixie Anne (because the priest insisted I also have a saint's name) McGirr.

As the first girl born since Clarinda's death, I imagine my arrival felt like a real blessing to my parents. My father certainly always made me feel as though I was his favourite.

I have no memory of living in Parkes, however, because the family moved back to Sydney in 1929 when I was only 2 years old.

I think my father was itching to get back into politics and needed to be where the action was in Sydney. Also he was a hugely successful businessman by then; Parkes may have been too much of a small town for him. I'm sure my parents, who were passionate about education, were also keen for their growing children to be educated in Sydney. Furthermore, we were a family of big personalities; I don't think Parkes would have been big enough for any of us in the long term.

We moved to 247 Ernest Street, into a house that looked out over Cammeray Golf Club, not far from the northern end of the Sydney Harbour Bridge, which had been under construction for six years by then. Indeed, we were living at "*Sunray*" – as my parents named that house – when the two halves of the iconic arch of the bridge touched for the first time on 19 August 1930.

*

When I was born, my eldest brother, Jack, was already 13. By the time I was old enough to play with my siblings, Jack was a teenager and doing his own thing so I didn't see much of him. The two siblings directly above me in age order were both boys, so there was an eight-year age gap between me and Patty, the next girl up. It was very frustrating being the baby of the family and having sisters who were so much older than me. My siblings would really give me the run around. The boys would say, "Go and play with the girls; we don't want you." But the girls would send me packing saying, "You're too young to join in; go and play with your brothers." I was stuck between a rock and a hard place; I had a rotten time, so I was absolutely delighted when my sister Nonna (named so for being the ninth child) was born in December 1931. I was four and a half, and I regarded Nonna as my very own. I helped look after her when she was a baby, and I couldn't wait until she could walk and talk so that I'd have someone to play with… and boss about!

Until Nonna was old enough to play with, one person I loved to spend time with was George, our cook. He adored me and would never tire of telling me about all the times he had to rescue me, when I was a baby, because I'd crawled away. If the person watching me took their eyes off me for a second, I was off. He'd find me outside, halfway to the woodpile, which was probably full of (potentially deadly) spiders. I was clearly a true Australian girl; I tried to go walkabout before I could even walk!

George had been born into a rich family, and had been left a large inheritance when his father died, but he was a compulsive gambler and had spent every last cent he had on the horses. George was just about ready for the scrapheap when my father met him. Dad gave him a lifeline by giving him a job and a roof over his head. It probably kept the old man alive because he always had food and shelter, even after gambling his earnings away. By this time, my father was often away for long stretches of time on business, travelling around his growing portfolio of properties throughout the state. I'm sure it was a comfort to Dad, knowing that George was at home with us during those trips.

*

Running such a large household must have been quite an ordeal, especially in those days. We had an ancient washing machine, but it was a terrible pain to use. Bed sheets were boiled in a massive copper tub that sat on a brick structure over a fire that had to be kept going. We had a woman who came in to do the laundry and she was marvellous at ironing. I can still remember the joy of getting into a bed made with her crisply ironed sheets on laundry day. There were no duvets in those days; it was just a sheet on top of under-blankets and then a top sheet with a big eiderdown over that.

George prepared all our meals. We always had a big breakfast that was available from 6am until around midday. We had a toasting machine, which was quite a rarity in those days, but it took forever. You waited ages to brown one side of the bread and then you had to turn it over and start again because you could only toast one side at a time. Milk and bread were delivered daily. My brother, Jack, always complained that, at school, they were made to eat the stale bread first. By the time they were finished with that, they had no more appetite for the fresh loaf, which would then be served to them, stale, the next day, and the cycle repeated. He couldn't stand how illogical it was.

"The fresh loaf costs no more than the stale one," he would say, exasperated. When he was at home, he wouldn't come down to breakfast until about 11am, timing it perfectly with the delivery of the fresh bread, which he would insist on eating.

Australia had suffered badly as a result of the Great Depression that followed the Wall Street Crash of 1929. You had to buy your bread by the slice during the worst times. People would come to our kitchen door begging for food. George would always give them a sandwich. He explained to me that some of them were really coming begging for money to spend on booze. He knew who they were because he watched them throw away the sandwich into the rough of the golf course opposite our house as they walked away.

George never drank himself; every penny he had in his possession would go on gambling. Well, almost every penny; he would occasionally give me a sixpence wrapped up in a piece of paper, which was absolutely precious to me. He would then take me down to the local sweet shop, and I would apparently stand there, staring at the shelves containing huge jars of sweets with my eyes almost popping out of my head. I'd start pointing to various jars asking for "a bit of this," and "a bit of that." Then I'd point to my favourite and ask for "a whole *bag* of that!"

Although he'd never married, George clearly adored children. He was like a second father to me. But that never diminished the closeness I felt to my parents, both of whom I adored; I had a wonderful relationship with each of them individually.

In 1931, *The Sydney Morning Herald* published a piece on my father that quoted him as saying, "It behoves every business man to get into politics." He was announcing his intention to run as the Federal Labour Party candidate for East Sydney. He was well known for his business successes by then and he was eager to conquer politics again. However, he was not destined to succeed in that particular ambition; he wasn't elected.

Dad's business success came at a cost. He would be travelling for days, all around the state, and it really wore him out. I remember him coming home after business trips absolutely shattered. He would more or less collapse as soon as he got home, taking to his bed for a few days to recover. My mother would then become quite preoccupied with looking after him. I remember how she would worry about him when he was in that kind of state.

My mother, on the other hand, seemed to have a never-ending source of energy!

At just 5'1", my mother's stature bore no resemblance to her feisty personality. She was a real force to reckon with, a true feminist who championed upward social mobility and universal welfare and health care. She campaigned passionately to help the causes she cared about, in particular the Sydney University Settlement. This was a project started by the Sydney University Women's Society in 1891 to help working-class people on low incomes by giving them the chance to integrate with and learn from the educated classes. They were focused, in particular, on helping the Aboriginal community, and the migrants who had come from the Middle East and Europe looking for manual labour. My mother felt strongly that, if you had the good fortune to come from a stable family with reasonable means, and you had half a brain, you had a duty to get a decent education. You then had a responsibility to help those less fortunate than you.

A passionate supporter of education, my mother established and presented the first "McGirr Prize for French" at St Aloysius' College in Milsons Point.

Rachel McGirr was always fundraising and raising awareness by making rousing speeches at events. She was a wonderful public speaker and regularly participated in radio broadcasts, often doing programmes to promote the Bush Nursing Association, which was set up in 1911 to help organise adequate nursing services in rural areas. Some places in Australia were so remote that it was hard to ensure they had access to adequate medical help. It was very exciting when we were allowed to stay up in the evening to listen to her on the radio.

My mother was always busy but she was still an attentive and affectionate mother, and I never felt neglected in any way. She was devoted to her family.

The press had always had a keen interest in our family because of my father's political career. The local papers reported everything he did. Whether he courted this attention to further his career, or he was a natural target for the press because of his political and business interests, I couldn't tell you, but the media interest extended to all of Greg's family. In April 1920, my mother was featured on the "Every Woman's Page" of *The Sunday Times*. There is a photo (unfortunately not clear enough for republication here) of her holding Jack aged 4, Muffie (referred to as "Mary" in the article, which is her middle name) aged 3, Gwen aged 2 and Patty aged 4 months. She is quoted as saying that having four children gave her "the opportunity of studying the psychology of the child mind, and the mental and physical needs of children". The article further states that "Mrs McGirr has unbounded sympathy with all mothers. She says she feels she has 'a bond of kinship with the army of noble women in Australia who are rearing fine families of young Australians in spite of financial obstacles.'"

This may all sound rather antiquated to us in today's world, but this was Australia in the 1920s where women and children really had an uphill battle to be valued and recognised as having a significant place in society. I'm so proud that both my parents were leaders in that fight. They were ahead of their time in that respect. They debated different issues fiercely, and had opposing political alliances (my mother always voted for the more right-leaning parties – the United Australian Party, which later became the Liberal Party – while my father was a life-long Labor man) but they were absolutely united on their core values.

Although Rachel McGirr had not been born a Catholic (and her own mother made no secret of the fact that she wasn't the biggest fan of her daughter's choice of husband and religion) she grew to love the Roman Catholic Church and got very involved with the Catholic Women's Association. For her charity work with them, she was awarded the Cross of Leo (*Cross Pro Ecclesia et Pontifice*), a Pontifical award given by the Pope to lay persons and clergy who give service to the Church.

In February 1937, Mrs Rachel McGirr, of North Sydney, was awarded an O.B.E. (Order of the British Empire) for her welfare services in the Commonwealth of Australia in the King's New Year's Honours list. That year, the list had been announced a little later than usual because Edward VIII had abdicated on 11 December 1936 and presumably they wanted to give George VI a chance to take up his new position as King of England before announcing the list.

What an honour for my mother! One that was well deserved.

In those days, many of the people from the British Commonwealth who were awarded honours lived in remote places. When they were notified that they had been awarded the honour, they could choose whether to have it sent to them by mail, receive it from the local official (in Australia this would have been the Governor General) or travel to London to be presented with it by the King at Buckingham Palace.

My mother loved the British monarchy and never failed to remind us that she had been born in Queen Victoria's Golden Jubilee year (1887). I don't imagine she thought too long or hard about how and where to receive her award!

3

A Birthday in Paris, 1937

Having decided to make the trip to London to receive her O.B.E. from the King, my mother reasoned that five-year-old Nonna was too young to be separated from her mother for several months. I was a few months away from my tenth birthday and my mother thought it would be a good idea to take me along as well, to help look after Nonna. She felt I was young enough to miss a few months of school without it affecting my academic progress too much.

I remember feeling tremendously excited as we prepared for our trip. I am sure there was a fair amount of jealousy felt by our older siblings.

My mother, Nonna and I left for Europe on 21 April 1937 aboard the SS *Orford*, an Orient Line passenger liner that had famously carried Don Bradman's cricket team "The Invincibles" from Australia to England along with the Australian Davis Cup tennis team in 1934. The journey took us around six weeks. Spending all that time on board a ship wasn't the nicest experience but there were some redeeming highlights. I remember going through the Suez Canal and seeing the long lines of ships passing each other as they travelled through that impressive feat of nineteenth-century engineering. And we met a formidable British nanny on board. She was looking after several children and she kept in touch with my mother when we arrived in London. We joined her for a day during our stay and she showed us around some attractions in central London.

Arriving in London was terribly exciting. We docked at Tilbury on 3 June and stayed at the Arundel Hotel on the Strand. We were too young to go to the ceremony at Buckingham Palace, which was a few weeks later, so I was left in charge of Nonna who spent most of the trip feeling very unwell. My mother was always sending me out to get food for her, thinking that there might be some particular thing she could eat to make her feel better. I wasn't surprised Nonna felt sick; I felt a little queasy myself the first time I tasted the drinking water. It was awful compared to our water in Australia. Obviously this was long before bottled water was readily available!

According to an article in *The Sydney Morning Herald* from 31 July 1937, we made a telephone call home at some point that summer. In the piece, Muffie describes speaking to our mother and mentions her surprise at how clear the long-distance line was. Reportedly we had spent time in Ireland staying with a "Lady Broderick" whilst on our travels and had also stayed with "Lady Game". We also spent "a weekend at the Duchess of Marlborough's home", so we were obviously moving in some upper-class circles!

After London, we went for a tour around Europe. I have a wonderful photo of me, Mum and Nonna standing on the tarmac before boarding a flight to Paris. It was the first time I had ever been on an aeroplane and I remember how excited I was. Compared to air travel these days it was all very glamorous, and there was nothing like the security we have now. We were able to stand very close to the aircraft to have our photo taken. In those days everyone dressed very elegantly to fly; air travel was a huge privilege, a real event. When I see people travelling in tracksuits, old t-shirts and comfy shoes these days, I wonder what they would have made of the times when you wore your best clothes to board an aeroplane. When we got on board, we could see the pilot and the flight deck. We were able to watch our altitude go up and down on a meter attached to the cabin wall. Flying was much more thrilling back then… although, of course, far riskier!

One of my most treasured memories of my whole childhood is sitting with my mother and sister at a café in the corner of Place de la Madeleine eating a fabulous birthday cake that had been ordered and made especially for me by the French pastry chefs. We looked up in awe at *L'église de la Madeleine*, the huge Roman Catholic Church that dominates that square with its imposing Corinthian columns and classical statues. We had never seen anything like it.

After Paris, we went on to Germany, visiting Berlin and Munich, where we were extremely excited to see a real hippopotamus that was being kept in a giant bathtub in Munich Zoo. As a family we absolutely adored visiting zoos; they had a very special place in our hearts because my father had been instrumental in establishing Taronga Park Zoo in Sydney, which was opened in 1916. For his generosity, he had been given a lifetime pass for the whole family, so going to the zoo was a regular family outing.

We spent time in Naples, too, from where I assume we boarded the ship home, arriving back in Sydney towards the end of October, after being away for six months… a very long time for a little girl to be away from her home and family. I remember the excitement I felt in anticipation of seeing my father in particular; I'd missed him terribly and couldn't wait to tell him all about our adventures.

My mother, however, had slightly more sobering stories to tell. She was shocked by the heavy presence of soldiers in a town we stopped at as we travelled from France into Germany. I believe it was Nancy, which is not far from the border. She told my father that there were soldiers everywhere. She also described how, when we were in Germany, we had visited a place where they had laid wreaths to commemorate all the colonies they had lost during the Great War, 20 years earlier. I think my mother's view was that they symbolised Germany's intention to rebuild its empire and she was genuinely afraid that another war was on the horizon.

Undeterred by my mother's fears about an impending war in Europe, my father planned his own world trip the following year, deciding to take Patty with him, who had just turned 18. At that time Muffie and Gwen were studying law and medicine (respectively) at Sydney University. Patty wasn't planning on going to university and my father wanted to present her at Buckingham Palace, as a debutante; he had become friendly with the Duke of Windsor (the title Edward VIII was given after his abdication) when the future King of England had travelled to Australia in

1920. Dad had also recently been made the Vice-Consul for Brazil, standing in for the Brazilian ambassador to Australia who had been recalled due to his ties to the Nazi Party. This gave my father diplomatic papers and I am sure he had several political contacts he wanted to meet around the world. Although he hadn't been elected to Federal Parliament in 1931, he was still an ambitious politician and it was a great opportunity to build an international fan base. He was presumably working on his next strategic move in the political arena.

Dad and Patty left for Europe on 19 March 1938 on the *Strathmore*, a P&O liner, and docked in Plymouth on 29 April. They also stayed at the Arundel Hotel, where Nonna and I had stayed with our mother. According to Australian press reports from that time, they visited every capital city in Europe. They even visited Soviet Moscow.

We know that my father had a very unsettling experience in Vienna.

Hitler had occupied Austria since March 1938 and tensions were growing with the international community (leading to the Munich conference in September 1938, during which Chamberlain received and believed reassurances from Hitler that he was not going to claim any more territory in Europe as long as he was allowed to annex part of what was then Czechoslovakia).

My father was in Vienna for a cataract operation that had been performed by a very skilled eye doctor there. He and Patty were staying in a hotel while he recuperated from the operation. A waiter approached my father one day and said words to the effect of, "Mr McGirr, you've been very good to me and so I must warn you to get out of Vienna immediately... it is not safe for you and your daughter here." We are not exactly sure why the waiter felt my father was in particular danger, perhaps because the eye doctor he had seen was Jewish and the association with him was a risk in Hitler's occupied territory, perhaps it was something else my father was involved with, but he took the advice seriously and boarded a plane with Patty despite the fact that he had not fully recovered from the eye operation.

The threat turned out to be real because, before the plane could take off, everyone was made to get off and show their papers. My father and

Patty were only allowed to fly out of the country because he had those diplomatic papers as the Vice-Consul of Brazil.

Before Vienna, my father and Patty had visited Paris and were guests of the Duke and Duchess of Windsor, better known to the world as the former King Edward VIII and his wife, the American divorcée, Mrs Simpson. Edward had abdicated in December 1936 in order to marry her: a scandal that had rocked the British monarchy. After their marriage in France, in June 1937, the Duke and Duchess had taken up residence in Paris in a sort of self-imposed exile. There is a family rumour that the Duke was very keen to be considered as the next Governor-General of Australia and was hoping my father would help him secure the position. The Duke had certainly thoroughly enjoyed Dad's company on that tour of Australia in 1920. He was only 26 at the time (and also the Prince of Wales, as his father was still on the throne) so he was closer in age to Dad than the other dignitaries and politicians, who he probably found a little stuffy!

The Duchess of Windsor, Wallis Simpson, was very kind to Patty, taking her around the top couturiers and milliners, which delighted her. Patty loved fashion; she was very petite and always beautifully dressed. She regularly featured on the "Best Dressed Women of Australia" list. Her outfits featured elegant suits and dresses, usually accessorised with stylish jewellery and chic hats. She had the tiniest feet (a UK size 3) and had struggled to find shoes that fit her properly in Australia. She was thrilled to discover Rayne in London, the shoe manufacturer that had received a royal warrant for making shoes for Queen Mary (the wife of King George V). Rayne designed fabulous court shoes in every colour imaginable and later, when Rayne brought their shoe sample (only in size 3 to save weight on shipping) to Australia, Patty always had first choice of the new season as the company was delighted to have her wear their shoes at society events.

From Europe, Dad and Patty travelled to the US, arriving in New York on Patty's nineteenth birthday, on 24 November 1938, having sailed from Southampton on the SS *Normandie*. They stayed in the famous Waldorf

Hotel and enjoyed the opera season. Next, they visited Florida, and then stopped in New Orleans on the way to Texas, after which they travelled up to San Francisco. At some point during this trip, Patty was excited to learn how to drive a car and drove them a good part of the journey.

Dad and Patty arrived back in Sydney on 20 March 1939, almost a year to the day after they left. I remember eagerly waiting on the docks for them to arrive. We were thrilled to see them when they disembarked, but then dismayed to discover that we were not going to receive our gifts because the dock labourers (the "dockies") were on strike. Our luck swiftly changed again when one of the dockies saw Dad and recognised him. (My father had been the MP for the dock area at one point.)

"Don't you worry, Greg," he said, "We'll get your luggage off this ship right away." And off came my father's *seventeen* pieces of luggage that were stuffed full of gifts for all the family.

In those days, fur coats were very fashionable and Patty had bought several in Russia for all the girls. My own gift was a pink velveteen evening cape with a big white fur collar, which was probably rabbit – not something that would be so socially acceptable nowadays.

On his return to Australia, my father reassured everyone – based on the conversations he'd had with many smart political minds in Europe and America – that Hitler's ambitions had been contained and that there was no threat of war in Europe.

4

War on the Horizon

I looked up to my father enormously. He strongly believed that no matter how much money you had, everyone should be worthy of their place in society. And he felt that being qualified to do something was one of your best ways of doing that. If you couldn't get qualified to do something, you should at least find *something* you could do to establish your place in society. I think he felt that, ultimately, life is not about what money you have or earn, it's more about what you contribute to society. He respected anyone with a strong work ethic.

Dad was a big fan of the popular boxing promoter of the day, Jimmy Sharman. My father and Jimmy, and the men who partook in these boxing bouts, had all grown up together as kids, or at least were aware of each other's families. Most of the people in Jimmy's shows were from central and western New South Wales so they knew my father from Parkes. They travelled the country going to various country shows. They would invite people in the audience to try their luck at fighting one of the professional boxers, to see if they could beat them.

One of the biggest boxing bouts that Jimmy ran was the one at the annual Sydney Show.

We loved going to the big Sydney Show with my father. My mother never came. It was an exhausting outing with considerable distances to walk. But for us children, especially the younger ones, it was a huge highlight of our year.

The Sydney Royal Easter Show is a huge annual agricultural show at which farmers showcase their livestock and produce, which are judged for a range of prizes. It has been going since 1823 so for almost 200 years now. The show always opens on the Wednesday before Easter. We would go on the Thursday as it was still early on in the show's run and also many people wouldn't get the Thursday off. It started to get crowded by Good Friday and was probably packed over the weekend. There was always the Grand Parade, in which the top prize-winners displayed their award-winning livestock and produce. It could really boost your sales if you won an award at the Sydney Show so it was an important event for farmers, and still is today.

A family tradition that we relished was eating the famous "Sargent's Pies" – a typical Australian meat pie – for our lunch at the show. One year when we got home, Gregory told our mother that there were many "spies in the show". She looked alarmed until he said, "Yes, *Sargent*-spies." She wasn't amused, but we all thought it was incredibly funny and often repeated the family joke.

We enjoyed watching the demonstrations of various agricultural practices at the Sydney Show, for example sheep dipping. This is the practice of making sheep swim through a narrow trough called a "race" filled with a disinfectant mixture that prevents them from getting infested by parasites like ticks and blowflies. The sheep need to be coated from head to toe so you have to push their heads under using a long handle that has a curved piece of metal on it. They are fully soaked by the time they get to the end of the race, and in a desperate hurry to get out of it. Anyone standing too close also ends up coated in the disinfectant!

We were actually no strangers to this practice and were used to seeing sheep dipping take place on our farm, Pomeroy.

My father had originally bought Pomeroy so that my mother's mother – our Grandma Hermes – had a place to live. She had come to live with my parents some time after her husband had died in 1917 but I imagine our house began to get a little noisy and crowded for her as the family rapidly expanded.

Dad bought Pomeroy from a farmer he'd met who was retiring. It was just over the Blue Mountains between Oberon and Tarana. We children often went up there for the school holidays, but the train only went as far as Jenolan (where the world-famous caves are located). Someone from the farm would come and pick us up from the station. Sometimes we drove with our parents in the Rolls-Royce.

Dad owned a very smart Rolls-Royce, which he travelled around the country in, visiting all his businesses. It would have been too much to drive himself such long distances in a car that was quite a handful to manoeuvre (there was no power-assisted steering back then) so he employed a driver called Bill Rourke. Like George, our cook, Bill was a man who had fallen on bad times in life – in Bill's case it was because he'd been badly affected by the mustard gas he was exposed to in the trenches during the First World War. As with George, my father was keen to help a man who, otherwise, could have ended up in very bad circumstances.

The Rolls-Royce was known throughout New South Wales. One sighting of the rather rare car on the outskirts of a town, and word would go round like wildfire that Dad was visiting. Before mobile telephones there were town gossips; they were possibly just as fast!

When Dad was at the height of his political career, the Australian press had been quick to reveal his wealth. One publication (we are unsure which as we only have the newspaper cutting with the date) ran a story on 11 December 1926 with the headline, "Labour's Rich Capitalists" and singled Dad out in a subtitle that reads, "Greg McGirr's £3600 Car" with reference to his Rolls-Royce. The article goes on to mention that the *Labor Daily* (the official newspaper of the Labour Party) had recently featured Dad in a piece entitled, "Greg's Possessions", listing his property interests, which included several hotels and shops across New South Wales. While it was the "left of centre" party, it seems the Labour Party of the day was proud of its members (even ex-members) who were self-made men and contributed to the growth of Australia.

The actual Rolls-Royce I remember would have been Dad's *second* because the first one came to a rather sticky end when it was involved in a fatal collision near Lithgow in November 1931. *The Canberra Times* ran the rather oddly worded headline, "Two Killed in Terrific Car Crash" and went on to report that "Greg McGirr's Rolls-Royce was wrecked" when two vehicles collided travelling at high speed.

The story went that Dad had loaned the Rolls-Royce to a charity for a few days. They needed to transport a group of opera singers to a gala event in a country town somewhere. The charity had its own driver, so luckily Bill wasn't involved in the crash. They happened to be travelling on the very day that a new law was coming into force in Australia regarding the transportation of goods. Many loads that had traditionally been transported by road now had to be transported by rail, which had become a cheaper and more efficient mode of transport. The lorry drivers were furious about their loss of business and were holding wakes to mourn the "death" of their jobs. One of those drivers, who had been attending a wake and was presumably a little worse for wear after drinking, collided head on with the Rolls and several people were killed. The most macabre thing was that a black wreath that the lorry driver had tied to the front of his lorry ended up adorning the wreckage of the Rolls.

Many years later, by sheer coincidence, I met someone whose aunt was involved in that crash. He informed me of this as soon as he heard my name because he had never forgotten the name of the owner of the Rolls-Royce involved. He was astonished to find out that Greg McGirr was my father!

Those family trips to Pomeroy were not the most comfortable journeys, with so many of us packed in. As big as the car was, it still didn't have enough seats for everyone. I had to sit in a little cane chair that was squeezed into the rather spacious area between the driver's seat and the passenger seat. This made me cross as I felt it was rather undignified. When Nonna was no longer a baby and needed a seat, she took the makeshift chair and I was promoted to a proper seat, which I was very pleased about!

There was also no room for our luggage inside the car, so this was wrapped in canvas, to protect it, and strapped to the roof. Dad was constantly irritated about the amount of luggage my mother travelled with as it took so long to be strapped on and he was always impatient to get to the farm. One day, as we were speeding along, one of the bags came loose and fell into the road. Assuming it was our mother's bag, he instructed Bill to keep going.

"It's actually your bag, Mr McGirr," Bill informed him

"Stop the car, immediately!" my father shouted.

I must have been around six years old when we first went up to Pomeroy because I remember Nonna was around but still a baby.

We were all fascinated by the place, it was like nothing we'd ever experienced. There was a separate cookhouse because there was no electricity, so you had to cook in a big oil-fuelled oven and the heat would build up so much (in addition to the heat from the sun, which was exceptionally hot in the summer months) that you couldn't live in the same structure. They would only run the oven once a week. Most farmhouses in those days were built as two separate structures for sleeping and cooking in.

Our light in the evenings came from kerosene lamps.

I shall never forget the first night we spent at Pomeroy. We had finished dinner and we were all sitting around the fire. Gregory, who must have been around eight years old, was sitting on a little bench. Suddenly a bolt of lightning came down the chimney, went under Gregory's seat and exploded somewhere. We were terrified. The very next day, Dad had a lightning conductor fitted.

Before we got our own generator to provide us with electricity, we had a kerosene refrigerator so that we could keep our meat fresh for longer. But until we got that, we had to keep our meat in a "meat safe". I remember my horror upon hearing that, in Aboriginal culture, you didn't throw meat away if it went bad because if you kept it, eventually it goes so bad that it starts turning green… at that point, it's apparently safe to eat again!

At some point, my father started to expand and update the property. He had a whole second floor added, put a veranda on the front and built a little attic room that you accessed from an open staircase on the side of the building. Nonna and I loved sleeping up in the attic room because it had a tin roof; when it rained we loved to hear the rain hammering on it.

We were very pleased when the postal service finally improved and would actually deliver to us out there, but we still had to make it exceptionally easy for them. We had to build two letterboxes of a particular height on either side of the road so that the postman could approach from either direction and not have to switch sides of the road or get out of his vehicle; he could just drive up, lean out of his window and reach the letterbox, whichever way he was going.

We eventually got a proper toilet, too. This was a huge relief. When we first stayed at Pomeroy, the loo was just a pit in the ground with a seat built above it. As a child I hated sitting there because the place was crawling with giant tarantulas; you'd sit on the loo watching them, praying they didn't move!

I've never been a fan of spiders but my mother loved them, despite the fact that Australia is full of poisonous ones. She had a pet spider that built a nest amongst her china collection inside a window at our house in Sydney. I never quite understood her liking such small insects, some of which could kill you. They've developed good antidotes now, if you can get to a hospital in time, but in those days you had no chance if you got bitten by, say, an Australian Redback, one of the most venomous types of spider that exists.

Grandma Hermes loved living on the farm at Pomeroy. Her bedroom was just off the lounge in the front building. She was quite an eccentric and one year I remember her making seventeen Christmas puddings for no apparent reason other than she knew how much we loved Christmas pudding. I suppose we ate them throughout the year!

Country life took some adjusting to. We were all city slickers, used to a lot of home comforts, but we soon came to love life on the farm, too. It was a charming place, and when each of us was at university we would often take a few friends up there to experience the joys of Pomeroy.

Eventually, Grandma Hermes wasn't able to manage on her own so Dad hired someone to look after her and take care of things on a daily basis. Gordon was a former jockey from Liverpool. I remember how short he was; he was the height of a child but still a grown man! He maintained the buildings and ensured that Grandma was safe. And, to my relief, he took over the milk run. Before he came along, Gregory and I would be sent to collect the milk from the man who used to own the farm, who had moved to a more manageable place a mile away. A two-mile round trip was a long trek for us youngsters to walk.

Gordon also looked after our horses, which included Dad's huge grey horse called Speculation, my chestnut pony called Don and the old miniature Shetland pony that my father bought for Nonna. She was a retired trick pony and had been taught to do various stunts in the circus she had previously performed in. We called her Kewpie after the popular dolls of the day.

Kewpie dolls were rather strange-looking things with little plastic points on their heads. These were supposed to resemble tufts of hair but it just looked like the dolls had very odd-shaped heads!

Kewpie the trick pony was a pretty shrewd little thing. If a new rider got on her and she sensed any nervousness, she would walk on for a few yards, then throw the rider off and dart through a fence. I was thrown off like that a couple of times. The family would just stand there laughing, wondering who would actually make it through the fence first… Kewpie, or me running away from her! Luckily it wasn't too far to the ground when you came off the back of little Kewpie, so only my pride was hurt.

We had years of fun at Pomeroy. As well as the exciting sheep-dipping events, we loved to watch the travelling sheep shearers at work. They would travel around the country, stopping at farms to shear the entire population of sheep for a fee.

We had a large flock of sheep, which actually grew dramatically one year when we found 150 sheep that no one knew existed. They'd established themselves as a group in a previously inaccessible mountain area. They probably weren't best pleased to have been found!

Life on the farm was always such a wonderful respite from life in the city. In Sydney, we were all busy bees. As my sisters got older and started going to dances and social events, the press loved to follow them around and photograph them. Muffie, in particular, was very popular and glamorous, and never out of the society pages in the newspapers. I remember there was quite a rivalry between Muffie and our mother. Muffie wasn't a natural beauty but her face was full of character. She had an engaging personality and could be very charming.

Gwen was a force unto herself. She could be quite selfish and demanding. She'd never put herself out for you, but she'd expect everyone else to drop everything at a moment's notice to help *her*. However, she was also very self-conscious about how she looked and would trawl through all the photo albums removing pictures of herself.

I remember a particular incident when Muffie and I were sitting on our beautiful balcony at *Sunray* in Sydney. We had a lovely old rocking chair out there that caught the best of the afternoon sunshine. Gwen came to say she was going off to the shops and Muffie said there was something she needed but couldn't remember what it was. Gwen just wouldn't wait for her to remember. She said, "If you can't remember, Muffie, I'll have to go." Muffie got quite angry and said, "Oh, just go then!" And Gwen did.

Gwen studied very hard at Sydney University; she was reading medicine like our eldest brother Jack. Gwen was always very focused, and things had a way of working out for her. I remember one of her first jobs, after qualifying as a doctor, was in Goulburn, a small town in New South Wales. The local policeman met her when she arrived and showed her the car she needed to use to travel out to see patients in the more remote parts. Gwen confessed that she didn't know how to drive and certainly didn't have a licence.

"No problem," said the policeman, and promptly wrote her out a licence. "You'll pick it up quick enough," he said!

Muffie, who was reading a law degree, didn't have Gwen's discipline. She was completely distracted and rarely turned up for her lectures. She would regularly borrow lecture notes for her exams from her friend, Gough Whitlam, who went on to become PM of Australia (1972–75)! For a while Muffie got away with asking friends to answer for her when her name was called in roll call, but she got found out when she asked a male friend to answer for her. When they called out "Beatrice McGirr" and a deep voice said, "Yes, here," the gig was up.

She was only called "Muffie" in our family. To her friends she was "Beatrice" or "B".

But it wasn't all parties and glamour for Muffie; she was heavily involved in fundraising, and got involved on the committee for the new opera house.

Patty was incredibly practical and had such strong values. She fell into the shadows slightly as the older girls and Jack had such big personalities, but Patty had a beautiful, sweet nature. She was never belligerent, unlike both Gwen and Muffie, who could be. Gwen and Muffie were competitive and regularly got the praise they craved. Patty wasn't given as much credit for her abilities. There was always talk in the family, too, of how a big accident had really affected Patty when she was young. She got quite badly burnt in an accident when a vapour lamp (a contraption that would give off vapours to help children with whooping cough) got knocked over.

My memories of Patty are always of her kindness and the wonderful advice she gave me. I got tips from her on all kinds of practical matters. She was obviously a huge source of information when it came to fashion trends, and I valued her opinions of people; she was a good judge of character.

The boys were very different from each other. Jack really had his own life. We were all off to school before Jack got out of bed. He would have a very leisurely breakfast made by George around mid-morning. Jack was studying to be a doctor but his big love was sports. Raymond was exceptionally bright, something of a genius, but he was a troubled boy, very spoilt by our mother, and this made him quite demanding. Gregory wasn't academic but he was good with his hands and was always interested in farming, possibly as a result of all our trips to Pomeroy.

Nonna was a little spoilt but she deserved to be spoilt because she was just so lovely; she was treasured by all of us, but mostly by me. I loved her to bits and would do anything for her. When I was old enough to learn dressmaking, I loved making dresses for Nonna. It was like she was my own living doll!

With a growing family and an expanding business empire, my father was always on the road visiting his properties. We sometimes went with him on those trips.

I once learnt, first hand, that Dad was a shrewd businessman, but ultimately an honest one, when I went with him to visit a hotel he owned the freehold of. The tenant told Dad that the staircase at the back of the property needed to be replaced. Dad replied that he was sure it was fine (because he didn't want to spend money on it) at exactly the moment *I fell through it*! Obviously Dad had to eat his words and agree to replace the staircase immediately.

I always loved hearing my father's stories about travelling around the New South Wales outback. I particularly love the story of how he once arrived at one of his pubs in Quambone, about 200 kilometres north of Dubbo (and more or less the very end of civilization!) in a very hot and dusty state. He was extremely tired and told the manager he was desperate for a bath. A few minutes later Dad looked out of the bedroom window and saw a couple of men pulling up a fence. When he shouted at them, "What are you doing? I've just had that fence built!" they replied, "You said you wanted a bath. This is the only wood around these parts." (The only way to get hot water in those days was to heat it over a fire so they were intending to use the fencing for firewood.)

My father thought about it briefly before sighing and telling the men to carry on. When a man needs a bath – he explained, whenever he told the story – he has to have a bath!

As a young child, I don't remember being aware of money, or wondering whether we had much or not. Children generally don't give money a second thought unless they are made to think about it by their parents. The first time I got an inkling about our wealth was when a plumber, who was doing some work in our home, remarked to me, "Your dad's got some dough."

I think I was around 11 or 12 years old. That was the first time it dawned on me that we were wealthier than most other families.

Dad was generous to a fault. He'd had nothing growing up so he wanted his children to have everything. He didn't believe in hoarding money, he wanted us children to have it and use it as and when we wanted it. Mum and Dad set up a bank account for each of us, that they added money to over the years, to provide us with tuition and subsistence when we were each at high school and university.

While I was only ever on a strict allowance of £1 a week, if I asked Dad for anything he'd give it to me. I once went to Melbourne to visit Patty. She had moved there with her husband shortly after she got married. Dad gave me £300 for my little holiday. I went shopping on the first day and blew through it pretty fast. One frivolous purchase was a lizard-skin handbag. I'll never forget buying it. Having used up all my money, I telephoned Dad and asked him for another £300. He sent it straight away!

(Until 1966, when the currency was decimalised and changed to dollars and cents, we had pounds, shilling and pence in Australia, just like in the UK.)

In the early years of the Second World War, we weren't too affected in Australia, but as war raged on through the early 1940s, Japanese submarines started arriving in Sydney Harbour and things got serious, particularly for my father.

Unfortunately, Greg McGirr had not made himself too popular in Japan. He'd been there on a business trip around 1934 with a friend in the hotel business. Whilst being shown around the city by a group of businessmen, my father made a comment about Japanese women being very servile because they were always walking behind the men. It was taken as a great insult. My father's secretary's sister worked for a Japanese company in Sydney and discovered that my father was on some kind of hit list that Japan had created. If they had successfully invaded Australia, we reckon the Japanese would have taken him out!

War eventually affected us all. My sisters all had boyfriends who would often visit us. Before the war they were big, strong, handsome men. They went off to war and when we next saw them, they looked like skeletons. It was shocking to see how much the men who had fought in the war aged after their experiences. In particular, those who'd been prisoners of war in Japan had suffered terribly. The Japanese soldiers believed that, if you were taken prisoner, it was your moral duty to commit hara-kiri (a particularly brutal way of committing suicide) rather than remain a prisoner of the enemy. When Australian soldiers didn't kill themselves upon being captured, their Japanese counterparts would mock them and punish them for being so weak. They couldn't understand how a man could allow himself to live as a prisoner, and not do the honourable thing and take his own life.

With the increasing threat from the Japanese, in 1942 many schools decided to evacuate. My school chose not to evacuate, but Nonna's school did. We were at different schools because, wanting us all to maintain our individuality, my mother had sent us girls to two different schools. Daughters one, three and five (Muffie, Patty and Nonna) were sent to the Loreto School which was strong in the arts, while daughters two and four (Gwen and I) attended Monte Sant'Angelo Mercy, which was stronger in sciences, and testament to that is the fact that Gwen and I became a doctor and dentist respectively. Both of these Catholic day schools for girls are still going strong in Sydney at time of writing.

Obviously Muffie and Patty had left school long before 1942 so Nonna would have been on her own without any family around. My parents were worried that she'd be homesick so they decided I should go with her to their intended evacuation location: Springwood, in the Blue Mountains. It was a good thing I was sent along; I ended up helping the police retrieve Nonna and her friend after they decided to run away! I remember this dramatic incident quite clearly. At a certain point, one day, someone noticed that they were missing. When they didn't return by nightfall, the police were called. I was allowed to go along with them into the bush, which was very frightening as it is so very dark at night. Although I wasn't half as frightened as Nonna and her friend, when we eventually found them on a deserted path in Sassafras Gully. They were petrified, having been spooked by all the glow-worms and fireflies that light up in the gully at night. They never ran away again!

Living in Springwood for a while during the war wasn't too bad. For one thing, we actually saw more of our beloved father during that time. It was on his route out to his various businesses around the state, so Dad would often show up and take us out for a bush-fire lunch – an Australian style picnic. We would drive out to a place where the bush had been cleared so that there was no danger of starting an actual bush fire. Then we'd make a small fire and barbecue whatever meat Dad had brought with him.

In all, I think Nonna and I were in Springwood for just over a year. When we got back to Sydney after the war had ended, I went straight into my exams to get a place at Sydney University.

I was also ready to learn how to drive by then.

The man who taught me how to drive was my father's driver, Pat, who had replaced Bill after the war.

During World War Two, Bill resumed his duties in the armed forces (he wasn't fit enough to be a full army driver but served as a ministerial driver) so Dad had given up the Rolls-Royce and drove himself around in a Chevrolet, which was easier to handle. After the war, Dad hired Pat and also found a new and very special car. It was a Wolseley; an elegant car made by Nuffield, and one of only two that had ever been shipped to Australia.

So I learned to drive in the Wolseley.

Pat had no nerves whatsoever. He would take me into the centre of Sydney where I would frequently stall across tramlines. The tram would be coming towards us, its bell clanging frantically and I would start panicking thinking I wouldn't get the car started in time to move it before the tram hit us. But Pat would be unmoved, telling me I could do it, and sure enough I'd always get the car started again and move just in time. He was obviously a good teacher because I passed my driving test first time.

I had great fun driving my friends around. Sydney Harbour Bridge had a tollbooth and you had to pay a certain amount for each person in your car. I had one friend who never had any money. He used to hide in the foot-well, feeling rather clever that he had dodged the toll fare without being found out!

5

University Careers: a Family Tradition

As the war was ending in 1945, it was time for me to choose my degree subject. I had long planned to study medicine like my brother, Jack, and sister, Gwen, but places were very limited and I finally realised that there was no hope in the world of me getting into Sydney University to study medicine. My family suggested that I apply to study dentistry. I followed their advice and got a place.

When word got out that I had secured a place at Sydney University, *The Sydney Morning Herald* published the news under the headline, "University Careers: a Family Tradition." They went into detail about me following in the footsteps of some of my older siblings; they still loved any news about our family.

There were only seven women in my year studying dentistry. The others studied much harder than me. I was a bit preoccupied with my social life… and knitting!

By this time, knitting had become something of an obsession with me. Our Northern Irish housekeeper, Katie, had got me hooked. Initially she taught Patty how to knit. I was desperate to learn but Katie said I was too young. I wasn't even allowed into her room to watch. Eventually, after what felt like an eternity, the day came when Katie deemed me old enough to learn. From the day she started teaching me (when I was probably around eight or nine years old) I never stopped.

Katie eventually left us to get married but she'd come back and visit once a week, and I was always proud to show her my knitted creations.

The very first wool I bought was the most ghastly bright yellow colour. During the war it was hard to get any wool at all. If you wanted wool you had to use some of the ration points that were allocated to every family. My mother wouldn't hear of me using our precious ration points for wool when she had so many mouths to feed. The points were only to be used for food and other essentials, such as petrol. I found a way around this obstacle when I stumbled across a shop in the Imperial Arcade that sold wool as well as completed knitted garments. They explained that, if you agreed to knit a garment for them to sell, not only did you get the wool, but you also got a small payment. It seemed like an excellent plan to me, although there was a slight catch. The patterns were really difficult and fussy, and full of lacy bits and tricky stitches. And often they'd insist on giving you white wool, because a customer had requested it. This would be a devil to keep clean. But I got on with it; it was worth it to me to be able to keep knitting. I would do anything to knit!

Everyone knew my whereabouts from the "clack-clacking" of my knitting needles. One of my lecturers at Sydney University once stopped his lecture and walked up to me and said, pointedly, "I hope I'm not disturbing you, Miss McGirr."

"No, not at all," I answered pleasantly, missing his sarcasm.

I was promptly thrown out of that class!

I got through two years at the University of Sydney Dental School, with a few distinctions in some subjects, but I didn't pass everything and ended up having to retake a couple of courses. This didn't bother me until one girl on my course made a comment that stopped me in my tracks. She said, "You don't deserve to pass a thing; you're one of the laziest people I've ever met in my life."

I will never forget how much her words stung, but they did help to determine the course of my life.

My father's health had been deteriorating for some time and towards the end of the second year of my dental course, in 1947, my father's health took quite a serious turn for the worse.

Nonna had secured a place to start at Sydney University in 1948, but my mother had grown reliant on her help at home in looking after my father since his health had deteriorated. We all felt that our mother needed someone who could stay at home with her and help manage my father's care. The older siblings were mostly married or living in their own places by then. Having taken a slight hit by failing a couple of courses, I suggested that it would be fairer if I postponed my degree to let Nonna go to university, and I would stay at home and help take care of my father.

Dad had been diagnosed with a condition called "thromboangiitis obliterans", also known as "Buerger's disease" after the doctor who first described it, pathologically. The disease, which is usually brought on by the use of tobacco products, leads to the inflammation of veins and arteries, and the formation of blood clots, which can result in the amputation of affected limbs. If the blood clots travel to the heart or brain, they can obviously be fatal. King George VI, the Queen's father, was diagnosed with the disease and underwent major surgery, but he never stopped smoking, despite doctors warning him that he was jeopardizing his life. He eventually died at the age of 56.

When I think of all that travelling Dad was doing for work, *while* having that disease, I realise it must have been especially tiring for him. If you're unfamiliar with Australia and you live in a small country, you can't imagine the kinds of distances my father was travelling on a regular basis. He was forever on the road, travelling between his numerous establishments, and the quality of the roads would have been nothing like those we drive on today. And there was no high-tech suspension or air conditioning in vehicles then. Travelling by road took a real toll on your body, even if someone else was driving. My father smoked, but many people smoked in those days. The dangers were not nearly as well known and documented as they are now. Smoking was even *promoted* as having some health benefits.

A fairly experimental operation for sufferers of Buerger's disease became available at that time and my father agreed to have it. While he was recovering from the surgery, Jack was visiting and was in mid-conversation with him when Dad died suddenly. A blood clot that had formed during the surgery had travelled to his heart or brain and killed him instantly.

Greg McGirr died on 23 March 1949. He was 69.

*

Coming to terms with Dad not being around was very hard. He had been such a huge presence in our family and it was the first time we had lost someone so close to us. We had known of plenty of people who had lost loved ones during the war but, fortunately, we hadn't been closely affected. Losing Dad was my first experience of real grief.

We were determined to give Dad the very best send-off; he was very popular and his funeral was packed. My clearest memory, though, is of worrying about what I should wear. I had a dark suit but nothing to wear with it, so I knitted myself a black bib.

When I look back, I am grateful I got to spend what turned out to be Dad's final year so close to him. As much as that comment by my fellow student, about me being so "lazy", had hurt my feelings, I have to admit it did me a favour. It gave me some precious time with my father at the end of his life, and it allowed Nonna to go to university. It also meant that I ended up pursuing things that I might not have done if I'd carried on with my studies at that point.

And of course, there are certain people I never would have met if I hadn't taken that break in my studies…!

I could have gone straight back to university after Dad died, but I was still grieving and didn't feel motivated to go. I also felt I should stay at home and keep an eye on my mother. I didn't want her feeling lonely. George had retired by then. Grandma Hermes had come to live with us, but her health was failing, too. She died in December 1951 at the ripe old age of 92. Later on, my mother found companions to live with her, as was quite customary for a widow in those days, but in those initial months and years after she lost her husband and then her mother within a couple of years, I was my mother's chief companion.

While she welcomed my company at home, my mother also thought I should start doing something practical to fill my time. She kept nudging me to find something. I thought of getting a part-time job so I rang up a very classy family in the neighbourhood who I'd heard were looking for a nanny. The woman asked me what I could cook. I said nothing much, and that was when I realised I had no real practical skills whatsoever... apart from knitting.

Eventually, my mother suggested that I do the cookery course that my sister, Patty, had done at Sydney Technical College. I was reluctant at first, but she gently pushed me into it.

"Just call up and see what they say," she suggested.

So I did.

If the administrator I spoke to on the phone had said, "Come along in a couple of weeks," I honestly don't think I ever would have gone. But she said, "Turn up on Monday with a white coat, notebook and pencil."

So I did.

Going to cooking school was perfect for me at that point; it really helped distract me as I tried to get over the grief of losing my dad. I think it was good that I had a bit of a routine, and it was something completely new. Also, the girls and teachers on my course were all very pleasant people; I kept in touch with some of them for years.

I was on the four-year course and no one had completed the full four-years in over ten years (Patty had done the two-year course). I imagine many girls started the course but then left to get married. I was really determined to stick it out and, along with four other girls (out of the seven or eight who originally started) I completed the full course in only three years. We were so dedicated, they allowed us to "fast-track" the qualification. It was still only part time – about two days a week, I think – but I loved every minute of it and had never worked so hard at anything before.

Determined never to be branded "lazy" again, I also made an effort to get involved with groups and organisations doing charity work. This was obviously inspired by my mother's work. I served on several committees including the Sydney Opera House planning committee that Muffie had been part of. I also did some work for the Red Cross and the Sydney University Settlement project.

I cannot over emphasise how much those experiences, in the years after Dad died, really changed me and shaped my life. I came across all sorts of people I wouldn't have met otherwise. I learnt how various organisations were run and how committees worked. I was very warmly welcomed into these groups and it really built my confidence.

By the time I was ready to go back and finish my dentistry degree, I had really matured. I'd achieved something concrete by finishing my cooking qualification, and I'd had my eyes opened to a side of life I'd never experienced before. I had probably found myself for the first time; I'd struck out on my own and had found a sense of identity as an individual that wasn't just assigned by being a McGirr girl. I was soon brought back to reality when one of the first patients I saw after I returned to my dental studies at Sydney University was a girl who was star-struck by the fact that I was the sister of "Beatrice McGirr". The press was still mad about Muffie in those days, especially since she'd married Tom Bateman, a fellow doctor, in 1941. She had started her family while completing her law degree and had become one of the first women in Australia to join the bar.

My own love life was just getting interesting, too. I had met a fellow dentist in my year called Don. He was a bit of a ladies' man, and completely obsessed with cricket, but I was quite enamoured with him.

I also became friends with many of my other fellow students, including the star student in our year, Kevin Gardner.

We all admired Kevin's work; he had superb manual dexterity. He would occasionally help his classmates but I was never one of the chosen ones. I knew he didn't rate my abilities at all. Once, when we were learning to make false teeth – for which you had to make a plaster mould – I was in the plaster lab working on mine and I noticed that Kevin was watching me. I got my hammer and knife out to work on the set I'd made, but I accidentally hit the plaster too hard and smashed my carefully made mould into pieces. I was furious that Kevin had watched me do it. And even angrier when he said, "I could see that was going to happen." I couldn't believe he had stood there watching me when he could have stopped me from destroying my hard work!

I was so irritated and became determined to get Kevin to help me somehow.

An occasion soon presented itself. I knew I needed to get good marks on this particular exercise. We were given a model of a mouth and had to bend some wires to show how we'd straighten the teeth. I was hopeless at bending wires so I went to Don and asked him, "Would you bend these wires for me and then I can solder them together?"

He was obviously more than happy to help me. Before this, I had been to see Kevin and asked him, "If I bend these wires would you solder them together for me?"

To my delight Kevin had actually agreed.

I thought I'd been very crafty and was heading for top marks, but after Don bent the wires on my mouth model, I took it to Kevin (claiming, of course, to have done the wire bending myself) so he could solder them in place. He took the model from me and said, "I know exactly whose work this is and it's just not good enough." He then threw the whole thing out of the eighth-floor window of Sydney Dental Hospital window. For the life of me I couldn't understand why he did that. I was fuming!

I ended up failing that module because I had no time to make a replacement.

Kevin rattled me on another occasion, too.

At a Dental Students' Association meeting we'd discovered that we were heavily in debt. To pay this off, I suggested doing what my family excelled at; I said we should throw a big fund-raising party. I offered up my family's home as a suitable party venue.

Our house, *Sunray*, in North Sydney was perfect for entertaining. We had extensive grounds; we even had a tennis court.

I loved playing tennis, although I never had anyone to play with because my siblings were all at school at different times from me or they'd left home. Thus, I got very good at serving… and carrying buckets of balls from one end of the court to the other!

We also had a couple of peacocks that roamed freely around the gardens and a kangaroo that had taken up residence on the tennis court. They always caused huge excitement for guests.

At a students' meeting, we assigned jobs. The whole class was expected to come and help set up the party. Kevin dutifully came with his sidekick, John (another dental student who used to stick by Kevin's side wherever he went). They were very useful, helping to hang ornaments on a big tree at the back of our house and doing other manual jobs. They did everything that was asked of them. But they left well before the garden party started and never actually attended it. I was really quite annoyed. But I didn't have too long to dwell over it because we were completely sold out and the whole event was a huge success. I'd used my cooking school contacts to get a huge incinerator, which we adapted into a barbecue with a massive piece of steel inside it so that we could cook 20 steaks at once. We got some fellow students who were ex-servicemen to man this giant grill. People had bought tickets for the meal and there was probably a raffle as well. We easily cleared the debt and made some profit.

It was a fabulous party and Kevin's loss that he missed it.

I was very proud – and more than a little relieved – to graduate with a degree in dentistry at the end of 1953 (although, for some reason, we have always been called the class of 1954).

No one was surprised when Kevin Gardner won the coveted prize for oral surgery, which came with the offer of a teaching job on the University staff for one year.

Unfortunately, Don did not graduate with the rest of us and was going to have to retake the year. I was getting a little frustrated with Don by then. I felt we had been courting for long enough to warrant getting engaged. I was rather naïve back then and hadn't realised that Don was quite the womaniser and possibly not ready to settle down.

There were a few other clues as to why I should have had some doubts.

I was a touch jealous that my younger sister, Nonna, had just got married. She'd married her wonderful husband, Peter Willis, in 1952 and had confided in me that the best thing about marriage was that you could have sex. Having been raised in a strictly Catholic family, this was our Holy Grail.

One day, Don and I were out doing a bit of shopping and we walked past a department store window display. There were a couple of single beds in the window and he remarked that they would be perfect for a married couple, that they were a better option than a double bed. This didn't sound too promising to me. If you ended up in single beds after years of marriage, fair enough, but to start there didn't sound like much fun at all!

We also had real problems with Don's mother. She wasn't keen on me at all, on account of my religion. They were Presbyterian and when I met her for the first time, she was very cold towards me and said, "You Catholics want everything. You think you've got the keys to heaven!"

Don and I had gone to see his mother to try to get her blessing before we got engaged. I was keen to publish it in the local papers. After that meeting, I thought Don was going to defy his mother and propose, at least that was the impression he gave me. But he suddenly went a bit cold and said it was probably best to postpone getting engaged until after he graduated the following year. His official excuse was that he needed to focus on his studies but I'm pretty sure he was afraid of going against his mother.

The only option for me at that point was to get a job. The problem was, there had been a mass graduation from our year and I didn't fancy my chances against some of the other, better dentists. Dental jobs were hugely over-subscribed at that time. Sydney University was producing around 150 dentists a year but there was only work for about 50 of us. There were plenty of jobs, however, in the UK. The recently launched NHS was crying out for well-qualified doctors and dentists, especially after losing so many men during the war. Australians, New Zealanders and South Africans (the Commonwealth countries from which the UK recognised dental qualifications) were heading to the UK in droves.

Dentists in Australia who didn't get jobs often ended up doing manual work. Several of them had been working on building new roads. I certainly couldn't see myself doing that! Eventually I made plans with my friend Jill, who was about to graduate as a doctor, to travel to London in search of work.

*

On some level, I was probably testing Don. I told him my plans and said that, if he was serious about me, he could join me in the UK when he graduated.

Don never showed up.

But Kevin did.

6

A Woman Goes Walkabout

Before we left for the UK, however, the UK came to us!

We were thrilled and excited in Australia when, in February 1954, the newly crowned Queen Elizabeth II chose to come and visit us on her tour of Commonwealth countries less than a year after her coronation. She was the first – and only, since she is still on the throne – reigning UK monarch to have set foot on Australian soil.

My great friends, Yvonne and Rhoda McNamee, had travelled to the UK the year before and had told me all about how exciting it was to stand outside Buckingham Palace watching the coronation procession in June 1953. People didn't generally have televisions in those days so most Australians had only ever seen pictures of the Royal Family in newspapers, or possibly heard them speak on the radio.

The Royal Visit was a huge occasion for us.

I remember the celebrations very well. People were hanging out of trees to try to get a glimpse of Her Majesty as she arrived by boat into Sydney Harbour. My brother-in-law, Bing Molyneux, Patty's husband, was very tall; someone put a ladder up against him to climb up and get a better view!

There was a great deal of excitement and speculation over whether or not the Queen would wear a hat to keep the sun off her face. In the end, she did wear a hat that was cleverly designed to shield and show her face at the same time. It was made of black transparent straw and featured a brilliant pink and turquoise feather.

I was very fortunate and honoured to be invited, as a representative of my family, to the garden party at Government House in Sydney that was given in honour of Her Majesty. Members of my family had often been invited to big parties at Government House because of the charity work we all did. I'd been to the Governor's garden parties before so I must have been on some sort of official list. At that time I was the only unmarried girl in the family so I also could have been invited on account of all of that... especially since I had been a debutante.

We were one of those traditional families that "presented" their daughters at a debutantes' ball. In Sydney this was the University Settlement Ball, first held in 1933 (there was a gap during the war, from 1941 until 1946), which raised money for the University Settlement. In London it was organised by Queen Charlotte's Hospital.

It was a huge privilege to be "presented" to the Governor General, but with privilege also comes responsibility and it was our responsibility to help raise money for people who were in need.

I remember that, at the time of my debut, the Duke of Gloucester was the Governor General of Australia. We all wore white floor-length dresses with wide, full skirts. Mine was made of satin damask that was trimmed around the neckline with some gorgeous Brussels lace that had been bought for me especially for the occasion by my mother. It was beautifully made, with little raised shiny white flowers embroidered onto the material. I must have had an elaborate hair-do for the occasion because I remember someone commenting on how lovely my hair looked.

My debut was in 1946, during my first year at university (before I left to help out at home when my father was dying). It was the first time the event was to be held since the war ended, so there was plenty to celebrate. I think it took place in the Great Hall at the university. I remember a lot of bowing and curtseying, and dancing of course. There was a nice photo of me published in the *Sydney Telegraph*. They had also published lovely photos of Patty's debut at Buckingham Palace that had taken place during her stay in London with our father.

For the Queen's arrival in 1954, we all assembled for the garden party in the grounds of the Governor-General's house, Admiralty House, an extraordinary residence in Kirribilli that sits just below the northern entrance of the Sydney Harbour Bridge, looking directly across the Harbour at Bennelong Point, which was later to become the site of the new, iconic Sydney Opera House.

From the garden of Admiralty House, we watched the Queen being brought by boat across from the Royal Yacht, which had anchored in the Harbour. I didn't meet the Queen personally, but I wasn't too far away and it was all very exciting.

—

A few months later, it was time for me to set sail for England. I was excited but nervous. In particular I was worried about how much I'd miss Nonna. We had remained exceptionally close. She and Peter had a little girl by then: Vicky, who was not yet two years old.

Thinking it would help settle me and send me off on my travels with some reassurance, Nonna accompanied me on the first leg of the journey aboard the P&O liner that Jill and I were taking to London. Nonna sailed with us on the first short leg from Sydney to Melbourne, where she got off in order to travel back home.

We sailed on to Adelaide. When we arrived, I telephoned Nonna and was absolutely devastated to hear what had happened.

Nonna had telephoned Peter from Melbourne to tell him she had left the ship and was making her way home. In order to answer the phone, Peter had left Vicky in the bathtub where he'd been giving her a bath. Vicky had rolled over and drowned. By the time Nonna got home, her daughter was dead.

I am sure I must have fallen into a deep shock. I don't have a very clear memory of the rest of that journey or arriving in London. Being so close to Nonna, I felt that loss as deeply as if it had been my own baby.

Greg McGirr, photographed on his visit to the U.S.A. in 1938

Rachel Miller-Hermes, the Academic, c. 1906

Mother with Jack, Muffie, Gwen and baby Clarinda, c. 1920

Dad with me as a baby, Parkes, NSW, November 1927

Muffie, Jack, Gwen, Patty, Raymond, Gregory and me (on the chair), c. 1929

Mum and Dad at Randwick Races, early 1920s

Dad at Pomeroy, 1941

Mum and Grandma Hermes in Sydney, 1944

Me aged about 6 with Nonna, 2, 1933

Me at Monte St Angelo School, 1935

Mum, me and Nonna arriving at Le Bourget aerodrome, on our way to Paris, 1937

Me amongst the hydrangeas in Sydney, 1936

Dad, Nonna and me in Sydney, 1941

Me and Nonna, 1950

McGirr Family Christmas at Sunray, 1946

L-R Back Row: *George Bolam (family chef), Jack, Raymond, Greg Snr, Tom Bateman with Rosalind in his arms, Gwen, Trixie*
L-R Front Row: *Joyce McGirr with Carmel, Nonna, Muffie with Beatrice, Grandma Hermes, Rachel McGirr with Jocelyn, Patty with Philip, Edmund Bateman in toy car, Bing Molyneux with Alan, Greg McGirr on rocking horse.*

*Me and Mum just before
I left for London, 1954*

*Me on my Graduation
Day from the University
of Sydney, 1954*

PART TWO

London

7

Aussie Dentists in London

My first job in London was with a dental practice in Putney that belonged to a man called Lister Berwick. The practice was in a big house with a dovecote built into the eaves. I sent a picture of me standing beneath that dovecote to all my family as my first Christmas card from overseas.

This dental practice was the most traditionally English operation you could imagine. Every day at 4pm, the whole team stopped for tea. The dentists took it in turns to buy a cake for everyone. A pot of tea was brewed and we all had a cup of tea and a slice of cake while we shared what had happened that day in the practice and discussed anything exciting that was happening in the news.

The first thing that struck me – or rather alarmed me – when I arrived at that dental practice was how out of date everything seemed compared with what we were used to in Australia. For example, in Australia, we had been taught to take regular x-rays to look for signs of decay. But the British rarely took x-rays; and you could hardly blame them when you saw what they were expected to use. The Putney practice had an enormous x-ray machine that was completely out of date. In Australia we'd been trained to stand behind a lead plate to protect ourselves from over-exposure to the radiation. There was no such protection from this antiquated machine, and yet you could practically see the x-rays shooting out of it!

Dentists in the UK were also drilling teeth without giving patients any anaesthetic. People literally had to grin and bear it, or make the dentist stop when it got too painful. We Australian dentists introduced the use of anaesthetic in NHS dental treatments. If nothing else, the British people should be thankful to the Aussies for that!

Our dental standards were, in general, considerably higher than the UK's at that time and I think our contribution really pushed up the quality of dentistry in the UK, in particular for children.

Thanks to all the available jobs in the NHS, there were loads of dentists and doctors from Australia, New Zealand and South Africa living and working in London by then; the ones who'd been there for a while showed us new ones the ropes.

Jill and I found a little flat to share in Notting Hill and built a great circle of friends.

For our first Christmas in London, in 1954, we invited everyone over to our one-bedroom flat; we were all miles away from our families so it was comforting to be together; I remember it being a very merry gathering.

Throughout our time in that flat, people would regularly turn up and stay for a few nights on the sofa while they got settled, or moved on to the next location if they were just passing through. They could be family members, friends, or friends and family of friends; as long as we had some tenuous connection to them, they were welcome. There's a long tradition of Australians looking after each other and sharing accommodation with fellow Aussies overseas.

We really had so much fun in our first year in London. We had such busy social lives. I remember one particular Aussie dentist who took me out on a date soon after I arrived. He had been in my dental class. He was a little older than the rest of us as he'd been a serviceman in the war. He picked me up in his old banger of a car – which had wooden boards as its floor and was absolutely freezing because the wind rushed through the gaps – and took me to the horse races. His name was Dick Abbott and his son, Tony, became Prime Minister of Australia almost 60 years later!

I enjoyed my job, and all the socialising, but I also had itchy feet. I'd loved travelling around Europe as a child and was keen to do so again. The first place I wanted to go back to was Paris.

Having enjoyed my cookery course at Sydney Technical College so much, I was eager to do some additional training at the famous Cordon

Bleu School in Paris. I wanted to get the prestigious Cordon Bleu qualification, which was considered to be terribly chic in those days. I wrote to them and they said I could come to Paris for a three-week assessment and from that they could let me know how long it would take for me to train for my qualification.

I was very excited to step foot in the French capital again. I stayed in a little hotel off Avenue de l'Opéra and the first thing I did was go shopping. I was dying to buy some of the best cookware Paris had to offer; the kind of quality stuff that one buys and keeps for life. In particular I wanted a traditional French cocotte (a type of casserole dish, like a Dutch oven). I found a beautiful one and many other delightful items. The only problem was, I didn't know how I was going to carry it all back to London. Luckily one of my new friends, a really charming South African boy, decided to visit Paris with his friend while I was there. They drove over, taking the car ferry. I offered to reserve them a room opposite mine, which was on the sixth floor of my hotel. In return I asked them if they would take all my cookware back to England. They said they were happy to. We all went out for dinner on their final night and the boys wanted to stay out late. However, I said I had to go back to the hotel and get to bed as I had school early in the morning.

I knew the boys were leaving very early the next morning so I stacked all the heavy cookware up outside their hotel-room door. I went to bed but was woken up by a loud crash in the middle of the night, followed by a lot of shouting and swearing. They'd come home in the early hours, presumably with plenty of good French wine inside them, and had fallen over the pile of cookware! I went back to sleep hoping they weren't so cross with me that they decided not to take it with them, but it was all gone when I left my room in the morning and they delivered it safely to me in London when I returned.

I love that cocotte; I have made countless delicious dishes in it and it's still going strong today!

The assessment at the Cordon Bleu school seemed to go well. I struggled a little bit because it was all in French. We had learnt all the French cooking terms in Sydney, but we were only required to know how to spell them and recognise them written down. I had no idea at all how anything was pronounced, and French is not a language that sounds much like it's written, if you're a native English speaker, but I muddled through.

They were suitably impressed with my standard and said that I could get my qualification in three months rather than the full year it usually took. They had space for me to complete the three months of training the following year.

Back in London, I got busy with more travel plans. I had set my sights on travelling the length of the British Isles, from Land's End in Cornwall to John o' Groats, on the Northern tip of the Scottish mainland. However, my plans were seriously threatened by the rail strikes that plagued Britain during the 1950s when the trade unions were wielding their power. I was doing it in stages and I'd done the southern part of the route. I'd managed to hitchhike down to Cornwall with a nice man who had picked me up and driven me down from London (in the days when it felt safe for a woman to do that.) Now I was trying to work out how to get myself up to John o' Groats. I came up with rather a novel idea. I thought I'd buy myself a Vespa scooter. A motorbike didn't seem like my style but I rather liked the idea of a Vespa. They were all the rage then, especially for the modern, independent woman. Glamorous European actresses had been photographed on them. I rather fancied the idea of bombing around the country on a scooter.

I contacted the AA to ask them for the best route. In those days the AA (the Automobile Association of Great Britain) planned your route for you if you were going on a long expedition. They'd even find places for you to stay along the way if you asked them to. When I rang and told them I was planning to drive a Vespa up to Scotland, they told me I'd need a three-piece wetsuit. Growing up with my family plastered all over the society pages in Australia had made me rather fashion-conscious and nothing in the world was going to get me into a three-piece wetsuit. The AA said they wouldn't support my trip unless I wore one.

I saw my Vespa travel plans fading away.

But then a different offer altogether presented itself.

8

An Unexpected Proposal

Kevin arrived in London in early 1955 after he'd completed his year of teaching at the University of Sydney School of Dentistry. He experienced quite a shock to his system as he left at the height of summer in Sydney and arrived in London in the middle of the famous "Big Freeze" that gripped the country that winter, when there were record-breaking low temperatures around the country with many roads closed and communities cut off. The RAF had been drafted in to make drops of food and medical supplies over the worst affected areas.

When Jill and I came over, we took the Orient Line, a one-class ship, which meant you could mix with everyone. But Kevin and his friend Stephen had come on the P&O Line, which was a two-class ship. They found themselves the only young men in First Class, which was full of widows and young single women. They had rather a nice time socialising.

Shortly after he arrived, Kevin telephoned me and invited me over for dinner with a couple of our other Sydney University friends who had come over to London for work.

I travelled up to their flat in Wembley on the bus. I remember it being a long journey. These were the days before the Clean Air Act, when the smog was so bad that the conductor had to walk in front of the bus to make sure the road was clear!

Kevin and Stephen met me off the bus and we went back to their flat for a little gathering. During dinner they discussed their travel plans. They said they were planning to buy a Morris Minor and drive up to Scotland in it. Anne, a girl that Stephen was keen on, was travelling with them. It sounded like there was a fourth seat available (and no three-piece wet suit required) so I asked if I could join them. They agreed.

Kevin told me when they were planning to leave; it was around six months away. I gave him my address, and he gave me the exact date and time when they would pick me up.

I left feeling very excited about the travel plans, and I started putting things into motion, like booking time off from my job. But then I heard nothing from them for months and I started getting worried. Finally, I telephoned Kevin and asked if the plans had changed at all.

"No, nothing's changed," he said, plainly. He confirmed our arrangement, reminding me of the date and time they were going to pick me up, and warned me that it was going to be a tight squeeze for all of us and our luggage in the Morris Minor, so I could only bring one bag.

I was still worried that the plan wouldn't materialise for some reason, but I needn't have been. They arrived to pick me up bang on time and off we set for Scotland.

I don't think Kevin had a driving licence at that time – I remember his parents never drove or owned a car so it probably wasn't something he had prioritised, so I imagine Stephen did most of the driving, and I might have driven some of the way, too.

We covered an impressive distance on that trip. We made it all the way up to John o' Groats and, despite the cold temperatures, we were all impressed with the beautiful Durness Beach because the quality of the sand was as good as any you'd find on Australian beaches. Prior to that I'd been disappointed with the beaches I'd come across in the UK; most of them, like Brighton Beach, had been pebbly, with no sand to speak of at all.

We stayed in B&Bs, with the girls in one room and boys in the other. I began to wonder when Stephen was going to propose to Anne.

In one B&B, in Inverness, Kevin, Anne and I stayed up late after dinner; Stephen had gone to bed. It got quite late and Anne said she was tired and was going up to bed. When I said I would go too, she said she'd actually stay up a bit longer. I stayed up, too. This happened a couple more times before she finally *did* leave and I went with her. When we got up to the bedroom we were sharing, she seemed exasperated.

"Why did you come with me?" she asked me. "I was trying to leave you alone with Kevin."

"Whatever for?" I asked her, genuinely puzzled.

"Everyone knows he's keen on you and wants to propose," she said.

Well, you could have knocked me down with a feather. I had never entertained such a thought. I thought the purpose of the trip was to get Anne engaged, not me! I had only ever thought of Kevin as a friend. In any case, I thought, if he was keen on me then he had a funny way of showing it; he'd not been overly kind to me at university, always helping others but rarely me. He hadn't attended the big garden party I'd instigated. He'd more or less laughed at me as I broke my false teeth plaster mould. (It never occurred to me at the time that he might have been jealous of Don.)

My immediate response was to laugh and tell Anne that she was completely mistaken. It occurred to me that the boys might have made this up to put her off the scent; maybe Stephen wanted to make his proposal a surprise.

The next day, we started to drive back from Inverness and stopped off in Oban where there is a famous tower, McCaig's Tower, from which you get spectacular views of the coast and surrounding area. Kevin suggested that he and I go off for a walk. I was sure this was so that Stephen could be alone with Anne and propose to her.

When Kevin and I got to the tower, he turned around and said, completely out of the blue, "I'd like to marry you."

"What makes you think you'd like to marry me?" I batted back at him instantly.

"I've always known I wanted to marry you," he said.

I didn't know what to think or do. I was completely thrown.

"There are others, you know," was all I could think to say. "I'll have to give it some thought."

And we walked back to the car.

Not a terribly romantic moment!

When we got to Edinburgh the following day, Kevin left to catch a train back to London. Because, he said, he had to get back to work.

9

"A Good Grip on This Earth"

What I really needed was time to think things through. I didn't know how I felt. I had waited so long for an official proposal from Don and suddenly I'd got one from Kevin. I suppose I had felt a little spark for Kevin at some point – I certainly admired his dentistry work – but because I'd never had the slightest inkling that he had any intentions towards me, his proposal had come as a complete shock. I was possibly even a little cross that he'd never even given me a hint of anything like that. It was all so sudden; I really felt in quite a muddle. I also suddenly felt very alone and homesick. Usually I would sit up all night with Nonna and discuss something like this. I had never missed her more.

Fortunately, I had some more imminent travel plans. That would give me some breathing space, I thought. As soon as we got back to London, I did a quick turn around and was off again. As I left, I gave strict instructions to Jill not to let Kevin know where I had gone in case he tried to come after me. I needed time by myself.

My first stop was to a dentists' conference in Copenhagen where one of the topics up for discussion was dental implants. The Italians were at the forefront of this pioneering procedure, which was in its very early stages and still very experimental; people had lost half their jaws in botched implant operations!

After the conference I travelled from Denmark into neighbouring Sweden. I was heading to Finland, eager to visit the "land of a thousand lakes" – they estimate that they have almost 190,000 of them across the country! In Stockholm I decided to write to Kevin to turn him down. I sent him a short note saying, "I've given it some thought, but I couldn't possibly marry anyone while I'm so far from home. Life is too unreal over here."

I had a very rough journey on the boat trip from Sweden to Finland. I was sleeping on the deck and at one point this lovely Finnish girl, who later told me she'd once been an au pair in England and waxed lyrical about toast and marmalade, told me I was on "the wrong side" of the boat. I followed her to the other side where it wasn't so cold and windy. My kind travelling companion's family put me up for a night when we arrived, before packing me off on a train to Helsinki the next day with these beautiful red and white currants that they said were ideal for quenching thirst... and so they were.

I will never forget how kind the people in Finland – and indeed all of northern Europe – were; they would do anything to help a tourist, even go out of their way to help you find your destination. I think most people always treat tourists with great care and respect until the day comes when there's too many of them; then they resent them and start grumbling. That's certainly what happened in Sydney!

A sense of Australian solidarity was never far away on my travels. I met up with some girls from Sydney University in Stockholm. I told them that I'd bought a box of beautiful glassware locally and was worried about how to get through the rest of my travels without breaking any of it. They were travelling around Europe in a car and said they had room to put it on the back seat. They offered to drop it off with me when I got back to London. Not only was it incredibly kind of them, but think how different things were in those days, that you could go driving around Europe for a couple of months with a box of expensive glassware on the back seat of your car without fearing that someone would break in and steal it.

After Finland, I made my way back west to visit Norway. In Oslo, I met a new travelling companion, Pat Vinigan, at a youth hostel that was actually situated on a ship in the harbour. She'd looked at me as I walked on board with my rucksack and said, "Where have you been and where are you going?" I told her all about my travels up to that point and said that I planned to take a boat from Bergen up to the Arctic Circle. She said she'd like to join me.

Pat and I took the cheap seats on the boat from Bergen. We sat below sea level, surviving on tinned food that we heated on a small burner; our tickets didn't come with the catering option. However, we met a kind American couple, Mr and Mrs Grebe (pronounced Greebee), who started smuggling potatoes out of the first-class dining room for us.

We had first encountered Mrs Grebe, a retired schoolteacher, when a group of us were lying on the deck watching the stars. She was waving her hands around pointing out the various stars that could be seen in the night sky. We got the most spectacular view of the Aurora Borealis (the "Northern Lights") while we were lying out there.

Pat and I got off the boat close to the Russian border, in northern Norway. There was no way you could enter Russia at that time, in 1955, but you could get close enough to see the guards, which was exciting enough. We then hitchhiked back down to Oslo, which was a little hairy at times. One driver dropped us off in the middle of nowhere and we had to walk quite a distance before we found a farmhouse and got permission from the owners to sleep in their barn.

Back in Oslo I met up with Mrs Grebe (who had travelled back in a slightly more civilised style) for a coffee. Before meeting her I had gone to pick up my mail. In those days, you had all your mail held for you at a "post-restante" address, an address in a location you were travelling to that you could give people while you were en route, so that they could send letters that you would collect when you arrived. I must have put it as a return address on my letter to Kevin because there was a reply from him.

"I pay no attention to what you have to say from that distance," he had written. "I'll wait until you get back and we can talk."

I sat down with Mrs Grebe and told her all about Kevin.

"Well, he sounds like a good fellow," she concluded. "I can't see what you've got against him. What's the problem?" she asked me, acting a little *in loco parentis*. The only thing I could think of was that Kevin had a gold inlay on one of his teeth that was a little unsightly. I mentioned this.

"He could always get a crown," Mrs Grebe suggested, probably thinking I was a little shallow and vain to be worried about such a thing.

I was sure I could find a better excuse not to marry him.

"He's also got big feet," I blurted out. My mother had been a bit of a snob about the size of a man's feet, considering big feet to be rather working class. She was very proud of my father's small feet and I suppose it had rubbed off on me that big feet were not a positive attribute on a man.

Mrs Grebe laughed and pointed downwards. I noticed she had enormous feet.

"I have a pretty good grip on this earth myself," she said.

Mrs Grebe might have planted a seed but I wasn't quite ready to give up my position on the matter. When I got back to England, I rang Kevin. He asked me if I'd changed my mind. I said I hadn't; I still felt the way I'd explained in my letter. Kevin invited me to a party that he and Stephen were having anyway, which was a few weeks away.

By the time the party came around, my feelings had started to soften, and I was coming around to the idea of marrying Kevin. But it had been so long, I was pretty sure Kevin would have moved on by then. Just to be sure, when I got to the party, I asked Kevin if he'd changed his mind about wanting to marry me.

"No," he said. "Nothing's changed with me."

So I agreed to marry him.

So once again I discovered, as I discovered on countless more occasions through the course of our lives together, that if Kevin Gardner stated his intention to do something, whether it was to pick you up at 6pm on a Tuesday in six months time, or marry you and spend the rest of his life with you, he never, ever wavered from it. He was dependable to his core, a man of his word, with an extraordinarily good "grip on this earth".

I couldn't have wished for a better husband.

10

A Very Parisian Wedding

We planned a big engagement party in London with all our friends. I told Kevin about the plans I'd made to do a three-month course at the Cordon Bleu school in Paris but said, since we were about to start our life together, I wouldn't go.

"Oh, yes you will," he said, "if you're marrying me!"

When we got engaged, Kevin and I obviously thought about moving back to Australia. We wrote to our dentist friends about job prospects there but the replies came back warning us that the job market for dentists was still pretty dire. One literally said, "Don't come back; you'll starve." We discovered that highly skilled and qualified dentists were still doing manual jobs on projects like the Snowy River project, or working on major road schemes. We had one friend pulping paper in a paper mill. So we decided to stay in the UK, get married in Paris when I finished my Cordon Bleu course and continue working in London.

Paris was our choice of wedding location not just because it was geographically convenient (since I would be at the Cordon Bleu school in the run-up to the date) but my friend, Monsignor Clarizio, was also positioned there at that time as the chargé d'affaires for the Nuncio in Paris. A Nuncio is the Holy See's equivalent to an ambassador; basically like the Vatican's ambassador to a country. He kindly offered to help us with our wedding plans.

I had first met Monsignor Clarizio when he was secretary to the Papal Nuncio in Sydney. He knew my family well because he had been involved in the arrangements when my mother was awarded the Cross of Leo. (When Kevin and I announced our engagement in *The Times*, we mentioned my mother's award and they didn't know what LC stood for; they asked if it was "Legislative Council" and I had to explain the definition to them. I was amazed they had never heard of it.)

Over the years, I became friendly with Clarizio. When Don and I were considering marriage, he gave Don some Catholic instruction (behind Don's mother's back, of course!). Clarizio liked Don enormously, they became very friendly and Clarizio was trying to find a way to let us get married in front of the altar in the Catholic Church despite Don not being a "cradle Catholic", which was the normal prerequisite for this.

When I had spent those initial three weeks in Paris doing my assessment for the Cordon Bleu school, Clarizio had been incredibly kind to me and my friend Thecla Broderick from Melbourne, who visited me during that time. Thecla was a talented singer from a very musical Greek family who were real pillars of the Catholic Church in Victoria. Clarizio gave us the use of his official car, instructing the chauffeur to show us around but not to linger too long in the Pigalle area.

At that time, Clarizio was eager for Don and I to announce our engagement; as far as he was concerned, we were practically engaged already. I was a little embarrassed when I had to explain that I hadn't heard from Don since leaving Australia. I had even written to him from London, saying I needed to know what his plans were, because otherwise I was calling the whole thing off. I never received a reply so I had written Don off and was trying to forget about him.

I was rather upset at the time. When we had visited Don's mother, I thought we had left her house with him firmly on my side, not hers; I was sure he was going to defy his mother and propose to me eventually. I assumed the delay was only due to his needing to finish his degree. But when I look back, it's very clear to me that his mother had won all along; finishing his degree was just an excuse. Don just didn't have the guts to tell me. Also, ever the charmer, he was probably leaving his options open. Don's upbringing had been very different from mine. He went to the Presbyterian College in the wealthy Eastern Sydney suburbs. They typically started their sex lives earlier than we did. In my family, we believed in no sex before marriage. I got a real shock when I discovered how many people started their sex lives early, when they were as young as 15 or 16, and well before they were married.

As soon as I told Clarizio my situation, he urged me to give Don one more chance. He was sure that there was a practical explanation for the situation; either my letter hadn't arrived or Don's reply had got lost in the post on its way back to me. I think he felt I was misjudging Don, who he liked enormously. Clarizio suggested that I ask my sister Gwen, who lived in the same area as Don, to find out for sure.

I telephoned Gwen to ask her if she would just go and ask Don whether he had received my letter. She said that although, in principle, she didn't feel right interfering in other people's personal affairs, she did think it was very odd that Don hadn't replied so she agreed to ask him, simply to check that he received my letter.

Don told Gwen that he *had* received my letter. Then he said, "I haven't replied because I don't know how to reply."

That was a clear enough reply for me.

This all happened several months before the trip to Scotland with Kevin.

I never stop thanking my lucky stars that I ended up with Kevin and not Don. When I look back I realise that Don was just very much into himself. He was so keen to be popular, he could be a real people-pleaser, and that's probably what made him a bit fickle and unable to make a commitment. By contrast, Kevin absolutely knew his own mind and wasn't afraid to make his opinion clear; he was the absolute king of commitment! When Kevin said something, he meant it; when he made a promise, he kept it. He was kind, but his kindness was genuine, not a ploy to gain favour.

If I'd stayed in Australia and married Don, I would have had a very different life. My time would have been focused on making teas for the cricket club (as I had done on many occasions when we were courting) and entertaining Don's social circle. Cricket was Don's life. He used to do special exercises to make his wrists stronger for cricket.

Kevin had very large, strong wrists. It was always difficult to find watchbands that fit him.

I had a brief moment as a cricketer myself. Mollie Dive tried to get me involved with the Sydney University team. I tried batting against her, but I wasn't much use. However, I shouldn't be too down on myself because Mollie became one of Australia's top female fast bowlers! She played nationally for Australia from 1948–1951 and captained the Australian Women's national cricket team in their first Ashes win against England during the winter of 1948/1949. I never stood a chance!

While I was doing my three-month Cordon Bleu course, I rented a little room in Montparnasse that wasn't too expensive. There was nowhere to cook, but I would buy my coffee and croissant every morning from a local café, and we would eat whatever we cooked during our classes at school.

It was a busy few months, planning the wedding and completing my course. I finished at the top of my class. I was introduced at the graduation ceremony as Mademoiselle Girr as the French couldn't handle the "Mc" part!

Clarizio was a huge help with all our wedding arrangements. He explained that our order of service was to be the same one used for Grace Kelly's wedding to Prince Rainier III of Monaco – which had taken place just a few months before, in April 1956 – because it was the only English order of service he had available.

Kevin, like me, was a "cradle Catholic" because both his parents were Catholics when he was born, so there were no issues with us getting married in a Roman Catholic Church. We were able to have our service at the Chapelle Notre-Dame-de-Consolation in the eighth arrondissement.

I decided to make my cake in London before I left. I ordered all the dried fruit from Harrods. They asked me where I wanted the bill to be sent and I gave them the new address of where Kevin and I would be living when we got back from our honeymoon. I remember it was months before they sent that bill and I had to chase them up for it. It's funny now, to think of the notion of going to a store like Harrods and not having to pay for the goods up front.

When I arrived in Paris with my cake, the funniest thing was the look on the faces of the two chefs at the Cordon Bleu school. They didn't know what to think of my "wedding cake" because they have fresh cake for weddings in France. One of them was very puzzled, saying that it would go bad before the wedding. Then the second one said, "Ah, non, c'est le plum pudding Anglais." He was one of the best sugar workers in the whole of France and did the most beautiful pulled sugar roses for me to decorate the cake with. Unfortunately, as they didn't do tiered cakes in France, there were no cake columns and I had to sit each of the three tiers on top of one another.

Kevin and I got married on 7 July 1956, choosing the date because it was a week before Bastille Day, after which many people in Paris disappear off for their summer holidays. French law requires you to have a civil marriage before you have a religious ceremony (which is optional), so we had to go to "la mairie" (the local town hall) the day before the wedding in order to become legally married. Clearly this was not quite good enough for the Madame of our hotel. She would not allow us to share a bedroom until we were married in the eyes of God! We had invited her to the wedding so she knew it was not until the following day.

After the beautiful church service, we had a reception at the British Embassy, in a room that had been arranged by Clarizio.

Muffie organised a big party back home; all my family and Kevin's family went to it. I admit that I was a little sad not to have my family there, but I already felt so much sadness that my father hadn't lived to see me get married, so I suppose I just accepted it. Kevin's sister, Anne-Marie, was living in London at the time and was able to come to Paris for the wedding, so at least one of us had a family member there. And a girl I'd been at school with in Australia was living in Brussels, and was able to attend. We weren't lacking in guests, though, as we had so many friends we'd met whilst living in London and on our travels; I think we calculated that we had 12 different nationalities amongst our guests at the wedding. Jill was a bridesmaid along with my Belgian friend, Emmy de Klerk, a tall, elegant, beautiful woman, and a multi-linguist who was one of the first air hostesses on KLM.

We received a lovely letter of congratulations from Mrs Grebe and her husband. She had a big place in my heart because she was instrumental in helping me come around to the idea of marrying Kevin.

Just before the wedding, I travelled to Stuttgart in Germany with my friend, Ros Ranson, from the Cordon Bleu school, to buy a car, a pale blue/grey Volkswagen "Beetle". Ros and I drove it back to Paris, and then Kevin and I drove all around Europe in it for our honeymoon.

We started in the Loire Valley (the Chaumont-sur-Loire region). Kevin was very keen to go swimming in the river, however he hadn't brought a bathing suit with him. When we went shopping, we discovered that the only men's swimming trunks available in France were those tiny, close-fitting "Speedos". We'd never seen anything like them in Australia where men traditionally wore long, baggy shorts to swim in. We had to giggle because they were very revealing. Also, Kevin didn't realise that it was a tidal river so he had to wade out for ages before it was deep enough to swim in. The swimming mission wasn't the biggest success!

It was wonderful seeing so much of Europe together. There was no time pressure and we had a very relaxing time. The only disappointing part was Triest, on the border between Italy and Yugoslavia (as it was then, the region now being Slovenia), which was the furthest south we went. You could tell how beautiful it had once been but it had become very run down. It was sad to see it in all its "decayed glory".

We drove our Beetle all the way back to London but we couldn't keep it in the UK longer than a year or we would have had to pay tax on it as we'd bought it on an "export" basis. The easiest place to sell it was the German town of Aachen, which was just over the border with the Netherlands. Before the year was up, we drove it across to Amsterdam, taking the ferry, and then into Germany. When we arrived we were almost hampered in our efforts because there was one vital piece of paper missing (and the Germans are nothing if not officious!). However, the people at the garage where we had taken it said we could leave it with them. They said they would sort out the paperwork and sell it for us, and then send us the money. And they did. In those days, you didn't think twice about trusting people. These days, if someone said, "Leave your valuable car with me and I'll sell it and send you the money," you'd assume they were going to scam you!

11

A New Family

Our first marital home was a flat in Kelvin Court, a group of apartment blocks on Kensington Park Road in Notting Hill, in west London. We actually lived in the building next door to the one in which I'd lived before, with Jill, who had moved in with Kevin's sister, Anne-Marie.

Kevin and I needed to get back to work pronto as we hadn't worked all summer and had spent a fair amount of money during our European honeymoon.

We were both keen to start a family immediately, but we didn't have much luck to begin with. I struggled to get pregnant and had several miscarriages. In those days, having a miscarriage was a pretty awful experience. On top of the discomfort and sadness you suffered, any woman who suffered a miscarriage was treated with suspicion. Abortion was illegal in cases other than life or death emergencies, so it was assumed that, if you had a miscarriage, you'd probably caused it yourself. Kevin was a huge support when mine happened. As a child, he'd once come home from school to find his mother lying on the kitchen floor having a miscarriage, so he had some first-hand experience and was extremely sympathetic and kind to me.

Subdued by the miscarriages and desperately homesick, having not seen my family for almost three years, Kevin eventually gave me his blessing to make a trip to Australia by myself. I made my first return journey to Australia in 1958. I went by plane on the "Kangaroo Route" between London and Sydney, which took four days with two overnight stops on the way.

*

At this point in time, I was still holding out some hope that I would receive an inheritance from my father's estate. I had been waiting for almost 10 years.

When he died in 1949, Greg McGirr was one of the wealthiest men in New South Wales, with a significant number of pubs and hotels in his business portfolio. A local newspaper reported that he had "acquired hotels and shops in about 37 country towns in New South Wales in addition to large grazing interests" and that his estate was worth "£215,226". I'm told that, adjusted for inflation, this would be the equivalent of around 6 million Australian dollars today.

My older siblings had all received substantial sums of money while my father was alive. You could only give so much every few years (I believe the same is more or less true in many countries today) so he had given the money in age order as we "came of age". Gregory had received a large lump sum like the others, just before Dad died, but Nonna and I had never received ours. We had all been left property but Nonna and I were hoping that the estate would give us similar amounts to those our older siblings had received from Dad when he was alive.

One of my tasks on that trip back to Australia in the late 1950s was to investigate the matter and find out what was happening.

When I arrived in Australia, I discovered that the Australian Taxation Office (the equivalent of the Inland Revenue in the UK) had frozen my father's estate because they were disputing tax returns going back 20 or 30 years. They were claiming that there was undeclared income. They had imposed huge fines and demanded back taxes going back several years, and probate had been held up because of this.

I was shocked and extremely worried, but encouraged when I heard about a Chinese family that had been stuck in a similar situation. They had launched an appeal against the Tax Office's decision and had won. I contacted my older siblings and suggested we do the same. The problem was, for them, it wasn't as urgent. They had all received large sums of money from my father when he was alive. They had set up their lives already; anything else that came to them was gravy. For me, and for

Nonna, a lump sum – similar to the amount our siblings had received – would have made a huge difference to our lives.

We had a meeting with Muffie (the chief lawyer in the family) and her husband, Tom. Muffie felt Nonna and I had a good case to fight. She set up an appointment for us to see a lawyer, but this would have meant extending my trip, possibly even staying in Australia for an indefinite period of time while we got it sorted out.

I telephoned Kevin and told him the whole story and explained why I needed to change my flight and stay on in Australia. By then I think I'd already been away for a few months. Kevin said, quite calmly, "If you're not on that plane, don't bother coming back."

Now, if anyone else in my life had said something like that, I would have taken it with a pinch of salt, as an empty threat; I would have ignored them. But I knew Kevin well enough by then. He meant what he said; there was no changing his mind once he'd made a decision about something. And he wasn't being unnecessarily dramatic or even overly romantic. He quite fairly pointed out to me that he was due to start his Masters at the Eastman Dental Hospital and needed me in London to run our dental surgery.

I got on that plane.

I really think Muffie would have helped us fight our case. She was a brilliant lawyer and if she thought we had a chance, then we did. Sadly, she died in July 1960, of an asthma attack, tragically dying in Tom's arms just before he was about to leave for work. I was absolutely devastated to lose my big sister, and for the immediate future that killed my appetite for a legal fight, especially one thousands of miles away.

When I got back to London, Kevin and I refocused on starting our family. We got an appointment at a specialist fertility clinic. However, as soon as all the arrangements were made for me to undergo tests, I got pregnant and managed to keep it. I've heard this often happens, that as soon as the pressure is off, and you believe you've put the matter into someone else's hands, all the stress and tension goes away, and many women suddenly manage to get pregnant naturally and have a successful pregnancy.

I was still kept under strict observation because I developed blood dyscrasia, so towards the end of my pregnancy they kept me in hospital for long periods. Earlier in the pregnancy, while I was in hospital having tests, a lovely junior registrar doctor came to see me. I told him that Kevin and I were thinking that I should go private to ensure the best possible care during my pregnancy. He suggested I should be under the care of his boss, the consultant obstetrician George Pinker. We made an appointment immediately.

Dr Pinker took exceptionally good care of me and went on to became the surgeon gynaecologist to the Queen, who is just over a year older than me. He delivered several royal babies during his long career, including the Princes William and Harry.

Kevin and I were absolutely thrilled when, in early March 1960, we welcomed our first daughter, Sarah, into the world. She was very overdue so she was a big baby, and as a precaution I had to have a Caesarean. In those days they made a vertical incision; nowadays they are more mindful of a woman's "bikini line" and the incision is made horizontally and very low down so that it can be hidden in a swimsuit.

Sarah came out weighing a whopping 10.5lb. She was so big that when they put her in the nursery (where they would keep the newborn babies, allowing them to be viewed through a glass window by visitors) she looked like she was around 3 months old compared with the other tiny newborns. Sarah was also born with a big birthmark over one eye. They assured us it would disappear in time... and it did.

To our surprise, but delight of course, I got pregnant again very soon after having Sarah. Rachel was born just 13 months later, in April 1961. Back then, it wasn't generally recommended that a woman have a vaginal birth after a Caesarean but as testament to the excellent surgical hand of George Pinker, I was able to go through with a vaginal delivery without any problems. Rachel was a more manageable size, weighing in at around 8lb. She was born with a full head of black hair, which later lightened.

*

When she was older, I confessed to Rachel that she was our "experimental baby" in that we did everything differently with her, following some new radical advice that had been recently published. For example, one article suggested your baby would never catch a cold if they were exposed to cold weather from birth. During the winter months, I used to put Rachel in her pram and wheel her out into the garden, running inside myself to get warm again. Obviously, I would watch her closely. If I saw her starting to turn blue, I would rush out and bring her back in again!

There was also a new trend of giving babies vaccinations in the soles of their feet so that they didn't get the typical scars on their arms. I thought this was a marvellous idea. What we couldn't have known was that Rachel was allergic to the serum in the vaccination shot. Luckily our GP identified the reaction and switched to a different serum before there was any lasting damage.

The cold weather experiment certainly worked. To this day, Rachel never gets colds or flus, despite spending every day in her GP surgery. However, she is also oblivious to cold temperatures. Rachel could live in a fridge and it wouldn't bother her! Her husband and children constantly complain, and campaign for the heating to be switched on while Rachel insists it's not cold enough to warrant this.

After our third daughter, Joanna, was born in November 1964, I asked Kevin, "How many children would you actually like?"

"Two," he replied, deadpan. This was typical Kevin humour; he was really over the moon with Joanna's arrival. We were both delighted by the arrival of every child. I wouldn't have minded having a whole swarm of them. However, it was a bit of a nuisance going through the process of having them… so we stopped at three.

In late 1961, when Sarah was a toddler and Rachel was still a small baby, we took our first trip back to Australia as a family. More commercial airline routes had opened up by that time and we decided to make the journey via the US, which is how we ended up stopping over for a few nights in Hawaii.

We stayed in a hotel in Honolulu that was rather fancy; this was confirmed by the fact that Frank Sinatra and his entourage were also staying there! We encountered them several times in the hotel and on the beach. Frank was very taken with our two little girls and made a real fuss of them. They were particularly gorgeous, but I am possibly biased!

Having endured a cold, wet winter in London, it was lovely to be on a beach again. Kevin and I developed a routine; we would let Rachel sleep in her carrycot under an umbrella while we paddled with Sarah at the water's edge. On one occasion, we were walking back up the beach after paddling when we heard a baby crying, loudly. We arrived at our patch to find a very cross Rachel in the arms of a policeman who gladly handed her over to me. An American woman walking by commented, in a wonderful Southern drawl, "Now isn't that the fattest little baby I ever did see!"

We also stopped over in Tokyo on the way. We had bought a little fold-up pushchair for Sarah in Hawaii and this was the wonder of the moment for the Japanese mothers. Their custom was to carry their babies on their backs, as they had done for centuries. They were quite fascinated by this contraption, as they were by Sarah's ice blonde hair.

Our first stop in Australia was Melbourne to see my sister, Patty, and her family. I remember someone – it could have been Patty herself, or maybe her husband, Bing – picking us up from the airport and dropping us off *close* to our hotel, but not right in front of it. We had to struggle with our luggage, and two small children, down the road to our hotel. We got into our room and then realised we'd need to go out again to get something to eat. It was a huge effort getting the children around. I remember feeling rather stranded in Melbourne.

Next, we travelled to Sydney for Kevin's sister's wedding. I have a little newspaper cutting from the time, announcing our arrival. (The McGirr family was still newsworthy!) I'm not sure where it was from – probably a society column as it is titled "Hello" with a cartoon of a woman on a telephone, presumably sharing gossip – but it states: "Great excitement in the McGirr and Gardner families during the week with the news that Kevin and Trixie Gardner and their children, Sarah and Rachel, will be here on December 3. They'll fly from London for the wedding of

Anne-Marie – Kevin's sister – on December 9, and plan to return towards the middle of January. Trixie, as you know, was out for a while a couple of years ago, but it will be Kevin's first visit home for about seven years."

Visiting my mother, having not seen her for several years, was a shock. She was still living in *Sunray* with her latest companion, but her health had deteriorated rapidly. She had become very forgetful and I suspected she might have had a small stroke because she didn't seem herself at all. She had such a brilliant brain and had always been so sharp, but now she seemed rather confused all the time. When my brother, Jack, would go and visit her she would always give him a shilling for the tram home, forgetting that he was a successful doctor with a car *and* that a shilling wouldn't take you very far on the tram in those days. She was only 74 but she appeared much older. With hindsight, I wonder if Muffie's death had permanently traumatised her. I don't think anyone in the family was quite the same after that tragedy.

I remember on one occasion, my mother was talking to Kevin in the garden. She seemed to know who he was and talked as if she'd known him for years, despite the fact that she had only met him very briefly before (while we were just friends at Sydney University). She suddenly stopped him, mid-sentence and said, "What did you say your name was?"

"Gardner," Kevin replied.

"Oh, well, I mustn't keep you from your work, I must let you get on," my mother said, indicating the large garden that had been tended to by many a gardener.

Perhaps the saddest thing of all was that, after being such a devoted and enthusiastic mother, and the prolific bearer of children, herself, she suddenly had no patience for small children at all. Some of my nieces and nephews remember being rather afraid of her. Muffie and Tom's daughter, Beatrice, remembers "Grandma McGirr" being quite cold. This is partly based on her brother Edmund's experience. He was sent to stay with Mother in the aftermath of Muffie's death. He apparently had a miserable time. But my mother must have been grieving, too. Perhaps Edmund reminded my mother too much of Muffie, the daughter she had just lost. My cousin, Mary Fitzpatrick, Gwen's daughter, also remembers my mother could be quite cold. Both Beatrice and Mary felt as though my mother had adopted the stance that, "children should be seen and not heard", insisting – on group visits – that all the young children stay outside in the garden playing and didn't come in the house.

This is not how my mother was when I was growing up.

I witnessed the change in my mother's personality first hand, in watching her interact with my own children. Sarah was a typical toddler, curious and eager to investigate anything she could reach. She was forever walking up to a side table, on which my mother had displayed a large onyx ashtray, and reaching up to try and pull the heavy object towards her. She had to be retrieved from this precarious activity several times. Meanwhile, Rachel mostly slept.

"I like this one," my mother said, pointing at Rachel in her pram. "She's no trouble." (For a few more months, until she finds her feet and her voice, I thought!)

Sadly, this visit turned out to be the last time I saw my mother alive. She died in July 1969 at the age of 81.

Sarah had been born while we were still living in our little flat in Kelvin Court. When I got pregnant with Rachel, only a few months after Sarah arrived, we knew we urgently needed to find a bigger place. We bought a new-build house in Bayswater, just off Bayswater Road on Bark Place. We bought it "off plan", which meant we had to pay for it before it was finished, but this allowed us to add some specific features to suit our specifications. Kevin was always very practical and this had really rubbed off on me. I chose flooring and cupboards that would be best suited to small children, in other words that wouldn't cause any hazards or show grubby little handprints.

One very special piece of furniture that joined us in that house was a teak garden trolley/table that was made from the wood of the Otranto liner, the ship I'd travelled to England on in 1954, that had since been broken up. I loved that trolley and it was put to great use in the garden, although I was once extremely alarmed at witnessing one of its uses. I had left the girls – Sarah aged around three years old and Rachel around two – playing in the garden while I nipped indoors for something. Literally, a few moments later, I glanced out of the window to check on them and saw Rachel standing on top of the trolley dancing while Sarah pushed her along the garden path! I raced outside just as the trolley hit an uneven part of the path and witnessed Rachel flying through the air – fortunately onto grass so there were no broken bones.

I've often told this story when people suggest that life is easier with girls than boys. Not with my high-spirited daughters, I assure them!

I was also very forward thinking when I was choosing the house specs, and insisted upon having multiple electrical sockets. The electricians thought I was mad, but I was tired of unplugging electrical appliances and switching them around because I only had one or two sockets. I knew electrical appliances were the future and wanted to be ready for them all. In one room I had eight outlets fitted so that every appliance had its own socket. This is now quite normal so I wasn't mad at all; I was way ahead of my time!

An Australian newspaper article cutting I have kept from this period, in a section called "Today's Living", reports my *avant-garde* approach to decorating. They came and interviewed me for it, and took some photos of me with Sarah and baby Rachel in our new house. They were fascinated by my design ideas, mentioning that: "Stable doors in the kitchen and breakfast room, where Mrs Gardner also does her sewing, are a boon to a busy mother. With the lower section shut, she can work in peace while still keeping an eye and ear alert for the children."

The final bill for the house (for the purchase of it and all the design specifications) came in at about £12,000; it was worth every penny to have a custom-designed house. And it was a great investment because we sold the place only four years later for about £20,000. We could have got more if we'd waited as it wasn't an ideal time to sell, the property market was a little sluggish then, but we needed more space again because Joanna was on the way.

*

Our next house was probably my favourite home of all the London houses we ever lived in. It was a few streets away on the other side of Queensway, on Porchester Terrace. The house was a grand old Victorian home with a large garden that had a converted coachman's cottage – a small mews house with a separate entrance on the parallel street behind it – at the end of it.

We moved into the main house in 1964 and over the next twelve years we did extensive work to it. We built an extension and moved the kitchen into that, turning the old basement kitchen into a self-contained flat, which we rented out to various tenants over the years to help with the considerable mortgage payments. Before the conversion, there had been a heavy spring-loaded door on the stairs to the basement. You could just imagine how well it would have separated the upstairs and downstairs, where the servant's quarters would have been located.

We lived in the property as we did it up, so we lived on a building site for a long period of time; it was quite an ordeal keeping an eye on the children and ensuring they didn't go anywhere dangerous. The builders weren't much help in this pursuit; they had erected joists and positioned planks to allow them access to the basement while it was under construction and, one day, Joanna, who was around four years old at the time, managed to walk across one of the planks right under the builders' noses and out into the street. She gaily headed off towards Notting Hill Gate and was halfway there before someone (presumably rather alarmed to see a small child wandering down the street alone) stopped her and asked where she was going. Joanna held up a penny that she was holding and said that she was "going shopping". The kind Samaritan got in touch with the local police, who retrieved Joanna. Meanwhile, I was getting into a blind panic after realizing that Joanna was missing. I had called the police myself, who soon made the connection with the missing child they had in their possession. We were eventually reunited with Joanna and we all kept a closer eye on her from that point on!

Inspired by my last kitchen design, I researched all the very latest timesaving gadgets. I ordered a dishwasher that was the envy of all my female guests, and I had a waste disposal unit installed in the kitchen sink, which had a rather terrifying attachment for peeling potatoes – probably not something that would meet health and safety standards today. Both these modern contraptions were imports from the US and were the talk of the town in our local community. I also had a wonderful slate countertop installed that surrounded a total of four sinks.

My penchant for multiple sinks caused Sarah a moment of embarrassment when she went to a friend's house and, on seeing only one sink in the kitchen, naïvely asked the friend's mother, "How ever do you manage with only one sink?" She is teased about it to this day!

When considering the kitchen furniture, I really wanted a solid table that would be large enough to accommodate the whole family plus visitors. I couldn't find the perfect table so we commissioned one. It had an iron frame with a Welsh slate top, which was great for rolling out pastry on since it was cool to the touch; it was also heat resistant and strong enough to take heavy cooking pots. The children loved this table when they were young because they could cover it with chalk and it would still wipe perfectly clean. That unique, long table was the perfect, hardwearing kitchen table for a large, sociable family; it has moved with us from house to house throughout the course of our lives. In one house, because the children had all moved out, I decided I would have it moved to the top floor and use it as my desk, which didn't delight the removal men! When I moved to my present home, it had to be craned out through a skylight. We have since had it shortened, and the girls have some of the offcuts that were removed, so it really has been a huge part of our family and has served us all very well.

I would have been happy to live in that house on Porchester Terrace for the rest of our lives. Sadly, over the years, the area changed and became very noisy; it used to drive Kevin to distraction to be woken up in the middle of the night by some commotion going on outside.

We sold Porchester Terrace in 1976 with an arrangement that we could live in the mews house (accessed through Queensborough Terrace) for a year while we did renovations to the new house we'd bought in St John's Wood, on Loudoun Road, where we lived until the girls had all finished school.

I wasn't as keen on the area in north London; it was too quiet and clean for me, almost clinical. I missed the hustle and bustle of Notting Hill and Bayswater. I had loved being a short walk from the centre of things. But it suited Kevin much better; it was quieter and fractionally closer to work.

The dramatic story of our move from Bayswater to St John's Wood is quite the epic legend! The removals company actually ran out of vehicles and had to call around other companies to bring in reinforcements. We had accumulated rather a lot of stuff by then, including items of furniture that were impossibly heavy; and the removals men kept finding more and more items stuffed into the backs of wardrobes or piled up in rooms throughout the house. They told us if we ever moved again they would *pay* for us to use a different company!

Some years later, my nephew, Michael McGirr, gave me a mention in his memoir *Things You Get For Free*, describing his Aunt Trixie's house in London being so full of clobber it "made the V&A, Britain's national attic, look like Zen minimalism."

Without my mother and sisters around, adjusting to motherhood was quite a challenge. But I had built up a good supportive network of friends in London, and we still had a stream of visitors pitching up from Australia, who would always help out with the girls. I had no luck breastfeeding any of my children – just like my mother, who had found herself unable to produce milk for any of her nine children – so they were all bottle fed, which makes it easier for other people to help.

After Joanna's birth, one of the nurses from the hospital was keen to help me at home so we paid her to come in for a few days a week, which took the burden off me, with three little ones in the house. I was also extraordinarily lucky that Kevin was a real hands-on father; not all men were in those days (or are these days!) but Kevin was devoted to all the girls from the moment they were born and happy to do whatever needed to be done to take care of them. He and Sarah were particularly close because she was our first child. The day she was born, he arrived at the hospital with an adorable chocolate teddy bear, which of course we had to eat for her!

Watching Kevin with Sarah was so endearing. He taught her to sit up straight at the table, have nice manners and speak correctly. He loved teaching her big words and always gave her so much praise when she managed to pronounce them correctly. However, Kevin was very concerned when Sarah developed a bit of a stammer. He had also had one when he was young; in fact it had occasionally reappeared when he felt under pressure. Kevin really wanted Sarah to be a great orator like her relatives on the McGirr side of her family, and this stammer really worried him.

As Sarah's stammer worsened, I wrote to Nonna about it to see if she had any advice. Nonna wrote straight back and said she'd been through the stammer stage with each of her children. She said it happens to children when they feel under pressure to perform well. She told me that you have to drop *all* the pressure on the child.

I showed Nonna's letter to Kevin and he immediately took all the pressure off Sarah. As Nonna had promised, Sarah's stammer completely disappeared. The really interesting thing was that I don't remember Kevin stammering again much either. I suppose once he understood more about what caused it, he could manage it better.

Although Kevin had strong inner confidence, and absolutely knew his mind, he didn't wear his confidence on his sleeve. He was quietly confident; outwardly he needed a boost sometimes. I think he got that boost by becoming a father and the head of a household, but it had obviously also put some pressure on him. Once he saw what happened by taking the pressure off Sarah, I think he went easier on himself, too. It was just like with all the stress we had put ourselves under to get pregnant; as soon as we took the pressure off, by making an appointment with the fertility clinic, I got pregnant easily and successfully… three times!

12

The Demon Dentists of Old Street?

When we returned from our honeymoon, I went to work for a dental practice in Maida Vale that had originally been established by Alfred Moss (father of Stirling Moss).

In 1956, a shift in legislation meant that many existing businesses were sold off to qualified dentists, who continued to run them. Until the mid-1950s, anyone could own a dental practice and hire qualified dentists to work in it; the owner of the business didn't have to be a dentist. But after the General Dental Council – a self-regulatory body – was established in 1956, only qualified dentists could set up new dental practices, which they could do as sole traders or partnerships (this changed slightly in 2006, after which dentists were also allowed to form corporations).

In 1957, Kevin and I bought a practice in Old Street in Islington, at a time when the area was still very much the "east end" of London. It has since become central London's answer to Silicon Valley with fancy glass office blocks and trendy cafés, and I am told it is now the UK hub of the "tech" industry. But the area has a long, fascinating history. Buried deep beneath many buildings are the burial pits that were used for victims of the Great Plague of 1665. When we took occupation of the surgery, there was a new building going up right next door to us. The foundations had to be carefully excavated by archaeologists. As they recovered pieces of skeletons, they would display their findings by balancing the bones and skulls along the wall just below the surgery. The locals were fascinated with this. Kevin, with his wicked sense of humour, loved to tease our patients. Pointing out the skulls, he would inform them, "Sadly some of our patients didn't make it."

He abruptly stopped making these particular jokes after a rather alarming experience. A male patient was in the dentist's chair and when Kevin checked the man's records, he said, "What's this on your record about a heart condition?"

"Oh, no, I don't have a heart condition," the man replied. He either genuinely didn't know or he was in denial. Whichever was the case, he promptly had a heart attack in the chair! We gave him oxygen and rang an ambulance to take him to hospital. After that incident, Kevin was very wary of people at death's door. He would say, "If someone collapses in the street don't bring them in here because people will think it's our fault. We'll help them in the street but not in here."

Kevin was also unnerved by the friendly local undertaker, who was one of our patients. Whenever there was a funeral procession (which were done beautifully in Clerkenwell, usually featuring an elegant horse pulling the hearse bearing the coffin) the undertaker would tip his top hat to us as the procession passed by. He was only being polite but Kevin worried that people would think we had something to do with the death, that maybe we had a little arrangement with the undertaker. He didn't want people thinking we were the Demon Dentists of Old Street!

We were well aware that the area was home to some dubious sorts. In fact we were on the turf of the infamous Kray twins, the big organised crime lords of east London. I heard rumours that members of their family were patients of ours but I wasn't aware of who they were. What I *was* aware of was that in all the years we had that surgery we never had one break-in. You never know who's watching your back!

Who knows how closely we rubbed shoulders with the criminal classes back then? I recall one woman who came in for a set of dentures. She arrived for a consultation pushing her baby in a large pram. I went through various options with her and she opted for the most expensive. I informed her that the dentures she had chosen weren't covered by the NHS, and explained that they would be very costly. I redirected her to the ones covered by the NHS. But this woman was adamant that she wanted the most expensive ones and offered to pay for them there and then... in cash.

She promptly lifted the baby out of its pram, reached under the mattress and pulled out a pile of notes. We gave her a receipt and in a few weeks she had her new teeth. Several months later we spotted a story in the local paper and recognised her name. The woman's husband had been arrested for a robbery. The report mentioned that the police hadn't managed to recover all of the cash!

We were not far from Whitbread's brewery, and occasionally a big, burly man would appear on a large dray cart pulled by these magnificent draught horses. He would inform us that he had brought in the "Guvner's" dentures to be repaired.

They were all such characters in that neighbourhood. We'd often get women turning up for dental treatment with rollers in their hair and carpet slippers on their feet!

Our original address was 157 Old Street, but after some local redevelopment they renumbered the whole street and we became 169 Old Street. All the properties along Old Street used to be owned by St Bartholomews' Hospital (commonly known as "Barts"). It was a lively and sociable neighbourhood with a mix of commercial and residential tenants. The residents, many of whom lived in the rows of little redbrick houses, often sat outside on their doorsteps because they had no back gardens to speak of. But this was also where they socialised. In the summer they would all go off, en masse, hop picking in Kent. That was their way of getting a summer holiday, even though it was a working holiday. At least their kids got some fresh air and space to run around in. They would all come back in the autumn bronzed from spending long days outside in the summer sun.

When the girls were babies, I generally only went into the surgery for one day a week, to do a general anaesthetic and check that the white coats and towels got laundered, but I still did a lot of paperwork from home, so it was always a juggle.

We had a wonderful assistant in the surgery called Elsie. She had worked for the previous owner and said she'd stay on with us for six months to settle in. She ended up staying with us until the day we sold the practice, over 30 years later, when she was well past retirement age! My only problem with Elsie was that she was in charge of the diary. It was a real struggle to get Kevin to agree to take time off for family holidays, he was such a workhorse. I would tell Elsie to keep a certain week free, but Kevin would let her book appointments in. Eventually I took to ripping out the pages of the weeks when I needed Kevin to take time off so that the days were not even in the diary to write on and Elsie couldn't physically book in any appointments!

Elsie really felt like part of the family. I remember when she got the opportunity to buy the north London house in which she'd always lived as a tenant. She had one floor in a three-floor house. We said we would be guarantors on the loan she would need. It was a great investment opportunity. To my amazement she said she didn't want to buy the house. She said she didn't want the responsibility of owning the property as she couldn't face the thought of being a resident landlady with lodgers, and she didn't want to deal with the hassle of turning the house into flats to sell on. I was fascinated that someone would have that attitude; in my book, you should always take a good investment opportunity if it comes up and just accept the responsibility. Elsie had a totally different perspective; the huge responsibility was not worth the profit she stood to make.

We also had Pat working for us in the surgery, as a chair-side assistant. When we advertised the position, which didn't require any dental qualifications, Pat came to the interview in a very expensive two-piece suit – a smart skirt and jacket. She was extremely pleasant and very keen, so we gave her the job. We later found out that her mother had told her she had to have a quality suit if she wanted to get a good job, so they had bought the suit on a hire-purchase basis and were paying it off in instalments. Well, that had turned out to be a very good investment! As well as being an excellent chair-side assistant, Pat was great fun. She was with us for years before she left to get married.

Over the years, we had several dentists work for us, on and off. Ben was with us for several years. He was originally from Ghana and I was always fascinated by his stories. His father had been a Governor in Eastern Ghana at a time when the Queen was visiting. They had to rebuild a section of the Governor's residence in which she was to stay, so that her valuables could be kept in a proper built-in safe that couldn't be removed. He also explained that in Ghana you were always named after the day of the week you were born, alongside your other given names. I thought that was charming. But my favourite story was about how he took a turkey to his family in Ghana every Christmas. He would buy a frozen turkey just before he flew out, and by the time he arrived it would be defrosted to perfection and ready to go straight into the oven!

We had several African patients over the years. They always asked to have a gold tooth because it was a big sign of wealth. We had to explain to them that this was unfortunately not covered under the NHS!

Kevin and I both worked very hard, and we were careful with our money. We managed our finances well and saved our pennies. One excellent scheme we had going was my sewing-machine fund. If anyone wanted to have a tooth taken out but nothing else, we would charge them half a crown and we put all of these in a jar (once I'd logged them in the books of course!).

The money in the jar was to be used to buy me an electric sewing machine. I particularly wanted one that went forwards *and* backwards. Until that point I'd only ever had a treadle machine that you operated by pressing floor pedals up and down, to keep the wheel going round. I had been doing my research and was keen to learn all about the latest machines.

I went into one shop in Notting Hill to enquire about electric machines and a man in the shop showed me one. I asked if it went backwards and forwards.

"Yes," he said. "To make it go backwards you just pull the fabric towards you really hard."

Kevin was unimpressed when I told him that particular story; he thought the man had been trying to con me, so we went to the Singer shop and discovered you could borrow a machine for a week to try it out. I was delighted to get the machine home and set about making some nighties for myself. The electric machine was difficult to control at first; I ended up making a collection of stitches that went anywhere but in a straight line, but I soon got the hang of it. On the day that the man was due to come and pick up that trial machine, I wasn't quite finished making my final nightie. I told Kevin to keep the man occupied, to offer him coffee, to talk to him and entertain him, basically to do anything to distract him while I finished my nighties. I needed every minute I could get before the machine went back to the shop.

Kevin successfully distracted the Singer representative and I got to finish my nighties. When I handed over the machine, the man said that he always came early because people made him such nice tea and coffee, and would engage him in the most interesting conversations; he knew this was so that they could stretch out their time with the machines, but he enjoyed the hospitality. So while we thought we were getting a good deal out of him, he was actually getting a good deal out of us. The loan of the machine was a great sales tactic by Singer. I loved it and was inspired to save up for it (hence the half-crown jar). I was thrilled when I eventually got my own Singer machine.

Not long after we bought the dental practice, the GLC made a compulsory purchase of a large area of Old Street from Barts in order to provide new social housing and community facilities. This included the building we were located in. All the residents and business owners had leases and those of us in the affected area were offered a choice: either we could take financial compensation for the ending of our leases (we all had relatively long leases) and find new homes and premises, or we could remain where we were and be temporarily re-located during our particular building's renovation work. We would then be able to move back into our new upgraded building and enjoy the new facilities in the redeveloped area.

Of the 40 businesses, only 8 decided to stay and stick it out through the renovation period; the other 32 took the compensation.

I think, if we'd known what we were in for, we might have taken the compensation and washed our hands of the place. From the day the redevelopment work started, to the day we moved into our new building, took almost 15 years!

When I first inspected the plans, I saw a huge problem for our practice. The way the new building had been designed would mean that our patients would be forced to walk past the doorway of the corner pub to get to the surgery. I didn't think it was appropriate for families with small children to be passing a pub – potentially walking past merry revellers spilling out onto the street – on their way to and from the dentist. We vetoed those plans and they eventually came up with a better solution.

We bravely stuck it out through the construction phase. Our building was to be completely demolished and replaced with a new one that was being built behind it. We stayed in our old building while the new building was going up behind us. The plan was to demolish the old building once we were settled into the new one. The old building was already in desperate need of renovation when we bought the business, and it got progressively worse as we waited for the construction of the new building to be completed. Towards the end of this phase, it was really becoming quite derelict and virtually uninhabitable.

There was a giant skylight above the dentist chair and one day, during a heavy rainfall, it started to leak. A rather aristocratic woman was in the chair at that time and said, in a rather posh voice, "Oh dear, I'm getting wet."

Without missing a beat, and totally deadpan, Kevin said, "Nurse, get the umbrella, please."

After this, the builders covered the skylight up with a big plastic cover. Unfortunately, this sealed the skylight shut, permanently. This was a huge problem in the summer months because that skylight had also been our main point of ventilation. From then on, the surgery became a Turkish bath during the height of summer!

We also had issues with our Saturday appointments during summertime. When we first started doing Saturday appointments, we had regular timed appointments, just like we had during the weekdays. The problem was, if the weather was nice, no one would turn up until the end of the day and we'd be sitting around doing nothing all day. So we opened the surgery on a "first-come-first-served" basis on Saturdays, with no timed appointments. We let people know that we would close the surgery as soon as we'd seen the last person in the waiting room. If they needed urgent care, they knew they had to turn up first thing in the morning. If they waited until the end of the day, we were likely to be closed. This was much better for us as it meant that we weren't obliged to wait around for anyone: when the waiting room was empty, we could go home.

We always found it difficult to get our support staff to come in on a Saturday so we often brought the girls in to help us, giving them age-appropriate duties. Sarah, and eventually Rachel when she was old enough, would help out with reception duties, booking people in as they arrived and asking them to take a seat. We were a fully-fledged family business! And if we couldn't get a dental assistant on a Saturday, I would take on that role, although this had its problems. In those days, you couldn't get pre-mixed material so I would mix the amalgam for Kevin. He would say, "That's not the way I'd mix it."

And immediately I'd say, "It's fine. That's how I do it."

It wasn't easy to stop being a dentist and be a dental nurse for the day, especially when the dentist I was assisting also happened to be my husband!

Kevin had a marvellous "bedside manner" with the patients. He always put them at ease, chatting away (often about the cricket) as he drilled their teeth. He was very quick-witted and dry. People would come in a bundle of nerves and, as they got settled into the chair, Kevin would ask them, "How's your Spanish dancing coming along?"

He said this to all of his patients, indiscriminately, and they would all look at him, surprised and confused, then say, "That's not me, I don't do any Spanish dancing; you must have me muddled up with someone else." But by that time, while they'd been pondering why Kevin had asked them such a question, he'd got the injection in. It was a great distraction technique of his.

I'll never forget the day when one particularly nervous patient was lying in the chair and Kevin asked the usual question, "How's your Spanish dancing coming along?"

"Oh, very well, thank you," the woman said, "I won a prize last week."

For once, Kevin was left speechless!

When the redevelopment was finished, it was lovely. There were residential flats all around us and in some of the front gardens they grew these tall sunflowers. Kevin used to tease the dental nurses, telling them that a man came around stealing the seeds and cutting the sunflowers down. He'd ask them, sombrely, "Has the sunflower cutter come yet?"

The nurse in question would go running out to check, and of course the sunflowers were all still intact!

In 1990, when Kevin retired, we sold the practice after 33 years in business. We sold it to someone who was working for us at the time as he expressed a strong interest in buying it. We lived to regret that decision because he really didn't have the business skills to run a practice by himself, but we felt obliged to give him first refusal as he'd been with us for some time and seemed so keen. I think he lasted in business for about a year before he ran the practice into the ground because he was so incapable. It was a real shame; it had taken us a long time to build that practice and it was sad to see it dismantled by someone else.

However, no one could ever take away our treasured memories of those days in the Old Street practice.

The coldest winter in London, 1954

My first snowball. London, 1954

Hitchhiking to Lands End, c. 1955

Hiking in Finland, 1955

Gaining my Cordon Bleu qualifications in Paris, 1956

Our engagement party in London, 1956

Our marriage at Notre-Dame-de-Consolation in Paris on 7th July 1956

Enjoying our wedding reception with friends, 1956

Our civil wedding at the British Consulate in Paris, 1956

Kevin in Capri on our honeymoon, 1956

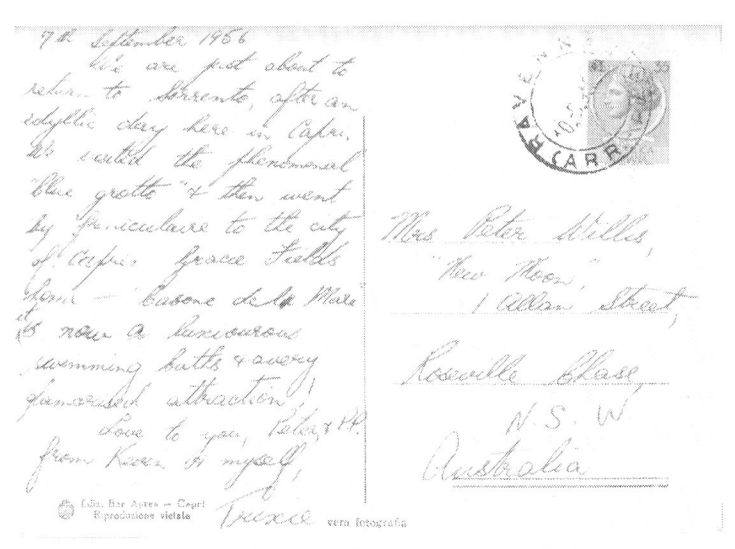

The postcard I sent to Nonna from Capri (during our honeymoon), 1956

At Flemington Racecourse, Melbourne, 1958

I was invited back to my old cookery school, East Sydney Technical College, to give a demonstration of making the Cordon Bleu's famous Duck à l'orange to students! Sydney, 1958

Motherhood... with a bewildered Sarah and a furious Rachel, c. 1962

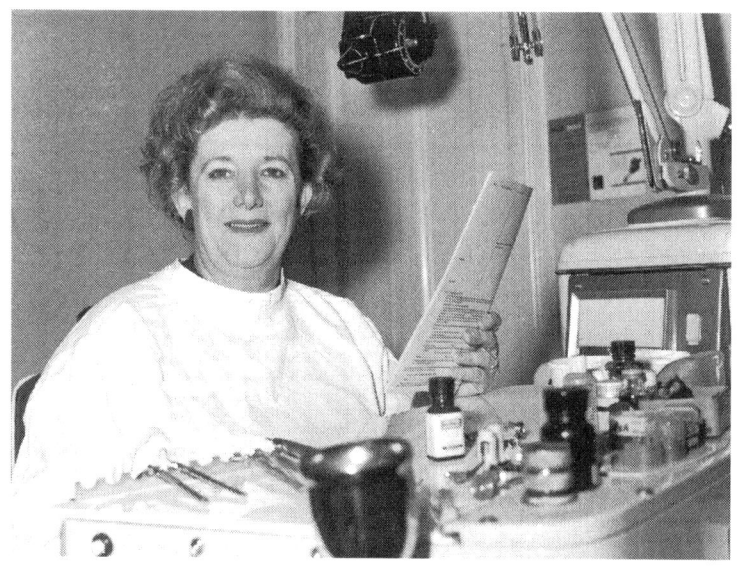

Life as a busy dentist in Old Street, c. 1968

Porchester Terrace in our kitchen with many sinks, 1970

Porchester Terrace with Kevin (and my favourite photo of Dad on my desk), 1970

Visiting Tokyo with Sarah, 12th January 1962

PART THREE

Westminster

13

A Frying Pan for Labour

Before going any further, in order to be completely transparent, I feel duty-bound to declare a past donation I made to the Labour Party.

Shortly after I arrived in London, a man knocked on our door and said he was collecting donations for a jumble sale to raise funds for the Labour Party. He asked me if I had anything I could donate. I found an old frying pan and gave him that. So, there you have it: the total contribution I have made to the UK Labour Party is one cast-iron frying pan!

Considering my family background, you might have assumed my allegiance to the Labour Party on arriving in the UK was a foregone conclusion. My father had stood and served as a politician for the Labour (later Labor) Party in Australia several times. Two of my uncles (Dad's brothers) were also prominent Australian Labor Party politicians, with Uncle Jim serving as the ALP Premier of New South Wales from 1947 to 1952 and Uncle Pat serving as an MP for the ALP and subsequently a long-time ALP member of the Legislative Council (the upper house) of the New South Wales Parliament. However, my mother had always voted for the "other side" (UAP, then Liberal) so it wasn't as if, as a family, we were expected to vote one way. My brother, Jack, had even supported the Australian Country Party, that later became the National Party of Australia. To be honest I hadn't been overly interested in politics as a young woman. No one was more surprised than me when my life veered off in that direction!

I have always been more interested in *people* than in politics *per se*; my interest in politics is only insofar as being a good politician enables you to help the most people. By chance I had ended up living in Notting Hill and then in Bayswater, which were both predominantly Conservative areas. I also carried that strong sense of social duty inspired by my mother's charitable work and the various committees I'd served on in Australia. So when my local MP asked if I'd like to get involved with some community work they were doing, I was only too happy to get involved. He just happened to be a member of the Conservative Party and so that's the party I got involved with, initially at a purely local level.

I first met our MP, Robert Allan, when he knocked on my door to introduce himself. I was particularly impressed because it was not during the time of an election. In my experience, politicians only went around knocking on doors and canvassing for votes at crunch time, but this man was simply coming around to introduce himself to a new constituent. I liked this very much because it meant you could really get to know the person without the pressure to vote or make any binding commitment. I began talking to him and immediately liked him.

Robert Allan had been elected in 1951 as the Member of Parliament for Paddington South, a seat he held until 1966 when he stood down to focus on his business activities. The Conservatives held the seat until the constituency was merged with Paddington North to become a single Paddington constituency, which went to Labour in the February 1974 election. Robert Allan was made a life peer as Baron Allan of Kilmahew in 1973.

I have kept a letter from Robert, dated 17 October 1962, in which he mentions our conversation, tells me that he's been busy at the Conservative Party Conference in Llandudno, and suggests various ways in which I could get involved with local activities in the Paddington area. He writes also to tell me that he was going to ask a Miss Rabagliati, an Alderman who lived in Sussex Gardens, to get in touch about the Old People's Welfare and ancillary services. From this connection, I found myself signed up to help out with lunch duty at a day centre for the elderly. I thought they might really appreciate having a Cordon Bleu cook on hand to help. However, it transpired that no cooking skills were required. My precise duty was to take prepared packets of whatever was delivered (usually some sort of meat casserole), throw them into a vat of boiling water, then fish them out when they were hot, cut them open and squeeze the contents out onto plates.

Boil-in-the-bag meals had become very popular in the early 1960s.

Four years at Sydney Technical College and three months at the Cordon Bleu School in Paris to end up reheating pre-packaged meat casseroles at a community centre. You can't accuse me of being too proud! I was rather relieved when I got pregnant with Joanna and told them that I was going to have to relinquish my duties because I was having another baby.

Miss Rabagliati was Chairwoman of the Paddington Women's Section of the Conservative Party. Their official office was on Westbourne Grove, a stone's throw from our house. Miss Rabagliati was a tiny, bird-like woman, but full of personality. She was fascinated with my Australian heritage and she asked me if I could do a talk about Australia for the members.

Through a letter of introduction from my Uncle Jim, I had met the Agent-General for New South Wales in London, a lovely man called Francis Buckley. He gave me, on loan, a set of slides that I showed to the group using a projector while I talked about life in Australia.

Francis Buckley had been so kind to me and adored the girls, giving Rachel a beautiful knitted toy lamb when she was born (that we obviously named Buckley). The first time I'd met him was when I had gone to Australia House to vote in the New South Wales elections. I was glad to meet a new ally in London that day but was annoyed to find that the seat in my Australian constituency was uncontested, so I need not have bothered going to vote at all. Although, if I didn't want to vote, I still needed to remove myself from the electoral roll (which you are allowed to do if you are no longer resident in Australia) because you are legally bound to vote if you are an Australian citizen.

I did remove myself from the Australian electoral roll before the next elections were due. It seemed sensible as I had become a UK resident and was out of touch with Australian politics. And it was better than missing an election date and getting into trouble.

The talk was a huge success and I was invited back the following year to do it again. Miss Rabagliati got me involved in other events organised by the Women's Section of the Conservative Party and I really enjoyed being a part of something. It reminded me of those years when I helped out with the Red Cross and got involved with the Sydney Opera House committee, and of the fundraising we used to do with my mother for the Sydney Settlement. I had so enjoyed the busyness of being involved with all those projects when I'd been in Australia. And I suppose I liked being around a lot of people, in a big group, because I missed my large, vibrant family.

At some point, Miss Rabagliati took me aside and told me that she had been "dying" to give up the Chairmanship of the group and had vowed to do it as soon as she found the right person to succeed her. I was flattered when she told me that she felt I was up to the job. She nominated me and I was duly elected. And since the Chairwoman of the South Paddington Women's Section of the Conservative Party also had a seat on the main committee of the local Conservative Party, I consider that appointment as my first real step into British politics. A whole new world had opened up to me.

Miss Rabagliati became a dear friend. When Joanna was born, Miss Rabagliati gave her a knitted poodle that Joanna treasured for many years. She was such a character, Miss Rabagliati. She lived until she was about 100, I think. The story of her death made me smile, when I heard it, even though I was sad to hear she had gone. Apparently, she had spent her final day on this earth at her grand niece's wedding. She had been up on her feet all night, dancing along with the other guests, seemingly as fit as a fiddle. When the party ended, she walked out into the street and dropped dead. At least she went out on a roll.

There was one more thing that cemented my support for the Conservative Party at that time in my life.

When that Labour Party member had knocked on my door asking for donations in 1955, I had asked him why I should vote Labour. He had been unable to give me an adequate summary of their policies, so I wrote letters to the two major parties asking them to explain their policies. I got an impressive reply from the office of the new Labour leader, Hugh

Gaitskell. At this time, the two major parties were fairly aligned in what was referred to as the "post-war consensus" but cracks had started to show in their starkly different approaches on how best to help the country recover from the devastating effects of World War II. Gaitskell, however, was still fairly (what we would refer to today as) "centrist" in his views, which suited me and I could have easily signed up to support the Labour Party but for one thing; they were completely opposed to home ownership for those in public housing. This was something that the Conservatives were pushing for. I had always been a strong believer in social mobility and progress, so I saw this as an essential way for people to better their lives. I think my firm support of this policy is what finally swayed me more towards the Conservative Party… more so, I would have to say, than my boil-in-the-bag duties!

14

The Road to Westminster

My appointment as the Chairwoman of the Paddington Women's Section of the Conservative Party was the start of a journey full of twists and turns and ups and downs that has led to me where I am today. At the time of writing, I have been involved in British politics for more than 50 years. It's quite extraordinary to look back over that time.

In my new position, I obviously had some involvement with Westminster Council, and as the 1968 council elections approached, I discovered that I had been added to the list of potential candidates to run for seats on the council. This was only the beginning of a long process. You still had to decide for yourself whether you wanted to stand, select which ward to run for (from a list of available constituencies) and then go through several interviews before you were officially selected to run for a seat.

The Conservative leader of the council at this time was Group Captain Sir Gordon Pirie and he was chairing the committee that would select prospective Conservative councillors. Sir Gordon was a highly respected leader who had overseen the merging of Westminster, Paddington and St. Marylebone boroughs when they were brought under one umbrella as the City of Westminster council.

Sir Gordon wanted all candidates to be pre-interviewed before they were officially put forward to the committee. He had made it very clear that he wanted people on the council who would be very proactive and really get things done, not just languish about having meetings about meetings. I had obviously made an impression during my time chairing the Women's Section of the Conservative Party for Paddington South because Sir Gordon rang me personally to check that I had made a seat selection and was intending to run! I told him that I was about to confirm my interest and had chosen to stand for the seat representing the Hyde Park ward. He seemed pleased with my answer and I got the impression that, had I not made my mind up or selected a seat, he would have asked me to stand, and suggested a seat himself!

I went through the interview process and got approved as a candidate. I fought a successful campaign and was duly elected as a Conservative Councillor for the City of Westminster in the Hyde Park ward.

In 1968, I also had three young children under the age of 10, a large house to run and was still working as a dentist in our blossoming business. I'm not sure how I thought I was going to manage it all, but it was like getting on a train that was hard to get off.

I had thoroughly enjoyed my involvement with the Conservative Party by this point and had become really passionate about politics. I had even applied to their selection committee to run for a seat in Parliament, but had been told, quite clearly, that I needed more experience first. I duly took any roles and responsibilities that were on offer.

I had already been involved with the BDA (the British Dental Association, the dentists' equivalent of the British Medical Association) for some time by then. This gave me plenty of experience and information that became especially relevant when I took a position on Westminster City Council's Health and Social Services Committee. I was also asked to become a Justice of the Peace and sat as a member of the Industrial Tribunal, which gave me invaluable insight into legal and employment processes. I had come on the scene just at a time when these bodies were very keen to add capable, professional women to their ranks. It was nice to be wanted and although I was possibly in danger of spreading myself a little too thin sometimes, I was eager to absorb as much knowledge as possible.

Being a Justice of the Peace was fascinating; you actually got to sit in court about once a month. There are always three magistrates. Usually the Chairman is legally qualified and the other two are not. Obviously I was one of the ones not legally qualified. I remember our Chairman's wife was from Canada, so we had our Commonwealth roots in common. The third member of our team was a retired British Army Major who slept through most of the proceedings!

One compelling case – that really stayed with me – went on for four days. It was a battle over the citizenship of a boy born in Egypt. The father was trying to take the boy back to Egypt, but the mother was desperate to have him acknowledged as a British citizen because she wanted to keep him in the UK. While I listened to it, I thought about how lucky I was to have both my Australian citizenship, which I held dear, as well as the right to remain in the UK, which I had been granted by then. Not everyone enjoys that kind of security and I always feel very defensive of people who have to fight for their rights to citizenship or residency.

My time on Westminster City Council gave me a tremendous education. I sat on many committees and learnt a great deal about all the administration and bureaucracy involved in running local government: all the plans that had to be made, the research that had to be done, the studying of reports and the endless discussions before decisions could be made. I had never been involved in anything so extensive and complex. I got a thoroughly interesting insight into the inner workings of it all.

I represented a very nice ward. The boundaries of the Hyde Park ward were Bayswater Road and Edgware Road, and the constituents represented a cross-section of society. I was absolutely devastated when I lost the seat in 1978 for a couple of infuriating reasons.

The first reason for me losing my seat was out of my control. They reshuffled the council and reduced the number of seats in the Hyde Park ward from five to three. By rights, I should have been one of the people who retained a seat given that I was the longest serving councillor, but I was pushed out. I was asked to fight for a new seat in the Little Venice ward.

The second reason I lost my seat on the council was all my own doing. My dear sister, Nonna, was visiting during the run-up to the elections; I got distracted by having the most wonderful time catching up with her and I didn't put quite enough canvassing hours in. I kicked myself when I discovered that I had lost the seat by just 54 votes. I was really very annoyed; I could have easily put in the effort to win those extra 54 votes. I don't think I've ever quite forgiven myself for making that error!

Losing my seat on Westminster City Council in 1978 was probably the greatest disappointment of my political life. I really was shattered by it. I had invested so much of my time and energy into the council by that time and it felt like leaving a family. Yes, I probably would have kept my seat had I been allowed to run, as before, in the Hyde Park ward, where I was known. And it really was unfair that they didn't let me keep one of those three remaining seats because I had served the longest and had generated the most votes. But, ultimately, I could only really blame myself for dropping the ball and not campaigning a little harder to secure the additional 54 votes that I needed.

The *very* worst part of losing my seat on the council was that I had been tipped to become the first-ever female Lord Mayor of Westminster. Being a very active member of the committees dealing with the health services and public housing had brought me a great deal of attention, and many people had spoken in support of my future appointment as Lord Mayor.

The conversations I had with constituents after I lost my seat were bittersweet. Many people told me that they had never voted Conservative until I stood. I remember one voter in Little Venice saying, "I voted for you because you were the only politician I saw doing the things they said they would." I felt huge support from people but was no longer able to help them. It was deeply frustrating.

When you don't get what you wanted in life, you at least get experience. From this experience I learnt that you have to have a "rubber ball" mentality in life. When you lose, or get disappointed with something, it's vital that you "bounce back" as soon as possible. There is no point staying crushed and getting down about things you can't change, you are no use to anyone in that state. You can feel the disappointment for a short while and lick your wounds, but then you *have* to move on. You have to channel your disappointments into being even more determined to succeed in all the future things you put your mind to.

I think this was one of the hardest lessons for me to learn in life.

I later discovered that you never know what might work out being best for you, or what might be waiting in the wings for you. Maybe, when you get a disappointment in life, it's because something much better – something you're more suited to – is just around the corner.

15

The GLC

Until 1965, the principal body responsible for governing London was the London County Council, which was the largest local governing body of its day. As part of the Local Government Act 1963, the Greater London Council (GLC) was created, taking responsibility for certain London-wide services and issues, with local administrative duties falling into the hands of the councils responsible for the 32 London boroughs that were established.

My only dealing with the LCC before its responsibilities were carved up was when we needed to apply for planning permission from them. Before we took over the Old Street practice, we had a little dental surgery in Bayswater. The roof of the garage had been "tanked". During the war, they put open tanks of water on top of several properties with flat roofs, such as garages, so that there was always an emergency water supply if the area was bombed. It was like having a little pond on top of the garage. When we applied for the planning permission to remove it so that we could build a second storey on top of the garage, people said we'd never get permission because the LCC was so notoriously difficult to deal with. But we did.

In my continued efforts to get as much political experience as possible – because I was still keen to be considered as a prospective parliamentary candidate for the Conservative Party – I found myself running for a seat on the GLC. In 1970 I was elected as Member for Havering, over on the east side of London, bordering Essex, which is about as far away from Bayswater as you could get within Greater London!

There were clear differences between the issues we dealt with on Westminster City Council and those that came under the GLC. For example, for the GLC, I was involved with reorganising the ambulance service in London. There had been real problems with ambulances losing radio contact when they went too far from central London. We campaigned for more money to improve the radio service. We brought in an outstanding man who'd reorganised communications for emergency services in Hong Kong.

I was also involved with the London Fire Brigade and was fascinated to learn about the different codes they used to signify the urgency of an emergency call-out – these codes would tell them whether lights and sirens were required, and if they could override traffic signals, or if the call-out was less urgent and didn't require such measures. In this role, I also had a pass that meant I had access beyond police lines when there had been a fire. The children thought it terribly exciting that I was allowed where only the police and firemen could go. It's interesting how children see fire as something exciting rather than highly dangerous, and potentially deadly.

I also found myself working with the police. I supported their efforts to make changes to improve the safety of their motorcycle training programme that took place in Enfield. This prompted me to campaign for greater safety standards around issuing motorcycle licences in general. In the early 1980s, I had some personal experience that fuelled my campaign further because my daughter, Rachel, was knocked off her motorcycle. I'll never forget the joy Kevin and I felt when we received a phone call from Rachel to say that, although she'd been in an accident, which involved her being hit by an oncoming car running a red light, she was thankfully unhurt. However, her motorcycle was a write-off. We had lived in fear of something happening to her since the day she got her licence.

When I took up this campaign, the police were very much on my side and were pushing for stronger safety laws for motorcycles.

However, not everyone agreed with me.

At a council meeting during which I spoke on this issue, a Labour councillor, John McDonnell, strongly disagreed with a point I was making. He stood up in front of the full GLC chamber and called me a "fascist in black leather." I was horrified. The wonderful David Pitt (later Lord Pitt), who was the GLC Chairman at that time, stopped proceedings immediately. He told John, "Either you retract that statement and offer an apology, or you leave this Chamber and you never come back."

I got my apology.

Being called a "fascist" by John McDonnell, whose extreme Marxist views have been well documented, was the ultimate insult to me. Nothing could be further from the truth. It was an unnecessary and unfair comment. I have followed his political career ever since and felt some degree of discomfort when he was appointed the Shadow Chancellor under Jeremy Corbyn in 2015. To me, this was a sure sign that Labour was swinging back to the hard left.

John McDonnell and I may have clashed swords on that occasion, but it was fairly rare for someone to react in that way to my efforts. In the less bombastic and militant members of the Labour Party I often found support. I have even commanded the respect of some Labour ministers over and above their own fellow party members. I remember one such incident when David Owen – then a Labour minister – showed such support for me.

Before David Owen left the Labour party to form the SDP (Social Democratic Party) in 1981, he was the Minister for Health from 1974 to 1976 in Harold Wilson's government. While David's stance could be described as more "centre-left", a hard left faction of the Labour party had taken control of the GLC in 1973 (and remained in power until the Conservatives, under Horace Cutler, won back control in 1977).

During those Labour-controlled years, it was a real struggle to be heard on the GLC if you were a member of the Conservative Party. You were often silenced for your party allegiance, even if your views were broadly in line with their ultimate goals. It was incredibly frustrating.

On this particular occasion, I was due to make a presentation to the Department of Health about whether we should have councillors on hospital boards of governors. It was basically an issue about how best to use local authority resources. I had done a huge amount of research and was well prepared for the meeting. However, just before we went into the meeting, the Labour leadership of the GLC informed me that I was not going to be allowed to speak in person. They were going to present my work themselves. I was furious.

So it was poetic justice when David Owen, in response to the presentation made by the Labour councillors, went out of his way to acknowledge me! He said, "Civil servants put papers in front of me to sign off appointments all the time, and they never mean anything to me unless I see a name I know... like Trixie Gardner." The GLC Labour councillors were quite taken aback that David knew and respected me.

Although there was no specific commitment at that meeting, we did, eventually, as a direct result, get councillors (one from Kensington & Chelsea and one from Westminster) onto the Royal Brompton Health Authority, which looked after the National Heart and Royal Brompton hospitals (the National Heart was eventually brought under the Royal Brompton).

What was even more impressive about David Owen acknowledging me at that meeting was that it came on the heels of a big disagreement we'd had over the issue of NHS beds in Plymouth. We hadn't even met in person before, but we had exchanged heated letters about paying for private beds in the Plymouth hospital. David argued that there should be no such thing as a "paid-for" bed but I thought there should be, because it could raise vital funds for the NHS. Despite our difference of opinion on this matter, it was clear (and became obvious on a later occasion, as I described) that David Owen still respected me.

The "paid-for" beds issue was a complex one. "NHS Tourism" was becoming a real problem in the UK. People would fly in from various countries to have their child born in the UK so that the child would qualify for UK citizenship and the mother would get the excellent maternity care on offer through the NHS. By rights, foreign states were obliged to cover the cost of any NHS services and treatments received by their citizens, but they weren't paying up. I think it was Libya that was particularly bad at settling its bills at the time, leaving hospitals with terrible debts.

The issue really shouldn't have been too complicated.

Whilst travelling in Europe, I once had to have emergency treatment in Sweden. They were very pleased to treat you while you were visiting the country, but you had to pay there and then. The NHS is a wonderful service but the system has always been exploited and not enough has been done to prevent this. The NHS should, by rights, be the absolute pride of our country, but it has been let down by being badly managed. People have been allowed to take advantage of it, and those who have more pressing needs, who have urgent health problems, suffer as a consequence.

I had always been frustrated to see those who are really desperate for help lose out because others take advantage of free services and use up precious resources. I remember when I first arrived in the UK, when the National Health Service was in very early stages, there were people who would have endless sets of dentures (false teeth) made. I remember one man having 40 sets made – far more than necessary – simply because the service was free and no one did anything to stop him. No one said, "You've got enough teeth!"

It was a loophole that the government could have easily closed. People had too much power, it was a "demand and be given" attitude. You run real risks if you have a free service that is not well managed and regulated. This is an ongoing problem.

The absolute saving grace of the NHS will always be the wonderful, caring people who work in it. I remember an elderly female GP who lived a few roads away from our first flat (so this was in the late 1950s) who had a surgery in her house. People literally used her waiting room as a place to get in out of the cold. She was so generous and never threw anyone out. She gave people a lot of comfort.

I've always been interested to observe that, when people make complaints about the NHS, it's rarely money that they are after; they all seem to be driven by the desire to ensure that no one else has to go through the bad experience that they have had. Very often it is a relative presenting the complaint because they have shielded the patient from the problem. The patient may not be in a condition to view whether the care was adequate or not.

My time on the GLC, and indeed on Westminster City Council, was heavily dominated by meetings about the health service. There were endless issues about how funding was distributed, with a constant pull between the health services and the social (care) services. Many people believed that the Social Services budget should come under the Department of Health, but they were directly under the control of the local authority and had to compete with the health service for funding. When I was Chairman of Health and Social Services for Westminster City Council we were faced with the choice of maintaining the care services or maintaining the buildings; we couldn't do both.

When public services are constantly vying *against* each other for funding, the system is not working at maximum efficiency. The battle for public money, for both the health service and social services, has always been a hard one. It is only made worse when they have to fight against each other. If they had joined forces and worked together, and shown that they could have managed their resources together, I think they would have got more. As it was, they were forced to compete. Whoever "shouted loudest" and piled on the most pressure got more funds. They were constantly pushing each other out of the way. This frustrated me because health and social care services are so intertwined and complementary to each other, they should be joining forces to apply pressure instead of fighting their own corners.

I wondered whether this was just something that the Conservative Governments had failed to address in the 1980s and 1990s, but when Freddie Howe (The Earl Howe) was the Opposition (Conservative) spokesperson for Health and Social Care in the Lords, a position he held all the time Labour was in power from 1997 to 2010, I asked him if this was still a big issue and he said it was. So Labour never fixed it either!

Certain health and welfare issues find it easier to get to the top of the list for attention than others. For example, the British Heart Foundation (the first charity to benefit from the government's "Gift Aid" scheme) always gets a lot of attention as it is so supported by the public. But there are very worthy and important issues that desperately need funding but fight to be heard.

Public health lies at the very heart of what makes me tick as a politician; it also underpinned everything that motivated the public lives of both my parents. You have nothing if you don't have your health; it is of primary importance to every single one of us.

Local government was not all about dry and serious matters, though. Once in a blue moon we got to rub shoulders with celebrities; or at least future celebrities.

One of our roles within the GLC was to issue late-night music and dancing licences. I was on a panel that considered applications. We had to weigh up the applicant's request against the impact the noise would have on local residents.

I will never forget Richard Branson striding in to an appeal hearing, a very charismatic figure in a white suit. He wanted a late-night licence for a show at a big London theatre that was going to involve various acts coming in and out of the stage door at the back late at night. There was obviously a concern that noise could spill out and disturb local residents.

He gave a very slick presentation to the panel, which included evidence from a sound expert from Switzerland who he had brought with him. We all received a very sound education in the physics of sound! Branson then had us chauffeured to the premises in question so that we could inspect the soundproofing efforts for ourselves. We were all offered a glass of champagne but we were obliged to turn it down or it would have been considered bribery. One of my fellow GLC councillors couldn't help himself, though, and took a glass. He consequently had to excuse himself from the panel!

We did eventually grant the licence and when I met Richard Branson again, many years later, I mentioned that I was one of the people who had given him a break in the early days of his business career.

*

I also sat on the Canals Committee of the British Waterways Board, a body set up as part of the government's Transport Act 1962 in order to clean up Britain's declining inland waterways. My role was to represent all the riparian (meaning that it contains an area bordering a waterway) boroughs in London. Many people assume the only waterway in London is the River Thames, but London also has a number of canals running through it. Branches of the Grand Union Canal connect with the Thames at various points, along with the Hertford Canal, the Limehouse Cut and the Bow Back Rivers.

The London canals had long been totally neglected and it was considered a real disadvantage to have a canal running along the back of your garden. In some areas, huge hoardings had been erected to stop people falling in. We ran a big campaign to raise funds to regenerate and upgrade the canals. Our first project was to redevelop the now world-famous market around Camden Lock on the Regent's Canal, which started its life as a handful of stalls and market sellers in 1974.

I am very pleased to say that the canals have become popular attractions in London rather than being treated as hazards or an eyesore.

I had a short period away from the GLC because, in 1974, I gave up my seat in Havering to fight for a parliamentary seat in the first General Election of that year, a story I will elaborate on in a subsequent chapter. However, in the 1977 GLC elections, I was asked to run again for a new seat.

The Enfield Southgate seat was considered a "safe" seat, as it was predicted to be held by a very strong Conservative majority, and so I was more or less left to do all my own canvassing; the party focused its resources on more marginal areas where they needed more bodies on the streets canvassing.

The girls were aged around 17, 16 and 12 by then so they were full of energy and enthusiasm and were a huge help in my campaign. I remember one huge estate we had to go round, pushing hundreds of leaflets through letterboxes, and I was worried as to whether they could last the course. But they seemed to love it, and got very adept at posting the leaflets through people's letterboxes then withdrawing their hands with great speed when they heard dogs barking, often narrowly escaping having their fingers nipped! They have always told me they have fond memories of us canvassing as a family.

I got around 20,000 votes to win the Enfield Southgate seat. This was a big majority. However, the Liberals, who liked to throw their weight around at that time, demanded two recounts. It was past 2am before my election was confirmed. I got congratulatory messages from several friends the next day saying they were exhausted from staying up half the night listening to the radio waiting for the official declaration!

The Conservative MP for the area at this time was Tony (Anthony) Berry. He was a very popular MP because he would knock on doors and visit his constituents throughout the year, not just when he was campaigning for re-election. He showed that he actually cared about his constituents and wasn't *only* interested in their votes. Most people were very surprised by this; Tony Berry impressed them, just as Robert Allan had impressed me when he knocked on my door outside of the normal General Election campaigning period in 1962.

When Tony had first run for Parliament, he had increased the Conservatives' majority, but it had been a real effort for him because he was naturally quite shy. I think he was very inspired by watching how easy I found it to talk to people, how I got onto their level, and spoke very plainly and honestly with them. After we started working and campaigning together I noticed he got better at talking to people.

Tragically, Tony was killed in the Brighton bombing, when the IRA planted a bomb at the Grand Hotel in Brighton during the 1984 Conservative Party Conference.

Michael Portillo took the seat in the 1984 by-election that was held after Tony was murdered. But Michael made a big mistake in 1997. He assumed the seat was safe and went out with his team to a different constituency, a marginal one, to help with canvassing there. Only a week before the election did the party realise they were going to lose the Enfield seat. Portillo came racing back to campaign for his seat, but it was too late and he ended up losing his seat to Labour in the General Election that returned a Labour government (led by Tony Blair) for the first time in 18 years.

Michael Portillo had discovered, as I had in the 1978 Westminster City Council elections, that there is no such thing as a "safe seat".

I think it's always foolish to make assumptions in politics. People need to know they are being heard. The minute they feel ignored, they will ignore you, and they have the votes that count! Enfield is a great general example of this; the seat has swung back and forth between Labour and Conservative a few times in recent years. The Conservatives took it back from Labour in 2005 but then lost it again to Labour in 2017. People want to know you are helping them. When they don't feel you are there for them anymore, it gives immediate weight to the opposition… it's as simple as that.

The minute you take something for granted, you run the risk of losing it.
That's not a bad motto for life!

I still have a strong relationship with the constituents of Enfield. In fact, the local Women's Section of the Conservative Party still asks me to visit occasionally and give a talk. I go up to speak to them every couple of years.

16

Blackburn, 1970

1970 was a very busy year for me... and for the country.

Thinking he had a good window of opportunity to capitalise on his perceived popularity after an upswing in the economy at the beginning of 1970 (which followed some shaky years at the end of the 1960s), the Labour Prime Minister, Harold Wilson, called a General Election in May 1970. And for the first time, I managed to get selected by the Conservative Party to run for a seat in Parliament.

In order to stand for selection as a Conservative Party candidate, you need to be on the Approved List of Candidates. These days you are assessed by the Parliamentary Selection Board by doing a series of tests that show your aptitude for teamwork, constituent correspondence, debating and so on. In my day it wasn't quite as sophisticated, but you still had to jump through some hoops.

When I first applied, in the late 1960s, Geoffrey Johnson-Smith was in charge of the Conservative Candidates List. He was known for never refusing to put anyone on the list. That is, until I came along! He told me I needed to get some more political experience, which I did. In some ways, I felt as though I had to try harder to prove myself, not only because I was an Australian citizen but also because I was a woman.

By the time I next applied, I was an experienced Councillor for Westminster City Council and was fighting a strong campaign for the GLC Havering seat. Richard Sharples had taken over the Conservative Candidates List by this time. He, conversely, had a reputation for not putting anyone on the list... again, until I came along! When he flatly told me that they didn't need any more candidates, I informed him that they most certainly needed me. (My political experience had clearly paid off; I was not taking no for an answer!) Again, he tried to dissuade me by saying, "Well, even if I do put you on the list, you don't have much hope of getting selected to fight a seat as they've almost all been selected now." But I was not to be deterred.

"Well I certainly won't get selected if I'm not on the list," I boldly pointed out. He finally agreed to put me on the list, pending my personal and political references. They still gave me one of the safest Labour seats in the country: Blackburn. Barbara Castle – a Cabinet Minister, as First Secretary of State, at the time – had held the seat for 25 years, since 1945 and was very popular. But that didn't put me off. I was ready for a fight!

Years later, I met Richard's wife, Pam Sharples (by then Baroness Sharples), who told me that Richard had come home the evening after our meeting and told her "I saw a really good candidate today." You really never know what people are saying behind your back: the bad and the good!

The announcement that I was contesting Barbara's seat attracted plenty of media attention; they had already been closely watching my work in local government.

The *Daily Express* came to take photographs of me at home in London, at Porchester Terrace. They used expressions like "...sitting in her mansion in Porchester Terrace..." suggesting that I was just a rich, privileged posh person. They never asked me about how we were juggling our finances to pay off our mortgage, or how hard we'd had to work to build our dental business. In those days people were indoctrinated with the idea that Tory politicians were all posh and not in touch with the real people. In my local Conservative Association, we were making a real effort to reverse that impression.

On February 19 1970, the *Daily Express* ran a story under the headline, "Here comes Trixie, the Tories' choice to challenge Barbara" and wrote some ridiculous things I would never have said, such as, "Mrs Gardner says of her opponent, 'She is attractive and petite. I would certainly like to have her trim figure.'" They seized on the idea that two females would be in some sort of catfight! I'm sorry to say that these were even more sexist times than we live in today. On the same day, *The Sun* newspaper, another national tabloid, published a picture of me on their front page, sitting in the dentist's chair in our surgery, with the caption, "You're next, Mrs Castle" (goodness knows what they actually meant by that!) and urged readers to read their story about "Babs 'n Trixie" on the next page where they announced, "It's a right luvverly, all-woman, scratch-your-eyes-out battle for Blackburn." They finished the article with two pointed paragraphs about my father. "Trixie Gardner's family has a political tradition. Her father was Deputy Premier of New South Wales," they said. "But he was a socialist." They obviously didn't spend too long doing their research!

Of course the most *important* piece of information that these "journalists" felt obliged to point out at any given opportunity, was that I was a blonde and Barbara was a red-head! What could qualify a woman for public office more than the colour of her hair?!

Of course, I couldn't have contemplated running in the General Election without Kevin's support, and he was 100% behind me.

We bought a small house in Blackburn while I was fighting that campaign, and I split my time between London and my prospective constituency. With three children under the age of ten, it was tricky, but we rallied around with the help of friends and family.

The whole family grew to enjoy the weekend excursions to the north of England. The local press were intrigued by us. I remember Joanna, who wasn't yet 6 years old, pointing out that the front door of our house was the wrong colour because it was red. She was well aware that the Conservative colours were blue! We soon had it repainted.

As I got to know Blackburn and its local community, I discovered that the area was very blighted. Several redevelopment plans had been put forward but the local people were not being treated fairly. As I dug deeper into the local politics I found out that, although the council was overwhelmingly Labour, they all seemed to be under the power of two leaders who were definitely on the side of the big developers and were making decisions to favour them. The Labour councillors were clearly very nice people but they were rather ineffective and seemed unaware of the true plight of the local people.

In general, the council seemed to be unfairly powerful with little opposition to proposed plans, or any true voice for the local people. Planning permissions were being granted without due care for the people who would be affected. If local people wanted to protest against a decision because it could lead to job losses or even evictions, they were completely unsupported. They couldn't even find any sympathetic local solicitors who were willing to go into battle against the council and big developers. If they were brave enough to fight, they had to go to solicitors in neighbouring towns because all the local ones seemed to be under the spell of the council leaders.

I also detected a fair amount of subterfuge going on because the most rundown areas were being hidden from journalists. When anyone from out of town came to visit, they were driven in a circuitous route from the train station to their hotel so that they wouldn't see the worst parts of town. They were then wooed with a tour of the better parts. It was all a ploy to display the great prospects and potential of investing in local development whilst the real problems were hidden from sight.

The more I discovered about local injustices, the more I was determined to win in Blackburn. I really wanted to do something for the people. But I was still relatively new to politics and I was idealistic. I was unaware of the limitations of what one could realistically achieve.

Our house in Blackburn was next door to a family from Uganda who had fled Idi Amin's regime. When we first moved in, we were sharing the water supply with them, which meant we had to leave the tap running for a considerable amount of time in order to get any decent quantity of water out. We eventually had to put in a separate water supply ourselves.

Kevin was particularly interested in how the Ugandan family worked together to do the DIY jobs. The husband was doing extensive renovations and as he worked he would ask his wife and daughters to pass him this and that; they always complied immediately. Kevin said he thought we could learn a thing or two from them and we teased him by saying he could stick to the DIY jobs and we'd do the cooking (which was just a joke as he was always teaching the girls practical things.) I think he paid me back for this by relinquishing "apple pie duty" to me.

Every Sunday, Kevin would make an apple pie from a recipe he'd been taught by his mother; they were wonderful. One weekend, for some reason (I think he was possibly unwell), he asked me to make the apple pie. Everyone loved it. The following weekend when the children asked him to make an apple pie he said, "No, I've signed off apple pie duty." And that was it; he passed the baton to me for evermore!

Although I was the qualified chef in the family, Kevin did do a great deal of the day-to-day cooking. Over the years, he had to develop his cooking skills because at a certain point, I just wasn't around to feed them!

"Someone has to feed and clothe the family," he would say, when I thanked him for taking care of the children so well.

When we first got married, it was quite an adjustment for me to start cooking for two. I'd never cooked for less than about 10 before because I had such a big family and had always thrown dinner parties for big groups of friends. Kevin also hated to have the same meal twice so I couldn't just cook a large quantity of something and reheat it the next day. He became a wonderful cook over the years and the girls really took to cooking, too. Kevin was particularly fascinated by the physics and chemistry of cooking, marvelling at how incredible it was that, if you choose exactly the right amount of each ingredient, mix it and put it in an oven for the right amount of time at a certain temperature, you end up with the perfect cake; yet if you left out or significantly changed only one element, the whole thing would be a disaster.

The big family joke was that if Kevin was cooking, he could make a whole meal in one pot. If I was cooking, it would take several hours and I'd use every single pot, pan and utensil in the kitchen. I would also recruit at least one family member as a sous chef to run around after me tidying and washing up.

"Your mother's cooking tonight," he would tell the girls when they got home from school, "so we'll be lucky if we eat before midnight, but at least it will be delicious."

I always loved cooking for my family but as my life got increasingly filled up with my political obligations, I had so little time. I was always looking for timesaving ideas. When the girls were at school but reasonably independent, I would put a casserole on to slow cook and they would gradually eat their way through it, reheating it during the week.

Some of my schemes were less successful.

Sarah decided she wanted to opt out of the school lunches that were available and take her own sandwiches instead. To get us ahead of the game, I decided we should make enough sandwiches for a full term of school lunches and freeze them. We made up a variety of different sandwiches. The fillings were peanut butter, jam, cheese, ham, or Vegemite (for me; Sarah hated the stuff and the rest of the family were relegated to using Marmite because my favourite Australian spread was very expensive at that time). We bagged individual portions of the sandwiches up, and put the whole lot into the freezer. Every morning we'd take a bag out and by lunchtime the sandwiches would have defrosted. This worked well for the first few weeks but freezers in the 1970s were not as powerful as they are today and the sandwiches were pretty grim by the end of term!

―

I campaigned tirelessly in Blackburn and actually believed I could win, despite Barbara's stronghold. I had heard plenty of stories about Barbara Castle. She didn't sound like your typical Labour politician at all. One story was that she would travel to Blackburn on the train dressed in fur coats but change out of them before she arrived so as not to give the impression she was too wealthy! But that was Barbara. One of her famous achievements was helping to bring in the laws against drink driving, despite the fact that she'd never driven a car herself. I already knew her husband, Ted Castle, who was a journalist, because he was the Vice Chairman on the London Canals Consultative Committee that I was on. I got along very well with him.

Ted Castle was instrumental in Barbara's success. He was her warm-up act. He would face the crowds with a megaphone, getting them excited about Barbara's arrival, shouting, "Barbara will be here to speak to you in half an hour."

It was very effective.

Whenever I appeared, conversely, I got a lot of abuse hurled at me.

"Why don't you go back to Australia!" they shouted. You really do need a thick skin to be a politician; it isn't for the faint-hearted!

Although I was unsuccessful in unseating the formidable Barbara Castle, I significantly reduced her majority. I got 19,737 votes and she got 22,473. It was a 6.1% swing from Labour to Conservative and the smallest majority – just 2,736 – she had received since she first won the seat (which was with a majority of only 489 to take the seat in 1955).

While Barbara was successful, the Labour Party as a whole was not. The 1970 election returned a surprise win for the Conservatives under Ted Heath's leadership and brought the Tories back to power after a break of six years. It was also the first election since the Representation of the People Act 1969 had extended suffrage (the right to vote) to all adults over the age of 18. It's surprising to think that inclusion of the younger population returned a Conservative government. I'm not so sure that the sudden inclusion of a younger portion of the population would do the same today.

To come so close to beating such a well-established MP, when I was a complete newcomer, was a huge achievement. One shouldn't look for excuses but I felt incredibly unlucky when a TV programme about me, which was due to air just before the election, wasn't shown at the time it had been scheduled to go out because there was a strike at Yorkshire Television. The journalist Austin Mitchell (who later became MP for Hull and was married to a woman from New Zealand) was very interested in my background and had made an excellent programme about me. In the end it went out *after* the election. Whenever I met people who had seen it, they said I'd come across very well. Many of them said they would have voted for me if they'd seen it before the election. Could it have made all the difference?

Many years later, I met Willie Whitelaw at an event. He had been the Opposition Chief Whip in the run-up to the 1970 General Election and became Leader of the House of Commons when the Conservatives came to power. He told me that they had underestimated me; if they had known I was going to have such a close fight against Barbara they would have thrown in the heavyweights to help with my campaign and given me far more support. He said he should have come up to Blackburn and helped me, possibly bringing Ted Heath himself along. It's a common strategy for shadow ministers, and even the party leader, to travel to marginal seats to boost the candidate's campaign. It reassures the constituents that the party fighting the seat really cares about them. It's the sort of support money can't buy and can make all the difference in convincing the electorate to vote for you.

It was frustrating to think about whether I would have had enough extra votes if the big guns had appeared in Blackburn, showing their support for me, and/or if that TV programme about me had been shown on time. I can only imagine how different my life would have been if I'd won!

17

Cornwall, 1974

Ted Heath's time in government was a particularly eventful one. British coinage went through decimalisation in 1971, and we joined the EEC (European Economic Community) in full in 1973. He was also in power when the situation in Northern Ireland reached crisis point. And Ted Heath was famously at loggerheads with the unions, which led to two miners' strikes. The second of these, in February 1974, had resulted in the infamous "three-day week" imposed on companies and the public in an effort to conserve energy. We were lucky because we had a gas fire and a gas cooker. We would invite the neighbours over to cook their meals. But everything had to be planned in advance. During scheduled "power offs" you were told not to open the fridge as you would let in warm air while it was switched off and unable to cool down again!

People were up in arms about these conditions, and as the situation escalated, Heath really had no choice but to call a General Election.

In 1972 I had been selected to contest another impossible seat. I was not best pleased with the situation. I only applied to be considered for North Cornwall because people in the party told me it would make a good impression on the selection committee. My so-called friends assured me that the selection committee would give me a better seat to contest, telling me that, "They will *never* choose a woman to contest the North Cornwall seat," and that I should just "go to the interview for practice." But I got caught out, because they *did* select me. I had to run against the very popular Liberal MP, John Pardoe, who had held the seat for eight years, and during a time when the Liberals were seeing a real resurgence in popularity in the polls.

What annoyed me further was discovering that the party members who had been advising me – suggesting I apply for the North Cornwall seat simply for practice – had ulterior motives themselves. Pushing me to go for North Cornwall cleared the way for them to be considered for much better seats that I probably would have been picked for had I gone up against them. I was always a little naïve to the underhand tactics that some politicians employed.

The selection process alone for the North Cornwall seat was almost unbearable. I had to go to countless meetings that they kept adjourning. I almost withdrew from the whole process at one point. I remember saying to Kevin, "If there is one more adjournment, I'm going to withdraw." But just after I said it they finally confirmed my selection.

I really was set up to fail in Cornwall and the travelling I had to do was horrendous, both in terms of time and cost. I kept a car at Plymouth station. I would take the train down and drive the rest of the way when I had to attend meetings.

The trains were not much fun at that time.

Lord Beeching, who was Chairman of British Railways then, had made considerable cuts (known as the "Beeching Axe") to the rail services and had stopped the trains that ran all the way down to North Cornwall in the late 1960s. There were a few sleepers that came through Plymouth but only one or two a night, so I had no other choice. It was extremely time intensive and was particularly unfair on the children, who were still quite young at the time.

Driving around the constituency was exhausting. It was over 60 miles from one end to the other. John Pardoe didn't even have a constituency office; he travelled around in a camper van bringing a "mobile constituency office" to people. For starters, I couldn't see myself doing that!

The upside was seeing such an exceptionally beautiful part of the country. Cornwall is truly stunning. One of its coastal towns, Newquay, was becoming very popular with Australians then because of the excellent surfing conditions. It wasn't a patch on an Australian beach town but, with its great surf, it was the closest thing England had to an Aussie beach.

The Aussies would turn up and teach surfing and lifeguarding skills. It gave the area quite a boost.

North Cornwall was also notorious as being the place where pirates would lure ships onto the rocks by flashing lights at them. Once they were wrecked and the tide went out, the pirates would go on board and steal the goods.

John Pardoe was something of a local celebrity. He had a beautiful singing voice and had become popular for singing at church services. I soon found out that, as well as being the wrong gender for the people of North Cornwall, I also went to the wrong church. I discovered this when I overheard someone complain to a member of the local Conservative Party, "You've made a *huge* mistake. Not only have you chosen a woman, but you've chosen a *Catholic*!"

The blow was slightly softened when I met a few people saying that they never thought they'd vote for a woman but were strongly considering voting for me.

I had encountered religious prejudice before in the UK. When I was out canvassing for my first council election, I was with a fellow party member who pointed to someone in our office saying, "Be careful of that woman over there, she's a Catholic." I hadn't mentioned any religious affiliation of my own at that point and thought it best not to bring it up from then on.

In Australia, the religious divide was even more pronounced. Originally, political parties were strongly split along religious lines. The most right-wing party, the Liberal party, was originally Protestant and fiercely anti-Catholic. The Labour Party (ALP) was the Catholic party. At the time I left Australia in 1954, my local MP was UAP (United Australian Party), which was made up of right-wing Catholics who wanted to leave the ALP to join the Liberals but had been rejected on account of their religion.

Catholics were no more popular in England.

After Queen Elizabeth I outlawed Catholicism, many Catholics were driven out of Cornwall by those loyal to the Queen. Many Catholics were killed because they would not renounce their Catholicism (in other words became martyrs to their beliefs). The Cornish Catholics continued to suffer religious persecution after Elizabethan times. Oliver Cromwell's Roundheads were of the Puritan faith and those loyal to King Charles I were mainly Catholics. As the Roundheads secured victory in the Civil War across the country, many Cavaliers made their way to Cornwall for sanctuary, although the Roundheads made life very hard for anyone who sheltered the Cavaliers. Cornwall found itself in a religious vacuum until the mid 1700s when John Wesley, the founder of Methodism, arrived with his preachers.

Roman Catholics have only been permitted in Parliament since 1829, and the move was not universally popular. The Liberals were anti-religion in general, but if you absolutely had to belong to a church, it had to be the Church of England.

Although the weather throughout the whole campaign was absolutely shocking – several times during the campaign we were almost snowed in – it did give me a slight advantage because it was generally very foggy when I went to mass on Sundays. The foggier the better so I wouldn't be seen going to the local Catholic church!

Throughout the constituency it seemed no one would hear a word said against John Pardoe. A friend of mine from the GLC got hold of a Hansard transcript of a debate in which John had said people sweeping the floors in hospitals should be paid the same as surgeons. But when I showed people, they said, "Oh, no, our John would never say something like that." I pointed out that Hansard was the official transcript of everything that is said in Parliament but they still refused to believe he had said it.

They do say love is blind!

Local loyalty to Pardoe was unmovable. I was so upset to discover that, after working hard to help a local constituent with a housing issue, he still displayed a poster for John Pardoe in his window. I was on my megaphone as we drove past this particular constituent's house during a drive we took around the local area in an effort to drum up support. When I noticed the poster, I grew rather irate and started shouting about how ungrateful people could be. Kevin gently suggested I tone it down!

At this time the Conservatives were using fluorescent pink posters with dark blue writing – very *avant-garde* for the time. We made a poster with my name on it that said "Vote TriXie", making the "X" larger than the other letters and inside a box, as you would see an "X" marked on a ballot paper. We put our posters everywhere, including on the sides of the car and in trees. I remember a poster hanging in a tree for several years after the election. I used to like seeing it hanging there and was a bit disappointed when the girls rescued it because they wanted to keep it at home for themselves.

I was fascinated to learn how different people in Cornwall felt they were from the rest of the United Kingdom, as different as the Welsh or Scottish felt in some cases.

There has always been a strong movement in Cornwall to give the Cornish an official status alongside the Welsh, the Scots and the Irish; some even want complete independence and the ability to make their own rules. Some would be very happy to run their own economy. I love the story someone told me about the pyjama factory. The authorities had decided that people needed employment all year round instead of just the seasonal employment they existed on during the peak tourist times. A firm in Europe set up a factory in Cornwall to make pyjamas and sent material over. The factory workers used all the material making pyjama tops, and forgot to portion out any of it to make any pyjama bottoms. I suspect they sabotaged the pyjama project on purpose because they didn't really *want* to work outside of the tourist season; they *liked* their four or five months off because they worked so hard the rest of the year!

People really were in their own world. A woman once told me that she was going "overseas" to her daughter's wedding. When I asked where – expecting her to say America, perhaps, or at least Spain, she said, "Devon." I soon discovered that many Cornish people considered crossing the Tamar River (that runs along most of the border between Devon and Cornwall) to be "going abroad". And an elderly gentleman we met once told us that he'd been up to London for heart treatment. He said he felt extremely out of his depth in the big city, like he was in a foreign country.

I will never forget meeting a woman who had a large growth on her lip that looked cancerous. I asked her if she had been to hospital and she told me not to worry as it had been "charmed". I told her two sons to get her to a doctor without delay!

And it was a delight to discover the smallest post office in the world at Piper's Pool. It was operated from the tiny living room in a woman's cottage. While it was slightly difficult to get through the doors, the post office was very efficient and people would queue patiently in the garden waiting their turn, and presumably catching up on the local gossip!

The best thing to come out of the Cornwall campaign was Trekenner, the picturesque little cottage we bought on a working farm near Launceston. Initially it gave us a place to bring the children to during the school holidays, but we kept it for years afterwards as a place for the family to escape to when we could. The girls absolutely loved it. They had been real townies until then and knew nothing about country life until we started spending time in Cornwall; they had only really experienced living in London, and a few short spells in Blackburn. I had so enjoyed time on our farm, Pomeroy, while I was growing up; I was thrilled when my girls got to enjoy some of that rural experience. And the family living on a neighbouring farm a few fields away had three daughters around the same age as ours. They had a marvellous time together, our girls teaching them about town life, and the Cornish girls teaching our girls everything about country living. They would disappear for hours to the nearby river.

ITV's popular current affairs programme at that time was *World in Action*. They decided to feature my North Cornwall campaign in one episode. They followed me across the constituency as I talked to farmers and smallholders, and visited livestock markets, schools and day-care facilities. They ensured their filming coincided with half term so that the girls were there; they were keen – as they always were with female candidates! – to show how the family were coping. They wanted to capture us eating breakfast. The children were more than happy to oblige but the excitement of being filmed soon wore off, especially for Joanna, who was appalled at having to eat a fresh bowl of cornflakes six times before the director was satisfied with a take!

On the whole, though, the whole North Cornwall election campaign was rather depressing. I knew I wasn't going to win against John Pardoe, who easily defended his seat and was re-elected by his devoted constituents, but you can't just give up. You have to put on a positive face and keep going.

As that election returned a hung parliament, a second General Election was called in October 1974. People suggested I run again but I really didn't have the appetite for it. I knew it was a seat that needed nurturing for several years if it was ever to return a Conservative candidate (and indeed the Conservative candidate selected for it after me, Gerry Neale, eventually won it, but not until 1979).

At the time, all I felt was relief that I *hadn't* won. I was perfectly happy to concede North Cornwall. I was glad when Gerry Neale eventually won it, but I preferred to have my Cornish neighbours as friends rather than constituents. I grew to love the people of Cornwall; many of them had been extremely pleasant and good to me during the campaign. The whole family enjoyed our time exploring Cornwall's beautiful countryside and pretty beaches. But I don't think we would have loved it half as much had it also been my constituency. With all the back and forth between Cornwall and London, I would have never seen them. They had all been so supportive and Kevin had done a spectacular job of holding the fort at home, as well as managing the surgery (in its dilapidated state as this was bang in the middle of the renovation project), but campaigning was always such a strain on all of them. After my defeat in Cornwall, I felt it was time to focus on my family and the responsibilities that I already had, rather than add more pressure and stress to our lives by running for Parliament again.

I decided I would give canvassing a rest for a while.

In the run-up to the 1979 General Election, the local Conservative Association were keen for me to put my name forward for selection to run for a seat closer to home: Paddington (later to become North Westminster). When I talked to Kevin about it, he said, "I'll back you anywhere except in this seat. I don't want you to stand locally where we live."

The seat had been held by Labour for some years by then and I think Kevin couldn't face seeing me lose a seat for a third time and then be unable to escape from the disappointment because it was on my doorstep. I saw his point completely, and so when it was suggested that I put my name forward, I declined. So I have to confess that it was a little galling to see John Wheeler win the seat for the Conservatives that year – albeit it by a very narrow margin that was accepted after two recounts – and hold onto it until 1997. But you should never say, "That could have been me." That gets you nowhere in life!

18

Europe or Home?

In the late 1970s, I was also being considered by another selection committee. The first European Parliament elections were due to be held in 1979 and, towards the end of 1978, I started going through the selection process to stand as a Conservative candidate in them.

In many ways this was the most gruelling process of them all.

As ever, Kevin was by my side, driving me around the country as I started hauling myself off to various selection committees. But this turned out to be quite the ordeal. The 1978–1979 winter was one of the worst on record, with brutal temperatures and exceptionally high snowfall. This was on top of all the public sector strikes and fuel shortages because the oil tanker drivers were striking. It became known as the "Winter of Discontent" and led to the downfall of James Callaghan's Government.

I remember one hideous journey out to Norfolk for a selection committee interview during a snowstorm when the exhaust fell off the car! I had to give Kevin the rather expensive coat I was wearing; it was all we had that he could lie on to go under the car to fix the problem. We were always a good team!

In the end I didn't get selected to fight for a seat as an MEP. Looking back I don't think there was ever a chance that they would have picked a woman for any of the seats I was in the running for. One of the seats that I interviewed for was won by Boris Johnson's father, Stanley Johnson.

I was secretly relieved I didn't get selected to run as an MEP. I had begun to wonder why I was even considering it. Why would I want to spend half my life living alone in hotels as the meetings moved between European cities, when everything I cared about – my family, my home and my city

– was in England? I had begun to feel it was time I made up for the years I'd missed.

Ever since the girls had been born, I'd been running around, juggling the Women's Section of the Conservative Party, Westminster City Council and the GLC, and fighting two General Election campaigns in far-flung locations, miles from our home in London. My family had always been so supportive of my career, and even enjoyed some of the exciting times, but I needed to redress the balance. The renovations to Old Street were almost finished, too, and I wanted to be around as we settled in to the new surgery.

I really wanted to take the pressure off Kevin, too. He had done a marvellous job of looking after the children whenever I had to be away, but it was my turn to pull my weight at home again. I needed to get a better balance in my life between my family duties and my work commitments. (Little did I know, then, what was in store for me around the corner!)

I had a few friends who did become MEPs. Some loved it, and some exploited it by claiming every penny they could, but I never felt any jealousy. I know it wouldn't have been right for me.

While I didn't become an MEP, I did take another political role that took me to Europe occasionally. In 1978 I had become the UK Chair of the European Union of Women (EUW).

The EUW was founded in Salzburg in 1953 by the Austrian MP Dr Lola Solar with the intention of helping women around Europe contribute to debate and stay abreast of European affairs. A combination of centre-right parties across Europe, it had helped British women in politics build good relationships with female politicians in the other European countries well before we officially joined the European Economic Community in 1973.

Diana Elles (later Baroness Elles of the City of Westminster) had become the UK Chairman in 1970, and was the International Chairman from 1973 until 1979. She was quite a big act to follow. She was a very strong woman, who had been a barrister before being made a life peer by Ted Heath in 1972. She went on to become a delegate to the European

Parliament and the United Nations, and chairman of the Conservatives' International Office. She served as an MEP from 1979–1989 and was a huge campaigner for women's rights. She famously launched the "Fair Share for the Fair Sex", a Conservative Party policy paper in 1969.

There was a little ripple of controversy when I became the Chairman. The woman who was the serving Vice-Chairman had been hoping her friend, who was a committee member, would take over the Chairmanship. But the Chairman of the Conservative Party, Peter (Lord) Thorneycroft was responsible for choosing Diana's successor and he had been a huge supporter of mine over the years. He thought I would do a very good job of building closer links with the Conservative Party.

Until then, the EUW had slightly stood apart from the Party and had been made up of a lot of different people with their own views. I suspected that many of them were not actually committed to the Conservative Party. This was confirmed when I met a woman whose husband was a long-standing Conservative MP. She said, "We're not really Conservatives, we're really Liberals."

I was quite shocked and replied, "No we're not, we are officially part of the Conservative Party."

I thought it particularly extraordinary that a woman whose husband was such an outstanding and prominent Conservative politician could say such a thing. I thought, if you want to join the Liberal Party, go and join the Liberal Party, but we are the Conservative Party. I thought it was rather discourteous of her – to the party *and* to her husband – to be involved in a high profile section of the Conservative Party and then be claiming to be aligned to the Liberal Party. I really objected to her disloyalty.

The person who was Chairman of the EUW automatically held the position of Vice-Chairman of the Women's Section of the Conservative Party so it was quite a prestigious position – and (contrary to whatever my Liberal friend might have thought) was therefore absolutely aligned with the Conservative Party. I felt it was important to get the Committee back on track. I felt like that was the responsibility that Peter Thorneycroft had charged me with in choosing me for the post.

So there were a few noses put out of joint by my election. Some of these women had been around a long time and had assumed one of them would be the natural successor to Diana Elles. I was treated as an outsider right from the beginning. I could tell their feathers were ruffled when the woman who was Vice-Chairman (the one who had wanted her friend to be appointed) announced my appointment by saying, "We've got a new chairman and *some* of you may have heard of her and some of you may not have." It was rather humiliating, especially as it was delivered to a very large audience; the meeting was well attended. She didn't even invite me onto the stage. I only ever addressed the group *after* I'd taken my position. But I tried to get on with it. I've never let things like that get under my skin. Not since my fellow student at Sydney University made that remark about me being lazy all those years ago; that comment definitely helped change my whole approach to life!

The EUW met about every six weeks or so, which felt manageable alongside my other commitments, but it wasn't long before I, again, got roped into taking on even more responsibility.

I was asked, in my role as Chairman of the EUW, to give a talk to the War Widows Association. They invited me to a gathering in Brighton where I was expecting to speak to a small room full of people. I was a little shocked when I discovered it was a big conference. I found myself on stage in front of a whole theatre full of people.

After the meeting I said to the organisers, "If I can ever do anything for you, let me know."

It was just a polite thing to say, but they took me literally and said, "Oh, thank you, yes, we would like you to be our President."

As busy as I was by then, I had to accept. Once I was in this position, I did suggest the post should only be occupied for three years and then there should be a change. Joan Vickers took over after me.

While I was President, we were successful in winning the right for war widows to keep their pensions even if they remarried. It was a huge issue and a very important victory for us. The War Widows Association really is an excellent organisation that I was proud to be a part of; it is as relevant and important today as when it was first founded.

19

"This One Looks Important"

Despite all the experience I'd gained since first getting involved with British politics in the mid 1960s, nothing could have prepared me for the letter I received at the end of March 1981.

It was an ordinary day in our bustling household. I was coming downstairs and Joanna had picked up the post from the doormat on her way out to school.

"This one looks important," she said, handing me a large white envelope before rushing out the door.

You can always guess the importance of a letter by the quality of the stationery. This envelope was made of the highest quality paper I'd ever felt. And it was larger than your average letter, but a particular size that I'd never seen before. On the front of the envelope was the confirmation that it had come from Downing Street, from the Prime Minister's office.

I took the letter upstairs to open it and could hardly believe what I saw. I called for Kevin to come quickly and we both stared at the letter, reading it over and over. It read:

> *Dear Mrs. Gardner,*
> *I shall shortly be recommending to The Queen the creation of a number of Life Peers in order to strengthen the Government's position in the House of Lords.*
>
> *The persons whom I shall recommend to The Queen must, for this purpose, be willing to commit themselves to an active role in the Lords. They will be expected to attend the House regularly and to speak for and vote in support of the*

Government's policies and legislation. I should be glad to know whether you would feel able to take on such a commitment. If you do, I should like to put your name forward to The Queen. I shall fully understand, however, if you conclude that your other commitments would stand in the way of your taking on this role.

I should be grateful if you would let me have your response to this letter, which should be treated in the strictest confidence, as soon as possible.

Yours sincerely,
Margaret Thatcher.

I really found it quite hard to believe. It was completely out of the blue. The last time I had been that dumbfounded was when Kevin proposed to me in Scotland!

Kevin planned a wonderful way to tell the children. That Saturday, he asked them all to come into the drawing room where he had a bottle of champagne ready. He'd made a homemade plastic double-sided photo frame into which he'd put Rachel's motorcycle certificate as she had recently passed her test. The girls were a little puzzled to begin with, thinking this was a rather over-the-top way of celebrating Rachel getting her licence. Then Kevin told them to turn the frame over and there they saw the letter from Margaret Thatcher offering me the peerage. He opened a bottle of champagne and we had a lovely celebration.

I wrote back immediately and soon received confirmation that I had been offered a "Barony of the United Kingdom for Life". What an honour!

The list of peers made by Margaret Thatcher was announced in the morning paper on 14 April 1981. There were a total of fifteen names on the list and, with the exception of the peerage offered to Diana Neave (who was made the Baroness Airey of Abingdon in August 1979 after her husband, Airey Neave was killed in an IRA attack) it was Margaret Thatcher's first list of peerages to be awarded since she became Prime Minister in May 1979. I was one of four women on the list. She had also chosen Felicity Lane Fox, Beryl Platt (an aeronautical engineer from Essex who had repaired aeroplanes during the war and who went on to chair a committee on equal opportunities) and Jane Ewart-Biggs, a very elegant woman whose husband had been assassinated by the IRA while serving as British Ambassador to Ireland.

It was all rather surreal. I went into work in the surgery as usual on that day. I was fixing the false teeth of a dear elderly patient and people kept popping their heads into the surgery to congratulate me. Finally, the old lady said to me, "I don't mean to be nosy but why is everyone congratulating you?"

When I explained, her face lit up in delight and she congratulated me, herself, exclaiming, "Gosh! I've never met anyone who's been made a peer. I've never even met anyone who's *met* someone who's been made a peer," which reminded me of a lovely line in a famous old song – "I've danced with a man who's danced with a girl who's danced with the Prince of Wales."

The lovely congratulatory messages flooded in all day, and for several weeks after, from our friends and family all over the world.

The press were as eloquent as ever, with the *Daily Express* announcing, on Wednesday 15 April 1981: "Fair dinkum – Dame Edna's made it!" later mentioning in the article that "unkind" people were calling me Dame Edna, and starting the piece with the words: "Most intriguing of the new crop of life peers must surely be this formidable Foster's lager drinking dentist, Australian lady, one Trixie Gardner." (I think I tried Foster's lager once or twice and didn't like it much.) But the most hilarious part was when they mentioned my past election fights and suggested that, "The Tories thought they could palm her off on the Cornish since her accent was even broader than theirs." Struth!

The *New Standard* newspaper showed barely more respect when they mentioned my peerage on Tuesday 14 April, getting my title wrong, and informing readers that I would be known as "Baroness Gardner of Parke*r*" before revealing that the most interesting thing about me was that I had two pet tortoises that I enjoyed talking to (true but hardly relevant to my political work!)

*

Getting my official title approved wasn't a smooth process at all. When I accepted the appointment, I was asked to attend a meeting with the "Garter King of Arms" at the College of Arms, which is located in a beautiful ancient building in the City of London. I was told we needed to agree on my title and decide on a design for my coat of arms.

I was quite overawed when first I arrived at the entrance to this historic building, which is located between Blackfriars and Mansion House, in the City of London. Even though it is very small, you're aware of its importance, and long history. The College is part of the UK's Royal Households and was founded in 1484 by Richard III.

I had been informed that I couldn't just be "Baroness Gardner" because the last Lord Gardner had died less than 100 years ago (actually 97 years before, but rules are rules!), so I had to be distinguished by a place name. I had to be the Baroness *of* somewhere.

After discussion with the family, I thought it would be nice for the place to be Parkes. I was born there, and my father was from there, and I thought the British would like the nod to Sir Henry Parkes, the "father" of the Australian Federation who had been born in Coventry, England in 1815.

I was promptly told this wouldn't be allowed because any place names that were used in titles had to be in the UK. I rather boldly said that I wasn't aware that Warsaw was in the UK (referring to the Baroness Ryder of Warsaw who volunteered to help the people of Poland during the Second World War and continued to do extensive charity work throughout her life). They sounded rather irritated as they explained to me that, while of course Warsaw was *not* in the UK, it had been extremely difficult for them to get that particular title agreed upon. Securing the official authority to use "Warsaw" in Sue Ryder's title had involved getting permission from a huge number of people. It had to be approved by the foreign city, obviously, and then personally by the Queen. They didn't want to go through the whole process again. They asked me to come up with somewhere else.

I left feeling rather deflated and went home to discuss some ideas with the family.

We came up with Baroness Gardner of Paddington because I'd been a local councillor of a Paddington ward. We felt this had a rather nice ring to it. This, however, was vetoed by the College of Arms on the grounds that there must be no "merriment" attached to the title. They felt it might remind people of "Pretty Polly Perkins of Paddington Green", an English folk song I had never heard of. (They obviously relaxed this rule, or someone new took charge, because in 1992, James Callaghan's daughter, Margaret, became Baroness Jay of Paddington. I'd argue it's hard to imagine a merrier title than that!)

We also considered "Baroness Gardner of Clerkenwell" as our Old Street dental surgery was in Clerkenwell. But my family made the very valid point that many people wouldn't know how to pronounce it. We were equally unenthusiastic about the idea of "Baroness Gardner of Southgate", which would have given a nod to where I held my GLC seat at that point. We could imagine people asking, "the south gate of where?"

Then fate intervened.

Before the College of Arms had turned down my first suggestion, I had done an interview for the *Today* programme on Radio 4. When they asked me what my title was going to be, I had told them I hoped to be "Baroness Gardner of Parkes" and explained the story behind it. ABC in Australia had the rights to broadcast BBC programmes and the interview had already gone out in Australia. The people of Parkes were apparently very proud of their new celebrity, the "Baroness Gardner of Parkes." My family had started to receive congratulatory letters from the people of Parkes and several newspapers had published the story.

I returned to the College of Arms and said it seemed I already had permission from the people of Parkes.

They begrudgingly agreed to follow the next steps, which included getting written permission from Margaret Thatcher, Malcolm Fraser (Prime Minister of Australia at the time), and finally the Queen.

Eventually it was approved.

I officially became Baroness Gardner of Parkes.

My title has not been entirely unproblematic since, though. Obviously getting people to spell it correctly when they've only heard it spoken aloud is an uphill battle. They're initially very confused that it's gardener *without* the middle "e" and parks *with* one.

Furthermore, the spelling variations have never stopped people confusing my names with the actual words they are derived from. I once wrote to a teacher of Joanna's on generic County Hall paper (while I was on the GLC), which I signed, Gardner of Parkes, which is the correct way to sign your official name when you are a peer. Joanna's teacher was impressed and said, "I didn't realise your father worked at County Hall". When Joanna said that the letter was from her *mother* not her father, the teacher exclaimed, "Oh, how interesting that a *female* gardener is responsible for all the parks and gardens at County Hall!" This amused Joanna no end.

Not many people outside of Australia have heard of Parkes; that is, unless they are space enthusiasts or saw the film *The Dish* about the Parkes Observatory.

There is a famous radio telescope situated on the outskirts of Parkes that was one of the recording instruments NASA used to capture pictures of the 1969 moon landing, allowing people all over the world to see Neil Armstrong become the first man to walk on the moon. Several people stopped me, shortly after the release of the film in 2000, to ask me, "Is that your Parkes, the Parkes in the film?" I was very pleased to tell them that it was, indeed, "my" Parkes.

I'm very proud that my title helps give Parkes a little more visibility. Over the years, Parkes has become somewhat overshadowed by Dubbo, the city that lies a little further north. After the war, Dubbo grew more rapidly than Parkes. This is partly due to the fact that there was a big RAAF stores depot based there – you can still see the huge disused buildings on the outskirts of the town. As a result, Dubbo's airport far outgrew the tiny airstrip in Parkes. It also had the better road links, being at the convergence of all the major highways, providing links to Brisbane, Melbourne, Sydney and Adelaide. The biggest boost to Dubbo's growth came in 1977 when the Taronga Zoo conservation organisation established "Taronga Western Plains Zoo", an open-range zoo on the outskirts of the town. These days Dubbo enjoys a healthy tourist trade. Parkes is still growing though, and has recently put itself on the map with Elvis Presley fans, holding a very successful "Elvis Festival" in January every year.

Wellington, NSW, is actually older than both Parkes and Dubbo but struggled to develop and remains a much smaller town today.

The last time I visited Parkes, in 2007, I was flown from Dubbo to Parkes after arriving in Dubbo on a flight from Sydney as there were no direct flights to Parkes. I was taken in a tiny prop plane that was so noisy, I was rendered deaf for several hours after landing. I can't recommend flying this route. I am told you can now drive it quite easily in just over an hour.

After all the delays with getting my name officially approved, the date for my Introduction to the House of Lords wasn't set until the end of June. The huge advantage of this was that it allowed enough time for two of my sisters to make arrangements to fly over from Australia. Patty came with her husband, Bing Molyneux, and my darling little sister Nonna came over with her husband, Peter Willis.

20

House of Lords, 1981

My formal Introduction to the House of Lords took place on 23 June 1981.

We had a lovely lunch in the Peers' Dining Room. As well as my sisters and their husbands, and Kevin and the girls, Kevin's sister Anne-Marie joined us, as well as some dear friends. My sponsors and their spouses, the Garter King of Arms and a few others attended the lunch, too. It was a wonderful gathering.

I must have got a little over zealous with my invitations because in the weeks running up to my Introduction I received a letter from Black Rod, the senior official in the House of Lords responsible for maintaining order and organising ceremonial events within the Palace of Westminster. Though polite, the letter was perhaps trying to hide some exasperation at the numbers I had added to my guest list. It read, "We have your list of guests duly registered, and will do our best to fit them all in somewhere in the Galleries. The numbers are, however, well over the top of our normal allocation of 15 so we shall need to dot them around. We should be able to manage provided we do not get a second Introduction sprung on us for the same day. But this is not anticipated so all should be well." I think there was a gentle warning in there, lest I thought I could add any additional names at the last minute!

After lunch, my family and friends were shown to the galleries so they would have a good view of the ceremony, and I went to get "robed" in the Moses Room (so called because of the painting on the wall of Moses as a baby, although it has since been renamed "The Grand Committee Room.") New peers are given robes on loan as well as a "tricorn" hat to wear. I remember worrying slightly about how my hair would fare under the hat as I'd had it specially blow-dried at the hairdressers that morning.

I believe hats are no longer worn.

We rehearsed the Introduction ceremony several times on the day, so I wasn't too nervous when the time came for the real event to start.

Wearing his official attire (as he wears for the State Opening of Parliament), the Garter King of Arms led the way into the Lords Chamber, followed by my official "supporters", Baroness (Janet) Young and Lord (Peter) Thorneycroft, and then I followed. They turned to the left and I carried on, stopping in front of the register. The Clerk to the Lords read out the "Oath of Allegiance" that I repeated, finishing with the words, "So help me God". I then signed the "Test Roll", which is a scroll parchment signed by all new peers on their Introduction. It really was like stepping back in time by a few centuries.

After signing the register, I proceeded through the Chamber with my supporters and the Garter King of Arms. As we approached the Woolsack (the seat of the Lord Speaker – a large wool-stuffed square cushion covered in red cloth), we all bowed and I shook hands with the Lord Speaker. After this, all the members cheered and I left the Chamber. I disrobed in the Prince's Gallery and was then shown back into the Chamber where I took a seat that had been assigned for me. (In the weeks, months and sometimes years after your Introduction, you have to fight for a seat, squeezing in beside other backbenchers, until such time as you feel senior enough to dare to move towards the front benches!)

We had a lovely tea party in the Cholmondeley Room after the ceremony and had photos taken out on the Terrace.

At the end of your official Introduction ceremony, as you are leaving the building, you are presented with your Letters Patent, with the Queen's seal, in a bright red leather personalised suitcase. Mine is quite substantial, about the size of a small flat-screen television! But I have heard this has reduced in size over the years. I love my official document, which is a beautiful, handmade inscribed parchment, showing the "E" for Queen

Elizabeth and the Tudor rose intertwined with the Australian Wattle flower, and setting out my full title, "Baroness Gardner of Parkes of Southgate in Greater London and of Parkes in the state of New South Wales and Commonwealth of Australia". And I was delighted that it stated that I was married to Kevin.

I gave my maiden speech on 29 June 1981, a week after my Introduction; I had been advised by my friend Tom Ponsonby – a fellow GLC councillor and hereditary peer as Baron Ponsonby of Shulbrede – to do so before the summer recess. You are told that your maiden speech to the House should not be on a particularly controversial issue and it has to be agreed in advance, so I made mine about the Zoo Licensing Bill, which was very fitting given my family's love of zoos. I described how much my mother, sister and I had enjoyed visiting zoos across Europe in 1937, especially our visit to the Penguin Pool at London Zoo.

I spoke in favour of the licensing scheme, but concluded by expressing that, "I should like to keep it simple, I should like to keep it central, and I should like to have it operated by one authority with the expertise to deal with this matter."

Kevin was in the lower gallery that day and after I finished speaking, I went to sit next to him, which was on the wrong side of the barrier that separates the peers from spectators. The doorman responsible for ensuring everyone sits where they are supposed to rushed over and, in an urgent manner, told me to go to my seat on the official benches.

There are so many rules and customs to learn when you join the House of Lords; it's like stepping into a whole new world. You have to learn to follow certain procedures and all the correct ways of addressing people. For example, when speaking in the Chamber, we address fellow party peers as "my noble friend" and any former bishops or archbishops who have been made Lords as "the noble and right reverend Lord. The serving bishops are also known as "the Lords Spiritual". Someone who was in the armed forces is called, "My noble and *gallant* Lord," and anyone who is in the legal profession, "My noble and *learned* Lord." My favourite address is the title used to address the Archbishop of the Church of England, who must be addressed as "the most reverend *Primate*, the Archbishop of..." This does make me smile as the word "primate" makes me think of monkeys!

When Lords get up to speak there is a pecking order. First priority is always given to the Lords Spiritual. If one of them gets up to speak, everyone else is expected to let them take precedence.

Another fascinating revelation I discovered was that some ceremonial elements still include Norman French expressions. This is because French was, for a long time, seen as the language of the "educated classes". So from the time of the Norman Conquest in 1066, until 1488, parliamentary and judicial business was conducted in French. The practice was re-introduced to some degree after the restoration of the Monarchy in the seventeenth century. For example, when we pass acts, the clerk makes it official by saying "*La Reyne le veult*" which, in Norman French means, "the Queen wills it".

When I first entered the House of Lords in 1981, it looked a little worse for wear. They had discovered that the heat from all the candles (that were traditionally used to light the Chamber for years) had dried out the ceiling. A big lump of the ceiling had consequently come loose. It had fallen and crashed onto the seat of Lord Shinwell who, fortunately, was not in his place at the time. After this, the ceiling was covered up for years as they carried out major repairs, fitting them in around the times that the Lords were sitting.

The refurbished ceiling was not finished and unveiled until 1984. According to Hansard, during the Centennial tributes celebrating Lord Shinwell's 100th birthday in October 1984, The Lord President of the Council, Viscount Willie Whitelaw said, eloquently, "It is fitting that this week we are sitting for the first time under the newly restored ceiling of this Chamber. It was, I am told, the boss above the seat of the noble Lord, Lord Shinwell, whose dramatic fall demonstrated the urgent need for the ceiling to be restored. I am delighted that the noble Lord is in his place today, but not nearly as delighted as I am that he was not in his place on the occasion of the fall. I hope that the noble Lord will be able to continue to sit in greater safety under the new ceiling, and that we shall continue to hear his inimitable contributions to your Lordships' debates."

Lord Shinwell died in May 1986, aged 101.

People don't necessarily find out how they were chosen to be peers, but I had an opportune moment to get a little insight into my appointment.

I happened to find myself sitting beside Lord Thorneycroft (who had appointed me as Chair of the European Union of Women and had been one of my supporters in my Introduction ceremony) in the Lords' dining room during teatime one day. Another peer at the table asked Peter (Lord Thorneycroft) if he knew how we had all actually come to be life peers. Peter replied, "I don't know your story, but I can tell you my own story and," he turned to me, "I can tell you your story, Trixie."

I was all ears as he went on to explain that he'd been in a meeting at Downing Street with Margaret Thatcher while she was making her very first list of life peers. She had three women on her list and was looking for one more female peer. Lord Thorneycroft had said, "I'll tell you a good woman for the job," and had then nominated me.

Peter went on to tell us his own story. After he lost his Monmouth seat (that he'd held since 1945) in the March 1966 General Election, the Postmaster General, Ted Short, had said to him, "How would you like to go to the other place, Peter?" and he was made a life peer in December of that year. (The "other place" is a euphemism for the House of Lords, used particularly amongst MPs in the House of Commons.)

When I thanked Peter, both for nominating me as a life peer and appointing me, earlier, as Chair of the EUW, he said, "You're one of my success stories, maybe my only success story," which was extremely flattering. He really was one of my biggest supporters and inspirations, and I had huge admiration for the work he did as Chairman of the Conservative Party.

Peter died in June 1994. His death was a real loss to the Party. And many people, including myself, felt a huge personal loss, too.

21

On Westminster Bridge

When I joined the House of Lords in 1981, you really had to figure things out for yourself. Compare that to today, when each new peer is assigned a mentor who guides them through all the procedures and customs during their initial few weeks. Another stark change to how things were in my day is that new peers these days expect to be given a desk right away. When I joined, there was a huge waiting list for desks; in fact it took me twelve years to get mine!

A desk in 1981 would have been *very* welcome to me because I ended up with rather more work than I'd bargained for.

I had assumed that, once I became a peer, I would automatically give up my seat on the GLC at the following elections. However, because the decision to abolish the GLC was made before the next elections were due to be held, those elections were cancelled and we had to stay on in our seats until the final day. For me, this meant a *lot* of running back and forth across Westminster Bridge!

Sometimes I wished I had a desk in the middle of that bridge – it would have made my life so much easier!

I was offered a locker near the dining room in the House of Lords, but this wasn't much good to me because I was always in such a hurry. When I had to leave, I had to go immediately, with no time to pick up anything I needed in a locker on a different floor.

I wasn't the only thing bouncing back and forth between two places. Control of the GLC was forever swinging back and forth between the two main parties. For a number of years it would be controlled by

Labour, and then it would bounce back to the Conservatives. Whatever one council did, the next one (led by the opposite party) tried to undo it. This can be an endemic problem when parties shift too far away from each other. When you start saying, "All the problems are the fault of the other side and now we have to fix them" – and both sides are repeatedly saying that – how can you make real progress? I think this is, again, another reason why so many people involved in politics today think we need major changes to the way we run things, so that we stop getting so embroiled in ideological debates and focus on getting the practical things done, of which there is a never-ending list!

In May 1981, Labour had just taken back control and was back under the leadership of Ken Livingstone, who I always got on well with. The original leader of the Labour group, when the election took place, was the centrist, Andrew McIntosh (later Baron McIntosh of Haringey), but he was ousted within 24 hours of the election in a leadership coup won by Ken who was voted in by the harder left members of the party.

County Hall soon became a symbolic – and literal – battlefield between "Red Ken" (as he came to be known) and Margaret Thatcher. Ken publically humiliated Thatcher by flying huge banners on top of County Hall publishing the number of unemployed in London. These were obviously in clear view of the Houses of Parliament and the figure was updated on a daily basis to show how the number of unemployed was rising. This stunt was undoubtedly the final nail in the GLC's coffin.

I'm not sure how, but somehow I managed to honour all my commitments during those busy overlapping years. I only went to the GLC when there was a critical debate or we were deciding on an issue where the vote was very close. Very occasionally there would be a clash where a debate I needed to attend in the Lords was scheduled at the same time as a GLC debate. On those occasions, I just had to decide which issue I felt was the more important.

In those days, there was a marvellous messaging system. Anyone could get a message through to a Member by calling a central number. The message would be written on a piece of paper and passed to you immediately. We also had pagers to tell us when we had to vote. These days, the service is more automated and most people communicate using mobile phones. I haven't exactly embraced these devices but I have graduated from an electronic typewriter to an iPad, and am rather proud of this achievement!

Despite a huge public campaign to save the GLC, it was officially abolished in 1986.

Thus I was a member of the Greater London Council for the remainder of its life. I was there for the final party, which involved much bittersweet merriment including a fireworks display at midnight, and the lowering of a flag on the Members' Terrace by Ken himself. It took place on Monday 31 March 1986, which was a bank holiday for Easter Monday, so that anyone who wanted to could attend the event on the South Bank.

I was among the many people who were very disappointed when the GLC was dismantled. The two-tier system is so necessary in London. And it did work. The GLC was a victim of the personality clash between Ken Livingstone and Margaret Thatcher more than anything else.

I remember with particular fondness all the people I met and worked with during my time on the GLC.

I was thrilled to meet the poet John Betjeman, who was Poet Laureate from 1972 until his death in 1984, while I was on the GLC's Historic Buildings Committee. When I told him my name, he said, "Trixie Gardner... Trixie Gardner..." He sort of sang it back to me, telling me it had a musical quality. Then he said he was actually familiar with my name as he remembered seeing it on a poster near his house in Cornwall many years after my 1974 campaign. Perhaps it was that one my daughters rescued from the tree!

Osbert Lancaster, the famous cartoonist, was also on the Historic Buildings Committee. He was such a gentleman and quite eccentric. I felt as if he was from a bygone age. I'll never forget his reaction when we were considering listing a building on Westbourne Grove. He said, "Absolutely not!" and went on to explain that when he was a baby, his nanny was pushing him along Westbourne Grove in a pram when a dog jumped up and bit him. From that moment on he'd declared a prejudice against the road! Sadly, he hardly outlived the GLC, dying in July 1986.

I was also disappointed when County Hall was sold off, reportedly for a bargain price, to a big developer who turned it into a hotel and aquarium. I missed visiting that building. It was wonderful to be so in the heart of things on the banks of the Thames with those fabulous views of the Palace of Westminster and Big Ben across the river, and the City of London skyline.

Of course the new GLA building is also very impressive, standing further down the Thames near Tower Bridge.

Labour had always promised to replace the GLC with a similar body and, in 2000, they launched the Great London Authority (GLA) with similar powers to the old GLC, although its members represent broader constituencies, such as the whole of west London. Constituents also get to vote in a variety of ways. Your first vote is for your named candidate – and first past the post gets the seat. Then you get to vote for a party and candidates from a "top-up list" get selected according to the percentage of votes cast for each party. So, for example, the Green Party has never won a seat outright but gets seats via the "top-up" (not unlike proportional representation) system.

You also get a vote to appoint the Mayor of London.

Ex-GLC members were invited to the opening reception of the GLA's new building near Tower Bridge in 2002. I ran into another ex-GLC member at that reception: Raine Spencer, the Countess of Dartmouth (later Countess Spencer). We were both looking around, comparing notes – such as, were the views actually better and how did the parking facilities compare? – with our old home at County Hall. She and I had also sat on Westminster City Council together. Raine became the youngest member of Westminster City Council, for the Conservatives, in 1952, when she was just 23. She was later on the GLC, representing Richmond, during the time I was there. I do remember she was terribly charming but could also be overdramatic. She would just go on and on from the backbenches without saying anything of much substance.

Most people are more familiar with Raine's famous mother and famous stepdaughter. She was the daughter of novelist Barbara Cartland and the stepmother of Diana, Princess of Wales.

I always thought fondly of Diana whenever I encountered Raine, with whom Diana had a very difficult relationship for many years; although reportedly they did make amends before Diana's death.

Princess Diana was a very special person. I clearly remember all the times I met her. Several of those times were with Kevin in an official capacity.

Kevin eventually followed in my footsteps and was elected as a Westminster City Councillor. I was extremely proud when he served as Lord Mayor of Westminster from 1987 to 1988, which made me Lady Mayoress. We met the Princess of Wales at several events during that time.

The very first time I met Diana was at Clarence House, several years earlier, not long after she was married, in 1981. Around 40 women who headed various organisations were invited to meet her. I was struck by how young she looked, almost like a schoolgirl. And she *was* incredibly young; she was only 19 when she got engaged and had just turned 20 a few weeks before her wedding day.

Most of us knew the protocol: that you don't speak to royalty until they speak to you. There was a lot of polite nodding and smiling. But then one woman, who either wasn't aware of the protocol or didn't want to abide by it, spoke directly to Diana, saying something along the lines of, "I believe you were in the Girl Guides, as I was, too." Well, it was like a light went on. Diana just came to life; the difference was remarkable. She looked delighted that someone had spoken to her, engaging her in a subject she was passionate about.

Another vivid memory I have of Diana was when she came to a swimming gala for children with special needs, organised by Great Ormond Street Hospital, that was held at the Queen Mother Sports Centre on Vauxhall Bridge Road near Victoria Station in 1988. I was attending in my official capacity as Lady Mayoress. This was at the height of the media frenzy around Diana and I remember the royal protection officers kept telling us, "Don't let the press get to her, she gets very upset."

We managed to keep the paparazzi at bay and once we were all inside the building, Diana seemed perfectly relaxed, realising that the press were nowhere in sight. What really struck me as extraordinary was that there was an elderly lady sitting beside the pool with an old camera. Diana walked up to her and said, "Would you like to have a photo taken with me?" The woman was absolutely thrilled. So I don't think Diana had an issue with being photographed, I think she just resented the paparazzi for hounding her and not respecting her privacy.

She could certainly be temperamental and she clearly struggled to keep up with the demands on her. I recall another occasion when we were attending a performance at the London Coliseum and she rushed in at the last minute, quite breathless. She was sitting in the front row of the Royal Box with Prince Charles. Kevin and I were seated with them. I was in the row just behind the Royal couple and watched as Diana's lady-in-waiting leaned forward to do up her dress that was still open at the back.

Diana did many wonderful things in official and unofficial capacities, and her death was devastating to so many people, but none more than those poor boys, Princes William and Harry, who lost their mother at such a young age.

I must also mention the few times I was fortunate enough to meet the Queen Mother. One occasion was when Kevin and I attended the Cheltenham Gold Cup. As we were passing the Royal Box we met Lord Porchester. He was delighted to see us and asked if we would come into the box because he urgently needed to go to the paddock. He explained that the Queen Mother was there and it was not done to leave her alone. Kevin and the Queen Mother spent a very jolly half an hour discussing the day's racing. She was a wonderful flirt!

The Queen Mother loved racing. When she was at the tracks, she liked to watch most of the race on a TV in the Royal Box until the final moments when she would come out onto the balcony to see the last length.

We also met her at an event in 1988 at the Royal College of Music when we all helped bury a time capsule in the foundations before a celebratory tea. She was particularly enchanting and relaxed that day and the young musicians had a marvellous time chatting away to her. She loved young people and I could see why William and Harry were reportedly so close to their great-grandmother!

22

Gardner's Question Time

Question Time in the House of Lords takes place after prayers at the start of every session (Monday to Thursday; there are no Questions on Fridays, when we sit at 10am). We have around 30 minutes when peers can ask Government Ministers to answer questions, verbally, that have been tabled in advance. The process of getting your question on the order paper is not an easy one so you have to pick your topics and timing with care. There's a very strict limit on how many questions each peer can ask per session. Currently, you can have six per parliamentary session. Apparently, I had something to do with this limit being set because, when I arrived in the Lords, back in 1981, when there was no restriction on the number of questions you could submit, I proceeded to ask so many questions, they tightened the rules!

On Tuesdays, Wednesdays and Thursdays, there are three slots for questions for oral answer, plus a topical question, which is balloted nearer the time. On Mondays there are four questions tabled for oral answer.

Submitting your questions is quite an ordeal. During our parliamentary sessions you have to submit them in person to the Table Office. With so few questions allowed per session and a limited number of slots available in the short 30-minute window allotted each day, competition is high. You have to start queuing up outside the Table Office from around midday (to be first in line when they open at 2pm). It's not much fun waiting around for the Office to open as there's an ill-fitting window in that corridor causing quite a cold draught! During the recesses you can submit questions for oral answer in writing and they will be drawn out of a hat and scheduled during the first four weeks after the House returns.

When your question is accepted, it is always scheduled for four weeks after you submit it.

Question time moves at a fair pace, and if you are particularly interested in the topic and want to question the Minister about it yourself, you have to be on the edge of your seat, ready to stand up and speak. The peer who has tabled the question speaks first, standing up and saying, "My Lords, I beg leave to ask the question standing in my name on the order paper," before reading out his or her question. The Minister responds, briefly. Then the peer may ask a supplementary question and the Minister will respond again. After that it's a bit of a free-for-all. Although we do try to share the floor fairly between parties so that one side doesn't get to dominate. And we always give way to the Lords Spiritual if they wish to speak. I'm not quite as quick up onto my feet as I once was, but if it's something I feel very passionately about, I do my best to hop up!

I usually sit in the second row right behind our Chief Whip, whoever holds that office at the time. I may be imagining it, but once or twice I could swear I've seen their shoulders twitch when I've bobbed up to ask a particularly pertinent question!

If you have any vested financial interest associated with the topic you are speaking about, you must declare it. Although, to save time, you only have to say "my interest is declared in the register" before you speak. There is an official register where peers are required to declare their businesses interests. For example, if Michelle, Baroness Mone, an entrepreneur with an underwear brand, was going to speak on an issue related to the clothing industry she would have to state that her interest has been declared in the register.

In 1998, Radio 4 broadcast an edition of *Gardeners' Question Time* from the Houses of Parliament. As a keen gardener, I was pleased to get the opportunity to ask a question on the programme. Because of this, and my reputation for asking so many questions, my fellow peers jokingly started to call our official sessions "Gardner's Question Time." I found this rather amusing!

*

The following are the issues that have been most important to me and that I have fought hardest for, either directly with an amendment or a bill, or in general whenever the topic arises.

Can I retain my Australian citizenship?

I have never given up my Australian citizenship; I have never wanted to. Kevin and I were both given the permanent right of abode in the UK, so there was really no necessity to give it up. When we first moved to the UK, if you wanted to become a British citizen you had to revoke your Australian citizenship, which I never wanted to do.

I was surprised – and very happy – to hear that it was not necessary for me to give up my Australian citizenship or become a British citizen to take my place in the House of Lords. However, when Labour came into power in 1997, they wanted to change the British constitution to require all Members of the House of Lords to become British citizens. This was chiefly to clamp down on people who were hiding assets in tax havens by taking citizenship of other countries. Ultimately it was all about money, about making sure that peers were not using any loopholes in citizenship laws to avoid tax, and to ensure that there was no conflict of interest while they were part of the law-making body.

By the time Labour's proposal finally came up, we were in the run-up to the 2010 election. We were given no time at all to debate it, which wasn't really right since they were trying to make a change to the constitution – a rather big deal! Constitutional changes are rarely made. But Labour were trying to push it through on their last day of power before the General Election of 2010, so they gave us a day to debate it and forced us to vote on it. Someone immediately got up and complained, saying it was something that should be given at least three weeks and we should refuse to debate it.

It's funny how, in life, you never know which of your experiences may turn out to be more useful than you could ever have imagined at the time. Years after hearing the citizenship case that I mentioned earlier, of the British/Egyptian child in the magistrates' court, I was able to use some of the information I had gathered from that case in the debate about peers being required to take British citizenship.

I was very aware of all the complexities and huge costs involved in changing your nationality; I was not keen on this law change at all. I wanted to speak against it but the Labour Chief Whip asked me, personally, not to. They were not confident of winning the General Election and this felt like their last chance to get the Bill through. Although I honoured the Labour Chief Whip's request, I rather regretted not using the tactic that my fellow peer and dear friend, Jean (Baroness) Trumpington had once used. When told that there was not enough time for her to speak (I think it was on the Gas Bill, regarding the privatisation of gas), she got up and said that she was just going to say all the things she *would* have said if there *had* been time for her to speak. I thought that was very clever! To be fair we had been sitting all night on that occasion. At one point we were told breakfast was being served in the dining room. But by the time we actually got there, we'd even missed breakfast, so goodness knows what time we ever got to bed.

On the citizenship debate, I could have got up and said that the Labour Chief Whip had asked me not to speak but that I was going to say all the things that I *would* have said had he *not* asked me not to speak, but I didn't!

The Labour Chief Whip knew my feelings because I'd shared them at a previous meeting on the issue. There were about 20 chairs set out at this meeting; a lot of civil servants were in attendance, but I was the only peer who turned up.

At the meeting, I'd proposed that we at least amend the Bill. My proposal was that sitting peers didn't have to become British citizens but should be *deemed* domiciled, and thus treated, for tax purposes, like any other British citizen. This would allow them to keep their citizenships while retaining their role in Parliament, paying UK tax just like any other UK citizen. That way, those of us who wanted to keep citizenship of our countries of birth could do so and still sit in the House of Lords. We would simply be deemed to be domiciled and be required to declare worldwide income as a UK resident.

So that was the Bill being proposed and voted on at the debate, with my suggested compromise as an amendment. I assume the Labour Chief Whip felt I had had my say by then!

There was a strong feeling that the debate should be pushed back to after the General Election, but Labour knew it would be thrown out if the Conservatives got in. Or it would at least have given the peers who wanted to avoid being UK tax payers enough time to re-arrange their finances to avoid as much tax as possible.

At one point, Lord Armstrong got up to speak. He'd been the head of the civil service and was once involved in a very famous case giving evidence in Australia in the John Stonehouse case. (John Stonehouse was a Labour MP who faked his own death by leaving clothes on a beach in Miami before fleeing to Australia to set up a secret new life.) Lord Armstrong said words to the effect of, "Before you decide to throw out this bill, I must speak up for the public services. We've waited 40 years for this. We don't have everything we want here, but it's better than nothing."

Someone got up shortly after Lord Armstrong spoke and suggested we adjourn for a short time so that each party could discuss it before voting.

While we were adjourned, Jack Straw, then Lord Chancellor and Secretary of State for Justice spent the rest of the afternoon going from party to party trying to get them to agree to the Bill with my amendment.

I had first met Jack in 1970. He was Barbara Castle's PA and campaign manager in Blackburn during that General Election. He had been a total newcomer in 1970 and although I had watched his subsequent rise through the ranks, I had not actually talked to him since that time, apart from the occasion when he came to open a refurbished gallery at the V&A. As I was being introduced to him, he said, "I know exactly who you are. You gave Barbara Castle the best fight she ever had!"

We spoke briefly about how there had been a lot of goodwill between Barbara and me, despite us being rivals.

Jack's efforts paid off and the Bill was finally passed at around 1am, in the last hour of the Labour government before it was dissolved in order for the General Election to take place.

So peers do, now, have to declare worldwide income and be taxed as UK residents, but – thanks to my amendment – do not have to become British citizens. Peers were given the choice to renounce their role in the House of Lords so that they were not taxed under the new law, and several wealthy peers chose to do this.

I was glad that my compromise was adopted but I didn't wholeheartedly support the Bill. I thought it was a double-edged sword. For example, I knew an Australian man living in the UK who was very interested in becoming a peer until this law came into force. He lost interest after this, as it would have upset his entire financial world. Even if he could have retained his Australian citizenship, it would have given him too great a tax burden. This is a shame as I think he would have been a good peer.

I later found out that Labour was specifically going after Lord Ashcroft (who had been a large donor to Conservative candidates fighting marginal seats) as he had taken citizenship of Belize in order to avoid paying tax on all of his assets that were thought to be around £1 billion. He apparently owned most of an entire Caribbean island.

You usually find that money is the motivation behind many heated debates!

I always try to speak when citizenship issues come up, and they come up a lot. I really do care deeply about people who are facing difficulties with their citizenship. I think it's fundamental for someone to have the citizenship rights that they are entitled to and want. Only recently, my optician told me that he had had his application for permanent residency rejected for no apparent reason. He is French and has worked for the NHS for 30 years, paying his taxes in the UK in all that time. He is exactly the sort of person we should be very grateful to have wanting to become a citizen, someone who is very well qualified, performs an excellent service and who *wants* to be here.

I offered to help him with his appeal. I gave his details to the relevant minister and was informed that we just needed to submit a few more papers.

The next time I saw him, I was very happy because he told me he'd got his permanent residency approved. Having said that, I was annoyed that the whole problem had only been an admin error. It was just a processing issue that had caused the rejection in the first place. I thought of all the people who had been driven into a panic because they found themselves in the same situation; how awful to go through the trauma of believing you are being kicked out of the country you believed was your home, and then to find out that the decision was simply an admin error! We have to do better than this. We have to become more efficient and accurate in these cases. The relevant departments need to communicate better with people, and the IT software needs to be up to the job of processing applications quickly and accurately.

Can we guarantee free NHS dental check-ups for all?

The hardest and most heartfelt battle I ever fought was against my own party's decision to introduce a charge for adult patients to get dental check-ups on the NHS that was initially proposed in 1988. This was obviously a deeply personal issue and to date it is the only time I have worked against a Conservative Government policy. I proposed an amendment to retain free check-ups for all, and tried to persuade others to do the same. I just could not support the introduction of check-up charges for adult patients. It was obvious to me that this would cause huge health problems. So many serious diseases, including oral cancer, can be prevented through early detection. I was very disappointed when the Government recommended that charges were brought in for adult check-ups. Going to the dentist isn't at the top of everyone's "to do" list; most people hate going. If you charge them for that check-up, they are even *less* likely to go. I knew people simply wouldn't get check-ups if they weren't free. And that could cost lives!

Lord Colwyn, another peer who had worked for many years as a dentist, was hugely supportive of my amendment, and Lord Ennals brought up the BDA's position on check-up charges. In his speech, he said:

> *It is clear where the British Dental Association stands on this matter. It believes that charging for check-ups will have a*

damaging and possibly disastrous effect on dental attendance. It says: "The price of a check-up may seem small. However, in charging for dental advice, alongside free health advice and health care that is offered elsewhere, the NHS would be making the clearest possible statement to patients and prospective patients that regular dental care is thought to be relatively unimportant. This may not be the intention but it is certainly the interpretation which many would put on the introduction of examination charges." The British Dental Association is strongly against the Government's proposals. One must ask oneself why the Government believe that they know better than the dentists.

In the end, my amendment was passed by the Lords, partly because I went into the library after lunch and rounded up everyone I could find to come and vote. Sometimes, after lunch, people settle in the library but I rallied them all together to listen to the debate and vote. We referred the Bill back to the House of Commons. However, the Government attached "financial privilege" to it, which means it becomes part of the budget and the Lords can no longer have any say on the matter.

I was furious.

I believe that losing this fight, to keep free dental check-ups available for all, was the beginning of the end for NHS dentistry. I feel that introducing charges for dental check-ups has had an *extremely* adverse affect on the dental health – and overall health – of the people of this country.

It has always been an uphill struggle to get people into dentists' chairs for regular check-ups and preventative treatments. Charging them for the experience is never going to help to get them there! There has been a constant eroding of free dental care that is provided in the UK. When everyone was entitled to a free dental examination under the NHS, people would take their children with them regularly for check-ups. Going to the dentist was a normal thing. Nowadays, as parents can't afford to go themselves, they don't take their children. By the time the children visit the dentist for the first time, they are older, full of fear, and usually have very poor oral hygiene. If you take children along for a check-up on a regular basis, when there are no problems with their teeth, they get used to the idea of being in the dentist's chair, and it will usually be a positive experience. If they never see a dentist until they are in pain, they will only ever associate the dentist with this unpleasant experience and will be reluctant to go and get regular check-ups in the future.

To this day, dentistry continues to be under funded and under represented in the UK and I will never stop campaigning in Parliament for better provision and changes. The future savings would be extensive. Why are we not providing everyone, for example, with the ability to get a very simple test that can be done to check for signs of oral cancer? This should be routine in every examination; it would save lives and huge costs to the NHS if we could catch oral cancer in early stages. Why has this never been adopted as a routine, free test?

We are still in a real crisis in the UK when it comes to dental care. On 18 January 2018, I asked a Question for Short Debate in the Chamber on the issue of child dental health. I was motivated by appalling statistics regarding the number of children in the UK having operations under general anaesthetic in hospitals for tooth decay. I highlighted the particular plight of children in Manchester, one of the worst areas for children's tooth extractions. I had found it very disturbing to read that, at one point, children in Manchester were taking up all the available paediatric general anaesthetic beds in local NHS hospitals in order to clear their deciduous teeth. A report a few months later, in April 2018, found that tooth decay is the most common reason for young children to be admitted to hospital. It found that, in 2017, children missed 60,000 days of school having teeth taken out. Public Health England data found that 39,010 teeth were taken out because of decay in 2016–2017, the equivalent to 141 every working day. Just over half were in children aged 5 to 9 but 7,530 were in children under the age of 5!

As well as the contribution of high sugar consumption (we can definitely see changes in the trends of tooth decay according to periods in recent history when sugar consumption was higher or lower), I believe there is a strong correlation between dental health and fluoridation schemes, especially in low-income communities. To date, only 10% of the UK's population are served by community water fluoridation schemes, compared with over 67.1% of the population in the US and over 70% in Australia (figures from 2012). Israel passed legislation in 2002 to require nationwide fluoridation of water but this legislation was repealed in 2014. In 2015, Ireland was the only country in the European Union with a mandate for nationwide fluoridation, with 71% of the population living in areas with fluoride added to their water supply, but there has been recent strong opposition to this and many local Irish councils have passed motions to end it.

There has been a long campaign in the UK to get fluoride added to water. There have been several water fluoridation schemes trialled but not enough, and those that are running are constantly under threat of being stopped. In March 2018, Lord Hunt (who is president of the British Fluoridation Society, founded in 1969) raised his concerns in Parliament about Bedford Council's proposals to end their scheme.

The issue of fluoridation has always been controversial. In the 1980s a famous case in Strathclyde ended with the council being stopped from adding fluoride to the water after a Glaswegian woman mounted a legal case against their plans to do so. However, while the council was defeated in maintaining their *power* to add fluoride to the water supply, the judge in the case rejected all claims that fluoride was toxic or linked to cancer.

As a dentist, I highly recommend taking fluoride for dental health. I took fluoride tablets during all my pregnancies because primary teeth start forming in the sixth week of pregnancy.

Dental provision in the UK was once the envy of the world. I will never forget Doctor Kiss, a Hungarian doctor who had fled Budapest during the Hungarian Uprising of 1956 and come to London. He was later granted the right to settle in the US. Before he left, he wanted to have all his crowns replaced under the NHS. In Eastern Europe at that time, they used what we called "jam pot crowns" made of base metal in stock sizes. They just chose one that seemed approximately the right fit and hammered it onto your tooth so you had great hunks of metal sticking into your gum, potentially causing terrible gum damage. Kevin fitted Dr Kiss with the most beautiful crowns that would have cost him a fortune in America, but were covered under the NHS. He gave us a beautiful teapot (not jam pot!) as a thank you present.

The academic requirement to become a practicing dentist in the UK has always been extremely high. The General Dental Council of the UK only recognizes qualifications from a few countries and universities. At time of writing, only degrees from selected schools in Australia, New Zealand, South Africa, Hong Kong, Malaysia and Singapore are accepted. Most of these must have been awarded before 2001 and in some cases earlier, or within a specific short time-period. Degrees from universities in the US or Canada have never been accepted. The GDC regularly sent out inspectors to universities to check the standards of those whose qualifications they accept.

When we arrived in the UK, we had to go and register ourselves with the General Dental Council, showing them our Australian qualifications.

I've always found it fascinating that for a country that has such high standards of dental training, dental health has traditionally been so poor. There used to be a trend in the 1950s and 1960s, especially in the north of England, of getting all your teeth removed for your 21st birthday and a set of dentures made. Most people had several rotten teeth by that time anyway, partly because of excessive sugar consumption. These days, dentists will do everything they can to save a patient's own teeth.

The best and worst part of being in the Upper House is that we have no direct powers; we are only an advisory body. The advantage of this is that we tend to work more harmoniously than in the Commons, always working together to come up with the best advice and revisions to legislation. But when our advice is ignored it can be frustrating, and in some cases heart-breaking, because we cannot overrule the Commons. We can send an issue back to the Commons twice, but if the same piece of legislation comes back to us for a third time, we are expected to pass it. That's the standard conventional courtesy. This back-and-forth process is known as "ping pong" as the bill or amendment keeps getting bounced back and forth between the two Houses. The Commons, by default of convention, wins if we can't agree.

If you plan to vote *against* your party, or introduce an amendment to the Government's legislation, as I did in 1988 on imposing charges for adult dental check-ups, then you are expected to tell your Chief Whip (whose job it is to tell you which way to vote on any issue) ahead of voting and explain your reasons why.

I could not be more committed to giving people the best dental care. The NHS was in its infancy when I first arrived in the UK and I have campaigned for better public dental care provision all my professional life. I was the first woman ever appointed to the Standing Dental Advisory Committee for England and Wales. Supporting public health care was in my blood; it was a family badge of honour that my father had been the first Minister for Health and Motherhood in Australia, and my mother had campaigned tirelessly to improve health services in remote areas via the Bush Nursing Association. It was my duty to carry on the good fight.

I saw the loss of free NHS dental examinations as us really failing the British people. But I fight on!

Can we get better education for all?

Ensuring everyone has access to a good education has always been a huge passion of mine.

We had a cleaner in the Old Street surgery who had three boys. She was more or less raising them and supporting them herself because the father was "a bit on the bottle" as we'd call a heavy drinker in Australia, back in my day.

These three boys were very different. One of the younger two was still sucking a dummy at 10 years old. People would say, "Take that dummy out of his mouth, he's too old for that!" But as soon as you did, the stream of expletives that came out of his mouth was so bad, you'd put the dummy straight back in again! Sadly, his language was probably the father's influence.

The eldest boy, however, had shown more promise.

The boys all attended the same local school and one day their mother was called in to see the head teacher who told her that her eldest son was exceptionally clever. He said the boy should be at a better school to give him the best chance of getting into university. I thought it was very fair and considerate of that head teacher to admit that the boy wouldn't get the right education in that local school. The mother took the advice and applied to have the boy moved to a different school. She was successful, and her eldest son went on to get a place at Oxford and even became captain of the University rugby team; he really thrived because he got a better opportunity and was able to fulfil his potential.

That family lived in a very poor area and had no money for private education; they were lucky that the talented boy got a good chance in life thanks to the head teacher spotting his potential.

In October 2017, during my speech in the House of Lords highlighting the benefits of social mobility, I spoke about increasing opportunities for people regardless of their background. I had been alarmed to hear from parents who told me they were finding it very difficult to secure a good education for their children… children who were showing real academic ability.

It is upsetting to think that gifted children may not get the opportunity to excel simply because of a lack of money. I feel it is terribly unfair that children aren't able to get opportunities if they are born in an area where there are poor-performing schools. I even remember noticing in 1974 that the secondary modern in Cornwall was getting much better results than our local secondary modern in London and it made me think, back then, about the problems of getting better opportunities for children.

My passion for education was really handed down to me by my mother, and my fight to get better educational opportunities for all is testament to my mother's legacy. She really believed that education gives you the best start in life, that you can overcome all kinds of difficulties in your background if you can just secure a good education. I was very proud of my granddaughter, Victoria, for carrying on the family tradition. After graduating from university, she spent some time working for "Teach

First", a wonderful organisation that helps improve teaching standards in low-income areas.

Can we ensure private landlords are regulated?

I always feel annoyed and frustrated when I witness people exploiting a system that is designed to help those in need, such as my exasperation when I heard of people ordering excessive sets of dentures on the NHS.

For many years I have been campaigning to ensure that landlords are properly regulated, that their properties are fit for purpose and that they are declaring their rental income, whether this is from long-term rentals or holiday lets. There is evidence that countless people are renting out properties, for long and short terms, that are not fit for habitation, and that many landlords are not declaring their rental income to the Inland Revenue.

Over the years, Kevin and I have invested our money and time in buying properties both for our own habitation and as investment properties that we rented out. I would usually research suitable properties but we would always make a joint decision before we bought anything. But no matter what we did, everything we did was always by the book. I have been shocked, over the years, by what I have seen property owners try to get away with within the rental market.

There was a time when the short-term renting of property was well regulated in London. Under the 1973 Greater London Council (General Powers) Act, a landlord had to get permission if they wanted to let out a property on a short-term basis. With the exception of a few unscrupulous ones, most landlords abided by the rules.

However, in May 2015, the Deregulation Act allowed landlords to let a property out for up to 90 days per calendar year *without* having to seek permission to do so. This may sound reasonable in theory, but it has led to untold problems because councils have found it impossible to impose any kind of control. They don't have the manpower to monitor every property to see if it has been let out for more than 90 days each calendar year. Also, landlords use a variety of websites to list their properties, so it's impossible to know, when they seem to have stopped listing on one, whether they are still listing on another. And it is very difficult to prove how long they are actually renting the property out for as most do not declare all their income. If you are renting out your property ostensibly on a "short-term" basis for 250 days but are only allowed to do so, by law, for 90 days, you can't declare rent from 250 days!

This legislation has pushed up rents considerably, exacerbating the housing crisis in London because properties are removed from the long-term rental market. My daughter knew a family that were evicted from a long-term rental property by a landlord who knew he could make far more money from offering short-term lets to tourists through Airbnb and other sites.

This practice is also having a detrimental affect on the hotel industry, and on the neighbourhoods where these short-term rental flats are located. Hotels are able to control the behaviour of their guests, to some extent. When people rent out properties on a short-term basis, they can have loud parties and dump rubbish on the street irrespective of collection day. By the time residents complain, the guests are long gone and it's almost impossible to track down the landlords if they decide to make themselves scarce. Many communities are suffering from damage caused by careless short-term renters who come and go, with no regard for their neighbours.

Hotels can't compete because they have to charge VAT and have higher overheads. Short-term renters only pay VAT on the agent's fee, not on the total amount. Also, hotels (and landlords with long-term rental properties) have stringent health and safety regulations to comply with, but there seems to be none that apply to short-term rentals.

A regulation that was supposed to make it easier for people to make some additional income from occasionally renting out their spare room, or their flat when they have to go on an extended work trip or holiday, has been totally abused. This has allowed people to turn short-term renting into a huge, unregulated business.

I do not understand why the Government allowed this to happen at a time when comparable cities like Paris, New York and Berlin were bringing in *more* regulations to protect residential areas and the hotel industry. I heard that Barcelona has banned short-term lets altogether, to protect its hotel industry, and that Los Angeles has recently imposed new laws that require Airbnb hosts to apply for a licence before they can rent out their properties. Why are we going in the opposite direction in the UK?

I have had direct experience of the plight of renters. A few years ago, I was contacted by a woman who was desperate for help because she had been made homeless. She had been in an HMO (a house of multiple occupancy where rooms are rented out on an individual basis) for 10 years. One day, she returned home to find that someone had stolen a lot of her belongings so she called the police. When the police investigated, they told her that the house was being let illegally; it had never been registered as an HMO rental property. When the landlord heard she'd called the police, he threatened her with physical violence if she didn't get out. The police told her to move out to protect herself and said they could do nothing for her.

This poor woman's situation just got worse and worse. She lived in some awful dormitories. While she was in one, a doctor she consulted about some health problems said she shouldn't ever go back there because it was clearly full of bed bugs; I imagine he'd seen that she'd been bitten by them. There was one safe place she could stay but only occasionally. It was a hotel that normally charged £60 per night, which she couldn't afford, but if the man who rented the basement went away, they would rent it to her for £25 per night. She finally found decent accommodation but had to get together a deposit and her rent is £250 per week, which is still very steep. She struggles to keep up with the payments, but at least she can sleep at night now.

We must give councils back some authority – a requirement to register all short-term lets. Westminster City Council has already said it is prepared to do checks with 24-hours' notice, so it should not inconvenience genuine landlords. But this needs to be resolved urgently as there is a real problem with property owners renting rooms to multiple tenants with no control over numbers. Some live in appalling conditions and often make unsafe renovations. In a block of flats where I own a property, there is a one-bedroom flat where it seems around 10 people stay at any one time. The flat owner installed a wet room but didn't plumb it in properly and every time anyone took a shower the water leaked into the flat of the 95-year-old lady who lived beneath them!

I obviously support the concept of private property rentals, in principle. We introduced an excellent scheme back in 1992, called the "Rent a Room Scheme" that allowed resident landlords to rent out rooms in their properties, helping put surplus accommodation to good use, and allowing landlords to make secondary incomes, and in some cases providing companionship between landlord and tenant. But the Deregulation Act went too far and has caused enormous problems.

I have spoken many times in the House about this issue. We urgently need to make changes to legislation, as other cities have been doing.

(Incidentally, I believe we have seen a similar problem with unlicensed taxis. Again, we need to re-introduce the regulations we once had. When I was on the GLC, I had responsibility for the licensed carriage office, which organised the training and licensing of all black cabs. Now, it seems anyone can operate as a cab driver, with very little regulation. I believe this potentially puts passengers at risk and is taking business away from genuine, licensed cab drivers.)

I am happy to say that there is a big review by the Law Commission looking into various aspects of property law and regulation. This does give me reason to hope for the best because the Law Commission always looks at things extremely thoroughly.

Can we limit the height that people can grow their hedges?

Inspired by a long battle that a friend of one of my daughters had with a neighbour, I put forward a Private Member's Bill called the "High Hedges Bill" in 2000 that was designed to limit the height that people could grow their hedges. This person's quality of life had been considerably diminished when his neighbours grew their hedges too high. In particular, they were growing a non-native fast-growing very dense type of hedging called leylandii. The hedging grew so high it cut out the light into his property and blocked his views.

I argued that we should make it illegal for people not to cut their hedges if they were obscuring the light and views of neighbours. If you can get it heard, a Private Member's Bill is a useful way to get a law passed quickly, especially if it is the type of issue that you wouldn't expect there to be any objection to.

I presented my Bill and, although it passed through the House of Lords, I was astonished and extremely annoyed when it was blocked in the Commons by an MP called Christopher Chope. Anyone who follows the news will recognise that name. He infamously blocked the "Upskirting Bill" that attempted to get a law passed quickly that would make it illegal to take photographs from beneath the skirt or kilt of an unsuspecting victim (I'd never heard of such a foul and absurd thing before). But far more seriously and outrageously, in 2018, he blocked a bill on outlawing the practice of FGM (female genital mutilation) in the UK. He is usually a lone voice objecting in the Commons Chamber, but one voice alone can stop a bill.

Chope says he blocks these bills because he objects to the whole principle and procedure of Private Members Bills. However, until the procedure is changed, this is how we do things and he should spend his time trying to make reforms to the procedure rather than blocking bills that would protect people's rights and even lives. I, and many others, think he has behaved disgracefully recently. Conservative MP, Zac Goldsmith, was reported to have called Chope's actions "appalling" and the Lib Dem MP Tom Brake said that Chope had "reached a new low" after he blocked the FGM Bill.

After considerable campaigning, the main legislation that I aimed to get passed in my High Hedges Bill was included in its entirety within the Anti-Social Behaviour Bill that the Labour Government passed into law at a later date. The matter was reported in an article in *The Times* in March 2004. The piece mentions Christopher Chope's objection and suggests that his argument that the law "... 'could have a more dramatic impact on the English landscape than the combined effects of the great storm, Dutch elm disease and the Luftwaffe's bombing' is among the most ludicrous comments made in this Parliament." The article concluded that, "The law now being introduced by the Government (after being championed by the unbelievably named Baroness Gardner of Parkes) ... is worthwhile, but modest."

Can we make our roads safer for everyone?

I have always cared deeply about road safety, probably inspired by my time looking into better safety for police motorcycle training in Enfield while I was on the GLC. I was instrumental in the introduction of "P" plates and certain restrictions for drivers on a provisional licence, inspired by the existence of them in Australia, where they are compulsory for all new drivers (in the UK they are still optional).

I have an ongoing campaign to bring in a safety shield on all large trucks. At the moment there is a law that says certain large trucks must have them but for others (at time of writing) – such as skip lorries and concrete mixers – it is optional; they can add the safety shields at their discretion. These safety shields prevent someone who is knocked down (for example off a bicycle, motorcycle, or even an unlucky pedestrian) by one of these vehicles from getting dragged underneath it and killed. A story that has highlighted the campaign came from a woman who was knocked down and dragged under one of these vehicles. She wrote a compelling article about how terrified she was as she saw the huge wheels coming towards her. (We know that it's the back wheels that kill you in these situations.) She had a very lucky narrow escape but it really gave weight to the argument that there should simply be *no* exemptions.

I have met with CEMEX, the big concrete company, several times, and they have agreed to put these shields on their concrete mixers voluntarily, but it should be written into law. I've got the House of Lords library checking into exactly which law needs to be changed to implement this. You have to know exactly which law needs to be changed, and how it has to be written, before you can proceed in a case like this.

I couldn't possibly tell you exactly how many questions I have asked in my time (although you could find the answer on the official parliamentary record, Hansard, which records every word ever said in Parliament). A few years ago I was one of a few peers asked if we would like bound copies of all our speeches. Mine had to stretch to over two volumes! I love my two beautifully bound books containing every speech I have ever made, from my maiden speech in 1981 to the latest in 2010 (when they published this book – I have obviously made plenty more since!) I spoke on a wide range of issues in that period, the book lists my speeches ranging from The Orange Badge Scheme (January 1982), Luncheon Voucher Concession (February 1982) and Educational Provision for 16- to 19-Year Olds (July 1982), to Disabled People: Mobility Scooters (April 2010) and NHS: Dog Attacks (April 2010).

The processes of government are very long-winded, and it can be excruciatingly painful when you are defeated on issues you care passionately about, but these processes are absolutely necessary to avoid rash or unconsidered decisions. All the back and forth between the chambers is necessary for us to revise legislation so that they work to improve the lives of people. I don't think this is a bad thing because it does give us all enough time to explore all sorts of related issues, and it often opens up points that people might not have thought about if the process was rushed. So as frustrating as it can sometimes be, it's worth our thorough investigation and all our patience.

23

The Long Table

Life sometimes has a funny way of giving you what's best for you instead of what you want. All those years of campaigning for seats on councils or for a place in the House of Commons only ever gave me, or would have given me, a seat for a limited amount of time until the next election came along, when I would find myself fighting for it again. As I experienced, you also have to navigate boundary changes. And sometimes, before you even start to fight the opposing parties, you end up fighting other keen candidates in your *own* party. It took me a long time to get over the fact that I'd been pushed into applying to run for the North Cornwall seat by so-called friends who were trying to get me out of their path so that they could apply for the good seats that offered much better chances for Conservative candidates to get elected. Not to mention the Westminster councillors who made sure they remained in their seats when the number in our ward was reduced, leaving me to fight for a new seat in a different ward. (I felt a little poetic justice had been served when someone told me that some of the people who'd pushed me out of their way to further their careers were eagerly vying for peerages. I imagine it must have been quite maddening for them when I was made a life peer!)

After all that campaigning, all that interviewing with selection committees and all that running around the country to fight for various seats, I suddenly found myself with a job for life. My seat in the House of Lords was mine for as long as I wanted (or behaved myself!) There would be no more campaigning, no more boundary changes, no more skulduggery… I had a permanent place in UK Parliament to call home. And even though I knew I would miss working directly for my own constituents, there was some comfort in knowing that I would *always* be able to contribute to improving their lives at some level.

I had dearly wanted to be an MP and I do believe I would have been an excellent MP, but was that position best for *me*? Maybe I really was better suited to my position in the House of Lords, where I could focus entirely on the work that needed to be done instead of worrying about whether I would keep my seat.

When you don't get exactly what you want in life, maybe you should take a step back and consider if perhaps it *is* actually the best thing for you and move on, rather than living with regret that you didn't get what you initially wanted.

I wasted no time in making my presence felt when I arrived in the Lords. My first job was to make sure we women weren't caught short when we needed the loo!

There were very few female peers at the time. The majority of peers were (male) hereditary peers and female life peers had not long been admitted to the House of Lords, so the bathroom facilities had been somewhat overlooked. I identified a perfect spot for an additional female toilet. It was a single loo next to the Printed Office. I soon discovered that this was not a popular suggestion. Bertie Denham (Lord Denham) was particularly partial to this loo.

The lady peers were asked to present their case to the House Committee and I was chosen to do the presentation. Lord Wells-Pestel spoke after my presentation and agreed that an additional toilet for the female peers was, indeed, a necessity.

Lord Denham was not amused!

Sometime later, Baroness Young (Janet Young, who was Leader of the House at the time) told me she had been at a meeting to allocate front bench roles. When my name came up, Bertie Denham said, "Not that woman! She stole my loo!"

I was even less popular after I interfered with the House of Lords catering. I was alarmed by the amount of fat that was left on the meat we were served, so I asked the chefs to trim it off, in an effort to make it healthier. The trial run of the new lean meat was met with absolute uproar. I was told that the peers liked their meat just the way it was, thank you very much; back then there was none of the awareness about healthy eating that is everywhere now!

One of the key differences between the House of Commons and the House of Lords, in my experience, is that in the Lords we tend to talk to people outside of our own parties more, whereas there is always this feeling of intense competition between "rival" parties in the Commons. I've never really understood that attitude. Yes, we all believe in different methods, but ultimately, we should all be on the same side: that of helping the country and its people prosper. We may argue about *how* best to achieve that, but we should always be working together towards a common goal: making people's lives better.

What helps us achieve a good amount of civilised discourse in the Lords, I feel, is the presence of our "long table" in the dining room. It is hugely symbolic of how we try to find common ground in seeking solutions to problems. Being able to sit anywhere at the long table means that we are constantly talking to different people in other parties and getting different perspectives. We are not so focused on the party line; we are more interested in getting the best *solutions* to problems. I think, in general, people in the House of Lords listen and then comment, while in the Commons it feels as though they are all desperate to get their opinion heard, often more for the exposure than because of their passion for an issue. It sometimes seems as though their agenda is more important than their duty of care.

The other reason we need more cross-party discourse in the Lords is that we need to present a united front in order to advise the government, so it's important for us to find a way to agree. It is not a place for big battles and oversized egos!

I have always thought it a pity that there is not a long table in the House of Commons, to give them more opportunities to mix with members from other parties, which would give them a broader perspective on issues, and prevent politics from becoming too polarised and partisan.

We actually had a similar table in the GLC dining room. You could always join the long table and start a conversation with anyone. There were smaller tables available if you needed to have a private conversation, but there was always lively debate on the long table. For the most part, in the GLC, we all got along very well.

The first long table I experienced was the one in my family home, in the big breakfast room in our house in Sydney. That table was the centre of our world. We were a vociferous, opinionated bunch, but we sat around that table until we'd ironed out our differences and had come to an agreement.

That is how politics *should* work.

The House of Lords has gone through tremendous change in the past 100 years and is still under much scrutiny and review. Until as recently as 1958, only hereditary peers sat in the House of Lords.

In 1958, the Life Peerages Act enabled life peerages (both male and female) to be created and for holders of them to sit in the House of Lords. The Peerage Act 1963 gave female hereditary peers the right to sit in the House of Lords but most of them weren't there long. The House of Lords Act 1999, introduced by Labour MP Margaret Beckett while she was Leader of the House of Commons and Lord President of the Council, removed all but 92 of the hereditary peers (including members of the royal family), and only one of those hereditary peers who remained in the Lords was a woman.

Hereditary peers still retain their titles but with the exception of the 92 who kept their seats, they are not eligible to sit in the House of Lords.

Labour only got this Act through because they allowed the Conservatives to keep the most hereditary peers. The Conservatives were allowed to elect 42 hereditary peers, 28 were elected by the crossbenchers, 15 were chosen by the whole house, 3 by the Lib Dems and just 2 by Labour. But Labour still saw this as a huge victory as it changed the dynamic of the House of Lords forever and made it much more open.

In 2000, the House of Lords Appointments Commission was established and introduced a very simple process for anyone to nominate themselves, or someone they wish to put forward, to be considered as a crossbench peer.

When you have a more diverse range of people with different backgrounds in the House of Lords, you get some very good points being made and hear many interesting opinions. In general, the standard of debate is very high in the House of Lords, and so is the level of courtesy. We take the attitude that legislation must be reviewed word for word, not in order to play party political games, but to make the law better.

A real challenge these days, of course, is sheer space for more peers. While some choose to retire, it is a job for life, so there isn't a high turnover.

Being a life peer carries a huge responsibility with it, and a very serious duty of care. You are chosen for what you have done in your life, your experience, and what you believe in. This is very different from being a hereditary peer who inherits a title by chance of birth. As a life peer, you have a life-long duty to put your skills to good use. One of the reasons I can't imagine myself retiring is because I see it as a life-long duty that I've been given. And that is a privilege I hold dear.

Even with so few hereditary peers left in the House, there are Members who want to do away with all of them. They want to stop the seats passing down to the next generation when the current hereditary peers die. Hereditary titles would obviously continue to be handed down to heirs, but they would no longer be eligible to sit in the House of Lords. Bruce Grocott (Baron Grocott) has brought a Private Members Bill to put this forward. He has a lot of support but there are mixed views. I think most people don't mind either way. There are equal pros and cons to the concept of hereditary peers, but Bruce has a very strong opinion about it and is in a real battle with David Trefgarne (the 2nd Baron Trefgarne) who is one of the 90 or so hereditary peers left with the right to sit in the House of Lords, and is a front bencher on the Privy Council. Baron Trefgarne has tabled amendments to block Bruce Grocott's Bill.

*

If asked to vote on whether or not to abolish all hereditary peers, I would probably abstain. If pushed to make a choice, I'd agree to keep them on condition that the whole system is reviewed. I do think it all needs a thorough review to make it more current, relevant and fair.

The advantage of reducing the number of hereditary peers is that the House increasingly becomes made up of a more broad section of society. And attendance goes up because life peers are more likely to turn up on a regular basis than hereditary peers, because they are more interested in the duty that has been bestowed upon them; while I think hereditary peers are more likely to see their position as an obligation that they do not necessarily have any true interest in.

Conversely, some people feel that the House of Lords Act 1999 cost us a lot of money because the hereditary lords were rarely in attendance and therefore didn't get paid. It's more costly to have a house full of life peers who actually show up every day! But I would argue the additional expense is easily worth the breadth of experience that is now evident in House of Lords debates.

Lords do not take a salary like MPs, but we get an "attendance fee" for every day that we sit. You have to come in for the whole day to get your whole fee. If you come in for half a day, you only get a half-day's fee. If you don't come in at all, you get no fee for that day. It's a non-taxable payment. We don't get an allowance, like MPs, for hiring secretarial and research staff. If we want to hire someone we have to pay for them out of our own pockets.

When I first arrived, we still had members of the royal family who were hereditary peers. Before they were mostly thrown out, I did hear one of them, the Duke of Gloucester, make a speech. The children were always excited to see the coat peg in the peers' entrance that was labelled "Prince of Wales". And I once found myself sitting next to the Duke of Marlborough.

"You don't come very often," I said to him.

"Yes I do," he retorted. "I come very regularly."

We were at the State Opening of Parliament, and he was proudly indicating that he came every year for it!

*

There are many other issues that are being discussed on the subject of House of Lords reform. For example, there is a suggestion that life peers should only be able to serve 15 years. I may have a self-interested bias but I'd have to disagree with that because I've so enjoyed my 38 years in the House of Lords. I feel you build up experience that helps you. After 15 years you are only really *just* getting going!

There is also a study being conducted into reducing the size of the House of Lords altogether.

I think some people have a slight misconception about how life peers are made, or rather *who* gets chosen to be a life peer and why. Some people I've spoken to have an assumption that most life peers were originally Members of Parliament, as if there is an automatic progression from the House of Commons to the House of Lords, but this is not the case at all. It is true that many long-serving and prominent MPs – in particular former party leaders and cabinet ministers – are made peers (for example Lord Heseltine, Baroness Boothroyd, Lord Tebbit, and Lord Kinnock). But this is not an automatic progression; they still have to be chosen.

Life peers are typically people who come from a diverse range of backgrounds, people who have been influential in industry or academia, perhaps, or associated with the party through local government positions (such as myself). Entrepreneurs and philanthropists, who have been generous to the particular party in power at the time, are sometimes chosen and bring with them a depth of understanding about business. It's valuable having these people in the Lords as they are not generally the type of people who would stand as MPs, so getting them into the Lords is the only way Parliament can benefit from their knowledgeable input.

Another misconception some people have about the House of Lords is that we have magic powers to produce things very quickly. In reality we have very limited "real power". Your local MP has more power that a Member of the House of Lords, and can do more for you, in an immediate sense, than any peer can. Where the Lords *can* be very useful is in generating awareness for an issue, especially something that is going to be a long battle. You can form an organization and start an all-party group to investigate and campaign for an issue if you can find a peer who is able to help you in that.

And we certainly do not have power *over* the House of Commons, as some people wrongly believe. In fact it is quite the reverse. The Upper House (House of Lords) actually has less direct power than the Lower House (the House of Commons), which is how it should be, because MPs in the House of Commons are *elected* by a democratic process, whereas most members of the Upper House are either there through inheritance or appointment (mostly the latter now).

Essentially, we are a "revising and advising" body. Our role is to look at what Parliament wants to do and then send back our revisions if we feel strongly about any aspects. And, as I mentioned before, we are not supposed to send anything back more than twice. If a bill comes back to us for a third time, we are expected to pass it out of courtesy.

We have party whips in the House of Lords, telling us how they expect us to vote, just as they do in the Commons. However, whereas in the Commons it is rare that MPs will vote against their party whip, in the Lords we are more inclined to vote with our conscience than to toe the party line, although if you are going to vote in opposition to your party whip, you are expected to tell him or her that your intention – as I did when I opposed the government's plans to charge adults for dental checkups.

If you keep voting against the party whip, the Chief Whip can issue you with a warning.

Sometimes we are specifically told we have a free vote, that we are having what is called a "conscience vote". On these issues, there is no whip. In other words, you can vote with your conscience rather than being asked to vote a certain way by your party whip.

The smooth passage through the House of all business does depend on having a strong Leader. We have a very good female Leader of the House of Lords at the time of writing. Natalie Evans is the latest of several female Leaders, the first being Baroness Young, who was one of my supporters when I was made a peer and the Leader of the House when I took my seat.

I think my favourite Leader was John (Baron) Belstead. He was very patient and courteous and got many bills passed through the House efficiently. I would love to see Freddie Howe (Earl Howe) become Leader of the House one day. He has been a very popular Deputy Leader since May 2015 and having been both Minister for Defence and Under-Secretary for Health in his time, he is very knowledgeable in many areas. He is one of the 92 hereditary peers who kept his seat in the House of Lords in 1999 and is the longest serving Conservative frontbencher, serving since 1991. Many of us think of him as the "father of the house".

The work that we get done in the House of Lords is, in fact, far more influenced by the Leader of our house than whichever party is in power. We are frequently challenging the policies that the government wants to introduce; that is our purpose. So it doesn't matter which party is in power, our role is to question, revise and advise. For this we always need to try to act as a whole body rather than allow ourselves to be too influenced by party lines.

When politicians have their own agenda and become focused only on keeping their jobs and keeping "the other lot" out of power, the political system doesn't work to serve the people. And the people will see that; they are not stupid. When the electorate witness politicians playing ego-driven games and getting locked into power struggles, they lose trust in politicians and the whole system fails to work.

Again, I think my underlying motivation for being involved in politics – to help people – probably makes the House of Lords a better fit for me. I can focus on the actual issues at hand rather than always worrying about whether I need to defend my seat against someone who might be trying to oust me!

In short, I think the absence of direct power in the House of Lords plays a very special part in the democratic process. It allows Members to be more independently minded and put the public before party, compared with the Commons where – because they are elected on party platforms, and are actively making legislation, they are more bound by the party whips. We can speak our minds and say exactly what we want without the risk of losing our seats. We tend to have far more cross-party discussion (thanks, in part, to our long table!) before we go in to debate and vote.

In both Chambers, the party in government or with the most seats in the House of Commons always sits on the right hand side of the Queen when she is in the Chamber (her throne remains covered at all other times), with Members of the opposition on her left. Because the Conservative Party has been in government and opposition and has switched between the two twice since I have been a peer, I have sat on both sets of benches in the House. It can be hard to adjust if you've been on one side for a long time. When Tony Blair won the 1997 election it was a switch to the opposition benches after I'd been on the government's side for 16 years. I then spent 13 years on the opposition benches.

On my first day back in the Chamber after the Conservatives returned to power in 2010, I went to sit down, as usual, on the opposition benches. A doorman came rushing over to remind me that I now sat on the government benches.

"You weren't the first today, m'lady," he said. "And I'm sure you won't be the last." We laughed about it.

Luckily he had caught me before I sat down or people might have assumed that I had crossed the floor and defected to Labour. I'm not sure many would have raised an eyebrow if they thought I had!

Because we need to discuss every aspect of the issues we review and advise on, our sessions can go on... and on!

In March 2005, when we were in Opposition, I was present for the longest sitting of the House, which lasted from 11.00am on Thursday 10 March until 7.31pm on Friday 11 March! We were debating and voting on the critical Prevention of Terrorism Bill. It wasn't much fun waiting around to vote in the early hours of the morning but it was vital that we completed all the necessary business. To mark the occasion, our Chief Whip at the time, Lord Cope of Berkeley, sent us each a card awarding us his "medal of thanks" (in the form of a sketch that also marked the fact that we were voting from 5–6am!) for our efforts.

The Lords has sat for some very long sessions since then but our March 2005 session still holds the record for the longest. A session in 2011 on the Parliamentary Voting System and Constituencies Bill lasted just 10 hours shorter... although it sounds like they had far more fun. I wasn't in attendance for all of it (for some reason I had to leave at midnight to get home), but I heard that ad hoc entertainment (like quizzes and talks) was arranged by some of our most creative peers, such as the famous children's presenter, Baroness (Floella) Benjamin, and our award-winning writer and actor, Lord (Julian) Fellowes. Some peers even took naps on camp beds that the Parliamentary Estate erected in their offices!

When I first came to live in England in the 1950s, I met an Australian correspondent. When I told him my name, he said he remembered my father fondly. He said, "I always remember your father because he was different from other politicians. The others would always begin by pushing their political agendas, but your father would always ask after my family first." That was Dad: a passionate politician but a family man first.

Like my father, I did not get into politics to push my own personal agenda. I have always simply wanted to help people.

I will never forget a woman we were trying to help while I was a councillor on Westminster City Council. She had a baby and nowhere to live. The only thing the Council could offer her was a temporary bed and breakfast hostel in central London while we looked for somewhere more permanent for them. She said she couldn't possibly take the room because it had no bath in it, only a shower, and she had to be able to give her baby a bath. She was also scared that, if she accepted it, they would leave her there and she wouldn't get somewhere permanent to live, even though she'd been reassured that the Council were doing everything they could to find her a permanent home.

I spoke to her myself and asked her why she didn't bathe her baby in a plastic bath that we could get for her. She had never thought of this before. No one had ever explained to her that you could bathe a baby in a plastic bath. She said she was very grateful to me for explaining this idea to her and that, because I had been so honest with her, she trusted me when I reassured her that the Council was looking for something better for her. She gratefully took the temporary accommodation (and plastic bath!) and was soon rehoused.

This was the first time I became aware of how, when people are in crisis they are too overwhelmed to think rationally and creatively. It was the most obvious thing in the world to me, to get a plastic bath to bathe a baby in if you only had a shower, but this woman was so scared, she couldn't see beyond the fact that, with only a shower in the bathroom, she wouldn't be able to give the baby a bath.

While I was involved in this case, I was reminded of a conversation I once had with a woman at a meeting of the Women's Section of the Conservative Party once. She talked about how, during the war, she'd had the responsibility of sourcing food for people who had nothing to eat. She said that people who had absolutely nothing, who had even lost their homes, wouldn't touch any food that was damaged in some way. However, people who were struggling, but at least had a home or safe shelter, would think in a more positive and practical way. If you gave them a potato that was only half rotten, or a piece of fruit that was partly damaged, they would cut the bad parts out of it and make use of the good parts. The people who had absolutely nothing just got into a blind panic; they couldn't think of how to use damaged food. They couldn't see past their overwhelming and immediate problem of having nowhere to live.

I have had a very privileged life. But I have always tried to understand the plight of people less fortunate than me. I've tried to put myself in their shoes and then I try to offer them the best practical advice I can think of. This approach runs through every single thing I do in my role as a Member of the House of Lords.

24

United Nations, IPU Visits and Plan International

In my long career in politics, I have particularly enjoyed the experiences I've gained from all the travel I've been required to do in my various different roles, both within and independently of the House of Lords. I visited various European locations with the EUW. I also had the privilege of being invited to go on several official delegations for the IPU (the Inter-Parliamentary Union) to places I doubt I ever would have seen otherwise. In 1982, I was appointed to represent the UK on the United Nations Commission on the Status of Women. I also voluntarily put myself forward (and was appointed) to serve as Chairman of Plan International, a charity that does incredible work to help people in developing countries.

―

The Inter-Parliamentary Union exists to foster good relations, at a parliamentary level, with other countries. I had only been in the House of Lords for about a year when I was sent on my very first delegation in June 1982.

I was very excited to discover we were to visit Iceland.

The UK claims to be the "Mother of Parliament" but the Alþingi (the Icelandic Parliament) claims to be the "Grandmother"; they have been debating policies since the tenth century.

We were taken to the famous hot springs that produce the geothermal heat used in greenhouses that, despite their weather, has allowed them to grow bananas since 1941. I found this fascinating. And I thoroughly enjoyed the several plane rides we took, allowing us spectacular views of Iceland's stunning glaciers and mountains. We were also shown the damage caused by the last volcano eruption in 1973.

In 1990 I went on a delegation to Cuba. Bruce Grocott – now Lord Grocott, the peer who has brought the Private Members Bill to phase out hereditary peers – was also part of this delegation. At the time he was Labour MP for Telford. We got along very well.

Cuba was fascinating. Since the revolution of 1953 it had remained fairly underdeveloped in terms of tourism so it felt sort of stuck in time. We went to buy some postcards to send home and they all seemed to be from the pre-revolution days.

We didn't meet Fidel Castro but we met his brother, Raúl, who eventually succeeded Fidel as President in 2011. There were those famous posters of Che Guevara everywhere. And of course we saw many references to Ernest Hemingway, who had a house there and spent many years in Cuba during the years before the US travel restrictions were imposed. Travel to Cuba for US citizens was heavily restricted for a long time, starting with the Cold War in 1961 and lasting until just recently in 2015, when President Obama visited the country. He was the first American President to visit Cuba in almost 90 years.

As anti-American as they professed to be, they never threw out the American vintage cars that they loved. You can just about see every vintage American car you could ever imagine in Cuba.

One major on-going bone of contention in US–Cuba relations has long been Guantanamo Bay. The controversy over the Americans keeping their naval base and military prison there continues.

I liked the Cuban people enormously; I found them to have such pleasant temperaments. My friend, Gloria Hooper (Baroness Hooper) with whom I share an office, has travelled to Cuba many times and is very vocal on several issues affecting the country. I have known Gloria for many years because I became great friends with her sister in the very earliest days of my political career. At the time, Angela Hooper was Deputy Director of the Conservative Central Office (a role for which she was subsequently awarded a CBE). Angela had the biggest heart and we became dear friends, bonding over a shared sense of humour. She always had a twinkle in her eye and we became like teenagers when we got together. Angela was Lord Mayor of Westminster from 1994 to 1995 and served as a councillor of Westminster City Council until her death in 2010. We all miss her terribly.

Gloria is a vibrant, intelligent and fascinating woman, like her sister. She speaks fluent Spanish, which helps her understand the many challenges that the people of Cuba are facing. She tells me they are currently in the process of restoring several ancient buildings. And they are doing very well in terms of medical research.

I believe they have also updated their postcards!

IPU delegations are a great way to meet your fellow politicians, with differing political persuasions, from both Houses, outside of the workplace. I became great friends with the Labour MP (and eventual first female Speaker of the House of Commons), Betty Boothroyd, because we were on our way to an IPU conference in Nicaragua in 1987. We had to make a stopover in Mexico on the way and she told me which hotel she would be staying in. I booked into the same hotel and we had a great time chatting over dinner.

And what an experience we had in Nicaragua.

On our first night there, the whole UK delegation went out to dinner at a restaurant that boasted a water feature with a decent-sized crocodile basking in it! To pay for our meal we had to present our cash to two people sitting at a table counting money. The value of their currency was changing by the minute; rampant inflation was reducing it to next to nothing. The following day some of us queued up at the post office to send some postcards home and the price of stamps kept changing as we moved up the queue. It was eye-opening.

At the main reception in Nicaragua, we met Daniel Ortega, the head of the Sandinistas and the communist leader of the country at the time. He had clashed with Ronald Reagan over the US President's strongly anti-communist support for the right-wing rebel Contras. Ortega mentioned to me that he would like to meet Margaret Thatcher. I advised him to let that be known, officially. He made the request to the British Consul at that very event.

Ortega eventually met Thatcher in London for the first time in 1989 and although she did come away from the meeting with "doubts about Nicaragua's commitment to democracy", Ortega seemed more hopeful and confident in the belief that Thatcher was not necessarily going to align herself with President Reagan, telling reporters that Mrs Thatcher "defines her own policy and is going to be fair in monitoring Nicaraguan developments." (*Source: Associated Press.*)

It is worth mentioning that the following year there was an IPU delegation (that I was not part of) to Nicaragua during their elections. The delegates were allowed full access to inspect the polling stations and concluded that the elections had been held in accordance with the best democratic processes possible for a country with limited resources. Daniel Ortega was narrowly beaten by Violetta Chamorro leader of the UNO (the National Opposition Union), which was a coalition of parties opposed to the FSLN.

That's democracy for you!

The IPU also arrange for delegations from other countries to visit us here in the UK and I will never forget the time the Russians sent a delegation to the UK in the 1980s, and the dinner we had with them at Claridge's.

The Russian hierarchy at the time was keen to increase their contact with the UK. This was in December 1984, an important time for Russia to be building relationships with the West. Some of the delegates told me that they had got up at 2am in order to make the flights and connections that would bring them to London.

I got a real taste of Russian charm at that dinner. One of the delegates was sitting opposite me with his chin resting on his hand, staring at me. After a while he said something to his interpreter who said to me, "He thinks you will make a good woman for him."

I swiftly replied, "I think my husband might have something to say about that!"

*

On another occasion around this time, I met Gorbachev. This was shortly before he became leader of the ruling Communist Party. He had come to the UK that winter to meet Mrs Thatcher and was invited to address both Houses of Parliament. I mentioned to him that I sat next to the female delegate from the USSR on the UN Commission on the Status of Women. He was delighted to hear this because the woman was a good friend of his. At the very next UN meeting, in February 1985, my fellow UN representative from the USSR, Gorbachev's friend, took me aside and said, "I will tell you this because you met him, although it hasn't been announced yet, but Gorbachev has just been made our General Secretary."

The news was formally announced in March, a month later.

The last IPU delegation that I went on was to Ukraine in September 2008. This was a very heated time for the Ukrainians who were internally completely split over whether to align more with Europe (there was huge support for joining the EU) or Russia. And considering Russia had just rolled into Georgia to support the separatists there, the more democratic/European Ukrainians were justified in their concern that Russia was planning to annex the area around the Crimean port of Sevastopol. The Russians were keen to take control of it because it was the only port in the Black Sea that did not freeze during the winter.

There was huge infighting within the Ukranian government and their coalition had just collapsed. I clearly remember sitting around the table with people from the Ukrainian government and being told that the pro-EU, pro-NATO Prime Minister Yulia Tymoshenko wasn't being allowed to run the country in accordance with her mandate. The whole place felt like a bit of a messy melting pot.

Outside of the political talks, we were able to spend some time in Kiev, which is a beautiful city, and were also taken to visit the city of Slavutych, around 150km north of Kiev. Slavutych was built in 1987 to re-house the residents of the city of Pripyat after they had to abandon their homes following the Chernobyl disaster. Pripyat is on the edge of the radioactive exclusion zone.

During this trip, we spoke to many Ukranian people who felt they had achieved a much better way of life than they had ever had under Soviet rule. The people of Georgia felt the same. The Ukrainians who felt this way became (and still are) desperately worried about ending up under Russian rule again.

In 1982 I was chosen to represent the UK on the United Nations Status of Women Commission. I believe that Jean Trumpington had suggested I take over from her, as she'd been the first representative. I remained the UK representative on the Commission until 1988.

I was honoured to be involved with such an important movement, especially at this particular time. After the first World Conference of Women held during the designated "International Women's Year" in 1975 in Mexico City, it was announced that 1976–1985 would be the "UN Decade of Women". In my role as the UK representative on this UN commission, I also attended the third "World Conference of Women" (the second had been held in Copenhagen in 1970) that was held in 1985 in Nairobi.

What was particularly interesting about that trip to Nairobi was that, while we were there, there wasn't a single beggar in sight, contrary to what we'd been told to expect in Kenya. But I stayed on for a while after it ended and Kevin joined me for a holiday. Once the delegation had left, all these beggars appeared on the street. Apparently they had been shipped out of town while the Conference had been in progress, to make a good impression on the delegates. I thought that was rather misleading.

The Commission had its major meetings at the UN headquarters in New York. Additional meetings were usually held in Vienna, which is a stunning city, but we always convened there in January or February when it is unbelievably cold. Although not the coldest temperature I have ever experienced. That was in Ottawa. My face got so cold walking back to my hotel from a meeting, I had to duck into a shop and wait in there long enough to thaw out a bit before I continued on my way!

I was always sent to meetings with someone from the FCO (Foreign and Commonwealth Office) to carry around the huge files of paper we were expected to have to hand, and who would – more importantly – ensure that I was following official Foreign Office policy. For example, I was once approached by a delegate asking me to support their motion. In principle I was happy to do so but I had to raise the issue with the FCO to check that it didn't conflict with UK policy, or cause any diplomatic upset, before I officially agreed.

On the UN Commission on the Status of Women, I was positioned between the Soviet Union's representative (the friend of Gorbachev's) and the United States of America. The delegate from the USA was Maureen Reagan, Ronald Reagan's daughter. We became quite friendly, even when I had been instructed to vote against a US proposal that the Commission should meet annually instead of every two years. The UK had told me to vote against this, assuring me I was in good company because the French and German representatives were voting against it. However, when we got to the conference I discovered that, on Maureen's instruction, President Reagan had spoken to France and Germany and they had changed their votes at his request. I think the UK would have been one of the only votes against the proposal. There was nothing I could do to change this; I was obliged to vote according to official FCO policy. Fortunately I didn't have to make my vote known as the decision was carried forward without a vote. From that point on, we met every year.

One year, after a meeting, Maureen suggested that we go for dinner and she mentioned a very popular restaurant. When we got to the place, having travelled there in her limousine, there was a huge queue of people outside. My heart sank because I'd been looking forward to experiencing this particular place. But the next thing I knew, we were walking to the front, ahead of the queue, and were let in immediately. Everyone at the restaurant seemed to know and love her.

Maureen had a little lame dog that she pulled around on a trolley. He'd fallen from quite a height out of a tall building and had broken his back. He had come very close to death's door and it was a small miracle that he'd survived. Maureen was quite devoted to him.

When Maureen and her husband Dennis visited London in October 1985, we invited them to lunch at our home in central London. We had no idea what a drama this would cause. A week before they arrived, eight security men came and checked out the surrounding area, in particular to look for any potential sniper positions! Maureen was always surrounded by security guards, at least eight of them (possibly reduced to four when she had to take an elevator!) I am sure this was partly due to the heightened fear in the US around political dignitaries, which had existed since President Kennedy was assassinated in 1963.

Maureen's security guards all sat outside in their cars while we had lunch. I did go out to offer them sandwiches but they declined. I assumed they didn't eat on duty. Or didn't have official clearance to trust my cooking!

I was so sad to hear of Maureen's death in 2001, when she was only 60. The first thing I noticed about her, when I met her, was what beautiful skin she had. That she died as a result of malignant melanoma seemed particularly cruel. I just found it tragic that her lovely skin had been a traitor to her in the end.

The UN Commission on the Status of Women exposed some critical issues facing women around the world, and gave a voice to women who had long been oppressed.

I also sat on a subcommittee, the Council of Europe Ad Hoc Committee on the Status of Women, which also met in Vienna. At one of those subcommittee meetings, a woman from Tanzania said to me, "I wish they would not send *money* to our country. If they send money we will never see it. But if they send practical things for our families, we could use them. For instance, if you send soap we could wash our children, but if you send money we will never get anything."

I asked her to make this point in a speech and she did. She made a very powerful speech and women from many other countries said the same thing was true for them. That woman from Tanzania eventually rose to quite a high-up position in the European Council.

*

Thanks to the Commission, the issue of violence against women was finally brought to light with Britain being the first country publically to declare it existed. I brought up the issue after visiting shelters for women who had escaped domestic abuse or violence in their communities. Until this point, no one had been talking about the issue, but once they heard that the British were prepared to admit that it goes on, one by one other countries spoke up and admitted that it was a real problem in their country, too. Previously, they had been afraid to speak up, out of shame. This shows you how important it is for a country like Britain to lead the way in matters that have been pushed aside or are being buried and hidden. We have a duty to highlight injustice. When Britain – a country perceived to be strong and powerful, and a leader for change in the world – is prepared to speak out, others have courage to stand up and speak out, too. We successfully brought a very serious issue out into the open.

Once the issue opened up, we discovered that there was a very strong movement to help victims of domestic abuse in Brazil. A local women's group had suggested that an entire page in their constitution should be dedicated to the protection of women, whereas the US felt it could be summed up in a few lines. Some countries had trouble coming up with any words at all because they said it just would not be accepted in their country.

I became further aware of the plight of battered women when I visited treatment centres and shelters through my work as Chairman of Plan International.

My voluntary involvement with Plan International (I served as Chairman from June 1990 to January 2003) was thanks to Paul Boateng, who was on the GLC with me. He was born in London but grew up, for a time, in Ghana. His wife, Janet, an exceptionally beautiful woman, was heavily involved with Plan and got me on board. This charity was perfect for me because they do so much to help people and they do it in really practical ways.

Emily, Baroness Blatch had initially been chosen to chair the UK branch of Plan International but was unable to take up the post when she discovered she was due to be appointed to a ministerial role in the

Government. She asked me to put my name forward for consideration. Before I did, I asked to meet the UK Chief Executive, Stephen Bingham, to find out more about the charity's work. He gave me an excellent, thorough briefing on the work that Plan was doing to help children in poor communities around the world. We agreed that I would be put forward and would attend the next board meeting to seek approval from the other board members. I was delighted when I was approved.

Through Plan, I visited many countries throughout Africa, South America and Asia to see the excellent work being carried out by the charity in many communities. I saw projects in India, Indonesia, Vietnam, Bolivia, Peru, the Philippines, Tanzania and Zimbabwe. I sponsored a child in Vietnam for a number of years and had the opportunity to visit the family several times to see how the money had helped them. They were ecstatic because they had been able to buy a new concrete floor for their dwelling, which meant that insects couldn't crawl up through the ground and into their home, and then eat all the grain in the bags on the ground. It was a very humbling experience seeing what a difference such a small, practical thing could make to a family.

I also saw what a big difference a little investment could make to people's lives when I visited a project that Plan had developed in Tanzania.

In Dar es Salaam, we saw the lengths people had to go to in order to get the most minimal amount of fresh water. We watched as a young child sat beside a hole in the ground that filled up with water at a painfully slow rate. He was using a little plastic pot – about the size of a small yoghurt pot – to collect the water. When the pot finally filled up, he would pour the water into a bucket and then start the painstaking process again. It must have taken him hours to fill that bucket. Later we were taken to a village where Plan had built a water pump. There, the children could fill a bucket with water in seconds. The families would still send the smallest children to collect water but at least they didn't have to sit around all day waiting to fill their buckets.

Similarly, Plan helped with water distribution in the Philippines. There was a community that got their water supply from a waterfall, but the people at the top were taking all the water and the people who approached the waterfall from below got virtually none. They built a pump to ensure that the people at the bottom of the waterfall got fair access to the water. The operation was a sensitive one, of course. You are dealing with people's access to drinking water, without which they will die; it was all carefully monitored by a Plan representative to ensure it was being carried out fairly.

On a subsequent visit to a Plan project in Africa, we visited a class where the children were having their lessons in an orchard, sitting on very basic benches. Some large pieces of timber were piled up nearby. They looked as though they could have been designed to erect a pre-fab schoolroom. I asked the teacher what the timber was for. She told me that it was a gift from the German branch of Plan International, but they were unable to use it as no one knew how to assemble the pieces. This really brought home the importance of supplying all the necessary instructions, and perhaps even a person to supervise, when donations of infrastructure are given. I asked the relevant people at Plan International to rectify the problem and ensure that it did not reoccur in the future. How frustrating if potential new facilities were being provided but couldn't be used as the instructions weren't being sent!

I always felt so happy to see people's lives improve, even in the smallest ways. Things we take for granted in the UK are unreachable dreams to many people in the world.

Whenever I stayed in hotels, I would always take the little bars of soaps they put out in the bathrooms. It used to drive Kevin mad because he argued we had plenty of soap at home. But then I explained to him that I was able to take the soaps overseas on my site visits to Plan International projects. I handed them out to children who were huddled around the new water pipes waiting to wash themselves. They were immeasurably grateful. After that, Kevin gave me his full support to continue being a magpie!

I was occasionally invited by other organisations to travel to some fascinating places. In 1986, I was invited to take part in an official visit to China for the Women's National Commission, an advisory non-departmental public body set up in the 1960s to advise the government on women's views. This was their first visit to China, to look at the country's schools, hospitals and factories. It was led by the Government Co-Chairman of the WNC, Dame Peggy Fenner MP. As our leader, she was allowed to sleep in Chairman Mao's bed when our delegation stayed at one of his official residences!

When we arrived in Beijing, we stayed in the All China Women's Federation housing settlement (similar to our council housing), which was a complex of wooden huts. They were basic but very comfortable. We came together in a central cabin for our meals and there was a great communal feeling.

Our focus was on seeing what life was like for women and children in China. While being shown around one primary school, we were impressed to be serenaded by the children singing "Happy Birthday" to us in English. We were taught about complementary medicines such as acupuncture and herbal remedies on a tour of medical facilities, which we found fascinating, but I wasn't convinced by their methods to induce labour. They made heavily pregnant women sit on chairs with heaters underneath, designed to loosen up the mother's muscles or perhaps to convince the baby it was warm enough to come out!

I remember the strange weather we experienced. A daily fog of sand blew in from the Gobi Desert. This gradually lightened to a sandy haze as the day wore on, but never completely lifted.

The Chinese are full of practical ideas. In one hotel, the mats in the lift were changed daily to tell you which day of the week it was. And Beijing was packed with bicycles, which gave people a cheap and practical way of getting around. I had never seen so many bicycles in my life.

We were shown many of Beijing's traditional sites and the parks, and we visited Xi'an to see the awe-inspiring Terracotta Warriors. After Beijing, we travelled to Shanghai (which I gather has changed dramatically since) and visited the Bund (waterfront) area to see all the buildings that reflect a huge variety of architectural styles from across the globe, designed to honour the diplomatic ownership of the property.

I returned to China with Kevin only two years later. As Lord Mayor of Westminster, Kevin was invited along with a British trade delegation.

We took Sarah with us on that trip. We were honoured with a banquet in the Great Hall of the People during which we were served a Chinese delicacy… sea slugs! We also visited the Great Wall of China, which was quite breath-taking.

I was quite sad to see that cars had replaced the plethora of bicycles in Beijing, which had increased the pollution in the city.

The Mayor of Beijing was very welcoming and hospitable to us, but he was also puzzled. He couldn't understand why he, as Mayor, represented the whole of Beijing whereas Kevin represented a relatively small area of London!

25

Being Conservative

My daughter, Rachel, has kept a copy of a letter I sent her while she and her husband were living and working in Australia for a short spell in 1993. It reads:

> *Today Maggie Thatcher's memoirs were released and she was signing copies at Harrods from 1.00pm to 3.00pm. The queue snaked back and forward, then ran right though the book department and into the street. Some people had queued from midnight, others a couple of hours. I did a bit of a Gregory Speck and so was through in 45 minutes. Maggie said "thank you" to each and every person as they passed and a woman just before you got to her was telling everyone "no dedications at all" and Maggie just gave a signature. When I arrived, Maggie said "Oh my dear, don't say you've been queuing. You need not have done that. I would have signed it for you in the House!" I explained it was for my daughter's birthday (if Jo had not requested it I would not have bothered) and then said "I would like it if you could put the date on it and she did, so that was the <u>only</u> one with that added feature. Harrods had to stop the queue long before people wanted to stop coming. I shall wrap it up and put it away for Jo's birthday in November. I will not tell Jo I got it signed until then but even the Evening Standard is full of the story of the crowds.*

Margaret Thatcher's name obviously permeated many Conservative meetings in the 1970s. I was well aware of her rise through the ranks of the Party to become the Conservative Leader of the Opposition in 1975. I had been to committee meetings that she had attended in her role as Secretary of State for Education and Science in Ted Heath's government and I was always struck by the fact that she would walk back to the House of Commons by herself after those meetings, which were held in the old Methodist Central Hall on the other side of Parliament Square. She would ask if anyone was walking back to Westminster and if no one was, she would just walk back alone.

I met her properly, face to face, for the first time when I went to a reception at Downing Street (presumably in my role as Chairman of the EUW and Vice-Chairman of the Women's Section of the Conservative Party) shortly after she became Prime Minister in 1979. I introduced myself and she just looked at me and said, "I know exactly who you are."

Thatcher was very switched on. She was on the ball with everything and worked incredibly long hours. Even though her famous phrase was "the lady is not for turning," she *could* be swayed, on any issue, if you could put forward a persuasive enough case. I once saw her start writing on the back of a napkin when someone was sharing an opposing opinion to hers at a lunch. She didn't want to miss any of the points. She was always willing to listen. She was very happy for you to argue with her, if you could really establish your facts, and if she saw a reasonable argument she *would* change her mind. But she had strong opinions about how to improve the country's economy and how to help people improve their lives. I don't think it's fair to say that she didn't care about people; she cared deeply. She just did what *she* felt would be best for everyone. And she didn't just talk about her ideas; she actually got things done. I know she became extremely unpopular for many of her decisions, not all of which I would have agreed with, personally, but she *did* bring about positive change at a time when the country was being crippled by union strikes. Those who supported her truly loved her; those who didn't despised her.

She divided a nation.

I always had respect for how hard Margaret Thatcher worked. She would sit and work on papers at all hours of the night. She was famous for championing family values even though she was married to a divorced man. Denis Thatcher had been married previously for a short time.

Margaret Thatcher was a scientist, having gained a degree in Chemistry from Oxford, and this also helped give her credibility amongst men. I wouldn't say she was an active feminist (as we would interpret the word today) in that she did not necessarily work directly to help women, *per se* (indeed, Harold Wilson and James Callaghan both had more women in their cabinets than Margaret Thatcher did) but I think she definitely did good things for the *image* of women at that time. Of course she was also famous for how she transformed her own image as she rose up the political career ladder, even totally changing her voice!

When Sarah left school and decided not to go to university, one of her first jobs was working at Conservative Central Office. She was there during the "Leader's Tour" ahead of the 1979 General Election and during the European elections that year, so she had some close dealings with the future Prime Minister. Sarah was actually in Central Office in Smith Square when the IRA car bomb went off that killed Airey Neave. She heard the blast and saw smoke rising above the rooftops.

Airey Neave was Thatcher's biggest supporter and really helped to get her accepted in the male world. It was thanks to Airey and Norman Tebbit that she got the backing of the male MPs, so that when she stood for the leadership, she got it. This made it even more devastating that Airey never got to see her become Prime Minster. The bomb had been planted under his car. It went off as he drove out of the Palace of Westminster car park after leaving the House of Commons for the day on 30 March 1979. Thatcher became Prime Minister just five weeks later on 4 May. Airey was the first Conservative MP murdered by the IRA, followed by Tony Berry (Sir Anthony Berry) in the Brighton Grand Hotel bomb in October 1984, and then Ian Gow, MP for Eastbourne who was murdered by a car bomb in 1990. Ian was the last MP to be assassinated until 2016, when Jo Cox, the Labour MP for Batley and Spen was stabbed and shot to death. Mr Justice Wilkie, who sentenced the perpetrator to life imprisonment, described the horrific event as a murder committed to advance a cause associated with Nazism. *(Source: The Guardian, 23 November 2016)*

The Brighton bomb was particularly chilling for me, personally. I will never know if a twist of fate saved my own life on that fateful night in 1984.

Originally I had been booked to go to the Conservative Party conference in Brighton that year. However, we were in the middle of moving house and I'd been given that particular day, the day the Conference was due to start, as the *only* day that the removals company could move us. We had been waiting for so long to move into the house we had been building, I couldn't delay the move any longer. I had no other choice but to accept the date for a move so I pulled out of the Party Conference.

Tony Berry was at the top of a waiting list to go to the Conference. When I pulled out he was given a place at short notice. He was in his hotel room in the early hours of the morning on 12 October 1984, when the bomb went off, and died in the blast. I have no idea if I would have been booked into the same room, or would have been as unlucky as him, but it has obviously played on my mind since.

Sarah was at school with one of Norman Tebbit's children; his wife, Margaret, sustained horrific injuries and ended up paralysed as a result of the Brighton bomb.

The threat of IRA terrorist attacks dominated the 1970s and early 1980s. Letter bombs were a particular fear and you always gave London's iconic red post-boxes a wide berth when walking past.

Kevin and I once had a close shave, when we were out shopping in Selfridges. We were evacuated because there was a bomb scare, so we went down to *Porcelaine de Paris*, a china shop near Marble Arch. Shortly after we left *that* shop it was blown up by an IRA bomb. In other words, the bomb wasn't in Selfridges at all, it was in this little shop we happened to go to after we were evacuated!

The whole IRA terrorist campaign just threw this country completely. No one had attacked the British establishment and government so aggressively and with such violent intent since Guy Fawkes plotted to blow up the House of Lords almost 400 years earlier. People didn't know what to make of it; the whole country was in shock.

Many British people didn't understand the historical context of the Irish troubles and the IRA's underlying cause, they just saw a terrorist group intent on killing British people and judged all Irish people by it (when in fact, the situation was even worse for those caught up in the troubles in Northern Ireland), so there was a huge anti-Irish wave that spread through the country and this led to a thirst for revenge and justice, which in turn led to wrongful arrests and unfair sentences. It is awful to think of the suffering of the people who served time in prison for the Guildford pub bombings when it has now been proved that they were totally innocent. The injustice of what happened is shocking. But people were incensed by the IRA's bombing campaign and needed culprits that they could name, blame and punish.

The Northern Ireland peace process has been a notoriously difficult one and I admire anyone who has been involved in securing relative stability in the region. The two sides are so extreme in their opposing views that it will always be a fragile situation. One can't forget the heated speeches made by the Presbyterian minister, Ian Paisley (who was made a life peer, Baron Bannside, in 2010, and whose son, Ian Paisley Jr is MP for North Antrim as a member of the Democratic Unionist Party). And for a long time, due to the extreme position taken by Sinn Féin, the voice of their leader, Gerry Adams, was banned on British television.

One of my relations on my father's side was a nun who lived in Ireland and showed no great affection for the United Kingdom. She did this by refusing to acknowledge my peerage, pointedly writing *Mrs* Gardner instead of Baroness Gardner on all correspondence. I wouldn't have minded if it was a personal snub, but I did feel that it was a pointed snub at the UK!

Kevin and I first met this relation of mine when we went to visit her on a trip we took to Ireland just before we were married. She kindly offered us lunch. For pudding, she got out a cake and a big bottle of Irish whiskey. Pouring a large saucer-full of whiskey over her cake, she encouraged us to do the same, explaining that we could all "make our own trifle". When we said we didn't fancy it, she thought we were respecting the fact that nuns were supposed to be teetotal. She quickly explained that you were allowed alcohol as long as it was in your food; in other words, if it was part of your pudding it was fair game – no matter the quantity!

Kevin and I later laughed over this. The truth was, neither of us were big drinkers. There's nothing I love more than a glass of champagne but I'm not keen on spirits. Kevin rarely drank. He might have had some wine on occasions and if he wanted a spirit, he might have had a small whiskey, but it was a fairly rare occurrence.

At the time of her death, Margaret Thatcher was quite alone as she was staying in a suite at the Ritz while she recovered from surgery rather than the residence she lived in for many years, which was a grand and impressive house in Chester Square. The owners of the Ritz Hotel, the Barclay Brothers, were very good to her.

I remember Mrs Thatcher for her determined stance on whatever she put her mind to... and for her appearance; she was always immaculately dressed. She took a great interest in her clothes. Once her political life got busier, she had someone who organised her wardrobe for her. Her dresser actually became a tower of strength to her.

And as a dentist, I couldn't help noticing that, after she won the leadership of the party, Margaret Thatcher got all her front teeth capped with very good crowns, so she had also found someone very adept at dental work.

She always surrounded herself with experts.

I have often been asked why I am such a loyal member of the Conservative Party, especially when my principles have often seemed more aligned with the left. But, as Kevin always said, "You can make more of a difference if you try to change from within." Also, I joined the party at a very different time. It is difficult for the younger generation to understand what politics looked like in the 1960s and 1970s. The Labour Party was a hard-left, socialist party controlled by the trade unions and was very male-dominated. In my day, it was hard for women to stand out and be heard in the Labour Party – although many brilliant women, such as Barbara Castle, Betty Boothroyd and Margaret Beckett did. For me, as well as it being half chance that the person who knocked on my door and got me involved with local politics was Conservative, I felt that the Conservative Party might be the easier place for me, as a woman, to stand out and make a difference. And, of course, there was the Conservative policy that stood firmly in favour of helping people in public housing to buy their homes, which I fully supported, while Labour vehemently didn't in those days. That was definitely one of my deciding factors.

In many ways I felt that, if you were an intelligent woman with a voice, and you wanted to be heard on many different issues, not just trade union issues, the Conservative Party was the more obvious choice. You simply had a better chance of being heard and getting ahead in your career.

As I have stated many times, I take my loyalty to the Conservative Party very seriously. With that major exception over the dental check-up charges for adults, I have mostly stood by my party, even when it does things I disagree with, especially since becoming a Conservative life peer, because that was the duty I was appointed to do: support my party. I will argue as much as I can in debates, and put forward amendments where I feel it is necessary, but when it comes to my vote (unless it is a free vote), it has to be for the party I represent. That is how I operate. I believe you should be honest and loyal.

When the woman from the EUW claimed to be a Liberal despite being part of an organisation aligned with the Conservatives and married to a Conservative MP, I was rattled. As I had been when a fellow Conservative Councillor on Westminster City Council had said to me once, "I'm really a Liberal at heart."

She said this privately to me and I was astounded at her disloyalty, particularly as she always expressed such right-wing views in debates. She was one of the people who kept a Hyde Park seat when I was pushed out to the Little Venice seat so perhaps I should have known that she wasn't to be trusted!

I don't care which party you belong to, if you want to belong to a party at all, as long as you stand by it and are open about your allegiance.

The only politician I know of ever to cross the floor directly from Conservative to Labour was Alan Howarth who switched to Labour and won a seat in Tony Blair's Government in the 1997 General Election. He became a Labour peer in 2005. His partner, Patricia Hollis, had been a life peer since 1990, becoming Baroness Hollis of Heigham. She had been a popular and very good Labour MP for Great Yarmouth, and also did a lot of charity work. I liked her very much. She sadly died too young, in October 2018.

I have always got along very well with many of my fellow peers, regardless of their party allegiance. For example, I am very friendly with the Labour politician, Alf Dubs (Baron Dubs since he was given a life peerage in 1994). We worked together on Westminster City Council. He has a fascinating history. He was born in Prague in the 1930s and was a "Kinder Child", one of the Jewish children who were brought over to the UK on Sir Nicholas Winton's "Kindertransport" to protect them from the threat of Nazi-occupied Europe. He has done tremendous work as an MP and as a Member of the House of Lords, most significantly his amendment to the Immigration Act 2016 to ensure that unaccompanied refugee children would be guaranteed safe passage to the UK.

The Home Office sadly abandoned the scheme in February 2017 after accepting only 350 of the planned 3,000 refugee children.

My daughter Sarah once had cause to question Michael Heseltine's political persuasion. The stunning landscaped gardens at his house, Thenford, are open to the public a few times a year. Sarah visited once with an All Parliamentary Group on Horticulture and Gardening. She was surprised to see a massive bust of Lenin (rescued from the former Soviet Union at the end of the Cold War) featured in one area, and amused when all the Labour members of the group lined up to have their photo taken with it.

I clearly remember when Michael hit the headlines in 1976. He grew furious when the Labour Government of the time won a battle over its plans for nationalising the ship building industry by a single vote (304 to 303). The Labour MPs started to goad the opposition Conservative MPs over it. Heseltine grabbed the sacred Mace (a five-foot long gilt club that dates back to the reign of Charles II, a symbol of the meeting of Parliament and of the authority of the Speaker) from its rack below the Speaker's chair and waved it at the Labour MPs in question.

He apologised unreservedly the next morning.

You will never agree with absolutely everything your party says and does, but I do agree with Kevin, it is stronger to fight to make changes from within. When policies are made that you don't agree with, you have a choice: you stand by them but continue pressing for changes, you change your party, or you give up politics altogether, keeping only your right to vote as a citizen (but then you have far less influence).

I believe the strongest position is to stand by your party's policies publically but to continue to campaign to have them changed or amended from within the party. When you do that, you must believe in what you are saying *very* strongly, that the cause is more important than your party loyalty. And your colleagues are more likely to listen if you are not known for being a serial rebel! You have to show overall loyalty but you are still there to keep checks on your party; you must give very careful consideration to everything that is put before you. Sometimes new proposed policies and changes to existing policies are presented very *plausibly*, in a way that make them seem as though they will benefit the country when, with a little digging, you find out that they won't. That's when you have to be prepared to fight back.

Years ago, when I was out campaigning and people would ask me to explain the difference between Conservative and Labour, I'd say, "If you take a Rolls-Royce, a Tory looks at it and says 'Oh, I wonder if I can work hard enough to get one of those,' but a Labour supporter gets out a coin and scratches the side of it." I always felt that many of the Labour supporters that I met were too focused on what they didn't have. You shouldn't be worried about what the other bloke has, you should be getting on with your own life and bettering yourself. People these days have far more opportunities than ever before; they need to make the most of them.

We don't see as much endemic resentment of wealth in most Labour supporters these days, but what I do see is people with a sense of entitlement; the idea that you can have whatever you want without having to work for it. We have much more equality of opportunity these days, which is wonderful, but I am worried that young people don't appreciate that they still have to put a lot of work into achieving their goals and gaining success.

For all my loyalty to the Conservative Party, I have probably still been one of its most outspoken members. For the most part, I will do my duty and vote with the whip unless we are given a free vote or "conscience vote", but if I think there are issues that are not being addressed I will not keep quiet for the sake of an easy life, my *overall* loyalty is still to the British people. I will always make my own views clear on an issue and try to persuade others to see my point before it goes to a vote.

My views don't always flag up that I'm a Conservative. For example, in the 1970 GLC elections, three of us were standing as Conservatives: Bernard Brook-Partridge (who later became a Chairman of the GLC), Shelagh Roberts and myself. Bernard and I had an interview with a young journalist from the *Romford Echo*. She questioned first Bernard and then me, taking copious notes on our opposing answers as we had very different views and opinions. At the end of the interview she asked me how I felt about my chances running *against* Bernard. She was astonished when I explained we were on the same side!

Many people in Parliament have told me that I "ask the best questions"; questions that are of interest to the whole house and provoke healthy debate around many important issues. Again, this is because it is always my first priority to help people. I don't like injustice, or deception; I think it's vital for the truth to be known. To this day I have Labour politicians telling me – as the girl who found me sleeping uncomfortably on the deck of the boat travelling from Sweden to Denmark told me – that I'm "on the wrong side"! But I think it's vital that we consistently challenge each other.

If we only side with those we agree with, and perpetuate only the popular views on our side, then we drift towards extremism… on both the left and right side of the debate.

This point couldn't be more relevant to what we witnessed happening in British politics in the early part of 2019. Several MPs left their parties because they felt they were not being listened to at all, that they were unable to speak out against the Leadership. They decided to become independents because they felt they could no longer, in good conscience, support the positions that their parties were taking on a variety of issues (particularly on Brexit, but also in response to unchecked anti-Semitism in the Labour Party and Islamophobia in the Conservative Party). This is a very worrying situation and there has long been a serious call amongst many in Parliament for a new centre-ground party because the two main British parties have drifted too far to the left and right with little tolerance of centrist views.

This situation reminds me of my father's actions in the 1920s. He left his original party, the Labour Party, when he fundamentally disagreed with its direction. But when he tried to run as a candidate for a new party – a party he had set up himself – he was unable to retain his seat. I am not sure what these new, independent British MPs will, in practice, achieve, but their actions have already indirectly affected some subsequent discussions and decisions in both major UK parties. Whether or not they end up having to join or re-join established parties in order to keep their seats, we shall see, but they have definitely shaken things up already.

One thing I am hugely in favour of is making voting compulsory, and of giving suffrage (voting rights) to everyone over the age of 16 (it is currently 18 in this country). I feel very strongly about this. Voting is compulsory in Australia. Even if you spoil your ballot paper because you don't agree with anything or anyone on it, you still have to go and vote, and be marked off the register as having done so.

I think we would see the most significant shake-up of British politics we have ever seen if we were to lower the voting age to 16 and make voting compulsory. Then people couldn't say, "I don't think I'll go out and vote, it's too cold and it's raining…"

—

When it comes to loyalty, I probably feel it most strongly for the Catholic Church, which has always been the foundation of my family's values and traditions. My mother had become a Catholic (having been raised without any particular religious affiliation) in order to marry my father and to ensure that all her children were considered "cradle Catholics". She was passionate about the Church and got involved with many of their local charitable efforts, which led her to being awarded the Cross of Leo by the Pope. But she wasn't in any way intolerant or non-accepting of other religions.

I have met a few popes in my time. During our travels around Europe in 1937, my mother took us to Castle Gandolfo, the Papal summer residence, to listen to Pius XI speak from the balcony. In 1982, when Pope John Paul II came to the UK, Catholic Peers and MPs were invited to Westminster Cathedral for his first celebration of Mass. I attended with Sarah. As the first Pope from a (then) Communist country (Poland), people were eager to see him. He was particularly charismatic so it was a rather magical experience. In 2010, Joanna and I were guests at Westminster Hall for Pope Benedict's address.

I wouldn't call myself a very religious person, in terms of my beliefs, but I am committed to my duty as a Catholic, and part of that duty is to go to mass every weekend. It is an obligation that I take seriously. Unless you are really unwell, not even well enough to go to work, you are expected to go. There's an exemption for when you are travelling. There is a saying that, "When you're travelling, you can eat meat on Fridays," (at home, we traditionally didn't eat meat on Fridays) and the same is considered to apply to going to mass, if you can't find somewhere to go near where you're staying.

I do enjoy the customs and familiarity of Church. I take communion every week, as is customary. You are expected to fast for at least an hour before. When I was young you were expected to fast all day, which was rather hard going. The Catholic Church is a big part of my life. I do go to mass out of obligation but I do enjoy it, too; I think I would feel quite bereft if I didn't go.

Kevin and I enjoyed going to church together throughout our lives. In the late 1960s, when I was on Westminster City Council, we used to go to Our Lady Queen of Heaven in Queensway.

But on this note I must make a confession!

There was a Chinese restaurant next door to the church. We went to mass every Sunday morning and one day, as we left by the rear door of the church, we passed the back of the restaurant where the kitchens were. I was alarmed to see large barrels of old frying oil sitting around and Peking ducks hanging by hooks just inside the door (presumably drying out). It didn't look too hygienic at all! First thing on Monday morning, I rang the council and spoke to the Environmental Health Officer who said he would visit later in the week. He was equally unimpressed with what he saw and closed them down until improvement works had been carried out to make the kitchens more sanitary. Mysteriously, 24 hours later, the restaurant caught fire and burnt to the ground. Unfortunately the blaze caused serious structural damage to the church and we had scaffolding propping up the building for several years after, as they carried out the essential repair work.

There was a lot of grumbling.

I obviously kept my mouth shut!

26

Being Australian

A girl born in a rural town in New South Wales, Australia, in the 1920s doesn't generally grow up assuming that she will, one day, be walking the halls of the Palace of Westminster being called, "M'lady".

I still pinch myself sometimes, even after 38 years!

In 2001, as part of an exhibition at the National Portrait Gallery to celebrate 100 years of Australian Federation, the Australian photographer, Polly Borland was asked to take portraits of Australians who had made a significant contribution to life in the UK. The exhibition featured people like Elle Macphearson, Barry Humphries (portrayed as his character, Les Patterson, even though he is better known for playing Dame Edna Everage) and (a naked!) Germaine Greer.

I was extremely flattered and honoured to be asked to sit for a portrait. However, the sitting got off to a rather bumpy start.

Polly liked to put people in unusual positions. She had taken a photograph of Alec Broers, the Australian-raised Vice-Chancellor of Cambridge University (who was soon to become Lord Broers), sitting in an enormous chair. He is not a big man to begin with and this seemed to make him look even smaller. Perhaps this was the image that gave her the idea of taking a photograph of me, in all my official robes… *sitting on Queen Victoria's throne in the Queen's robing room.*

When Polly told me this was her plan, I had to explain that it was completely out of the question. Yes, we had got special permission from Black Rod (as you always have to do if you want to publish anything) to take photos in the House of Lords, and they said that we were allowed to be *in* the robing room, but I knew the throne was strictly out of bounds. When Polly saw the elaborate throne she got very excited and urged me to sit on it. I explained that nobody sat on it; no one had sat on it since Queen Victoria had sat on it. We had quite a standoff for a moment. Polly didn't seem to think it was a big deal, but you have to respect the rules in the House, you can't just bend them to your will. We were already in quite a privileged position having been granted permission to be in that room and for her to publish a photo taken in it.

I do understand what made Polly so keen; that throne is quite spectacular. There is all this beautiful embroidery around it and what is called "stump work", where they embroider over little stumps of wood to give a raised 3D effect. I actually learnt about this from an Australian visitor.

The Australians officials in London have always loved celebrating the British monarchy. I once accompanied the Agent General for the Australian State of Victoria as he was being shown around that very throne room. He commented on the two lovely portraits of Queen Victoria and Prince Albert that are in there. He thought they were much nicer than the portraits that were hanging in Australia House. I suggested he ask Black Rod for copies. He did, and was delighted when he was presented with them. They were hung in pride of place in his office.

Polly was absolutely convinced she had permission to put me anywhere in that room but I obviously stood my ground. In the end, I suggested she ask Black Rod's permission. I assured her that I would sit on the throne if Black Rod gave permission. We went to enquire and I watched Polly's face fall as she was denied permission. However, they consented to her photographing me on the *steps* of the throne. And that's where she took a lovely picture of me. (In fact, if you do an online search using the terms "Polly Borland Baroness Gardner" you will see it on the National Portrait Gallery website.)

There are strict conventions in the House of Lords, and even if they feel inconvenient you must abide by them or fight to change them officially.

I knew how thorough the rules were because I recalled an incident when a peer had given a Japanese newspaper a photo that had been taken in the throne room, without asking permission for it to be published. The Japanese newspaper published it and someone saw it and mentioned it to someone official. The news got back to Black Rod and the peer in question was reprimanded.

I may have seemed intractable to Polly, but I believe that it is extremely important that you live by the standards expected of you if you are given a position of privilege and duty. Having said all of this, I was personally very relieved that they didn't allow her to position me on the throne; I think it would have made me look very small indeed!

When the portrait was finally displayed in the exhibition, there I was, adorned in my gold and red robes, which cascaded down the steps of the throne, while below me was the photograph of a naked Germaine Greer. The contrast couldn't have been greater!

I am always thrilled to be included in Australia-related events. In November 2018, I went to the celebration of 100 years of Australia House. It was a lovely event and people were extremely kind to me. Our family friend, Isla Baring, took me under her wing as soon as we walked in and kindly looked after me all evening.

All the big Australian celebrities and personalities were in attendance to celebrate 100 years of Australia House. On my way in, I was very pleased to see Barry Humphries in a rare appearance… as himself!

We weren't told in advance, but the Prince of Wales and the Duchess of Cornwall (Charles and Camilla) were guests of honour at the Australian House reception. Prince Charles was at school for a time in Australia so he has a huge fondness for my motherland. Charles isn't always the most dynamic speaker, but he spoke extremely well at this event; it was probably the best speech I've ever heard him give. He was very relaxed and made it very personal.

Isla Baring established the Tait Memorial Trust in 1992 in honour of her Australian family, who were big patrons of the arts. The Trust sponsors talented young musicians and dancers from Australia and New Zealand to study at the UK's world famous music colleges. Many of those who have benefitted from the Trust's sponsorship have gone on to become internationally recognised. For her contribution to the arts, Isla is a recipient of an Order of Australia (established by the Queen in 1975). She was awarded the OAM (Medal of the Order) in 2009.

I was very honoured to be awarded with another level of the Order, the AM (Member of the Order) in November 2003. I was thrilled to be invited to attend a ceremony at Buckingham Palace and be presented with my AM by the Queen herself as she rarely presents them in person (it is often another member of her immediate family – the Duke of Edinburgh, or Princess Anne or Prince Charles). Your moment in front of the Queen is so brief, but I managed to tell her, when it was my turn to step forward, that my mother had received an OBE from the Queen's father, King George, in 1937, and I could tell that she was really quite moved by the story.

I was very impressed with the way the Palace protocol staff mixed up the recipients for the event, ensuring that we represented a wide spectrum of society. You could find yourself talking to a film star one minute, a charity worker the next, and even an astronaut or two! All the guests mingled in the courtyard after the official presentation ceremony. With the nervousness around meeting the Queen over with, there was huge merriment as we took photos and chatted with fellow guests.

I was reminded of that first trip to London, when my mother received her OBE, on that very night when we were celebrating 100 years of Australia House. When the official part of the celebrations had ended, I decided to head home and I offered Isla a lift back to Notting Hill Gate, where she lives. As we walked down to my car, which I'd parked on a street that runs down from Aldwych (where Australia House is located) to the River Thames, I realized that we were on Arundel Street, the location of the hotel (that sadly no longer exists) that my mother, Nonna and I stayed in when we very first came to London on that trip in 1937.

What a wonderful thing and how appropriate!

I am always so happy when I am reminded of my roots. I saw someone in the House of Lords wearing a traditional Australian akubra hat once. I had to stop him and tell him the story of my father's akubra hat collection.

Dad had a tenant who could never pay his rent so he would give Dad an akubra hat in lieu of rent. The only problem was, the tenant was regularly short of money so Dad ended up with a large collection of akubra hats!

Ever since I've lived in the UK, I've tried to champion all things Australian. I was a leading member of the Cook society and their first female Chairman in 1996 (Sarah was their second in 2009), and in 2007 I was honoured to be awarded an Honorary Fellowship from Sydney University for my work in founding and developing the Sydney University UK Alumni Association.

I will always try to go out of my way to help a fellow Aussie and I once had a letter published in *The Times* for this purpose, to defend my fellow Australian, Bill Harney. Someone had been quoted in *The Times* as saying that they had written the very first book on "bush cooking". I wrote to say that this was incorrect. Bill Harney and his co-author had written the first book on bush cooking in 1960.

I knew all about this book.

I'd met Bill and his writing partner when we were all appearing on a TV interview programme in the 1980s in Melbourne. They were going on before me, or perhaps after me. We got on very well and they asked me to take some copies of their book back to England. I was happy to help them and managed to get Harrods to carry a number of copies. The boys were delighted when Harrods ordered a second lot of books because they had proved so popular.

My favourite "recipe" in this book was called "Rabbit on a Shovel". It reminded me of our days at Pomeroy. To cook a rabbit (they explain), you catch it, kill it and put it on a shovel, which you put into the fire. You don't even bother taking off the fur because it will mostly burn off in the cooking process. Then you can tear the cooked animal apart with your hands.

I was a big fan of the book, and it always proved a good talking point. I was once asked to speak at a Lord Mayor's dinner in the City of London. I mentioned the "rabbit on a shovel" recipe and people loved the story. I had people coming up to me for years afterwards saying they remembered my speech about a rabbit on a shovel.

*

Having been here since 1954, I must be one of the longest permanent UK residents who is still an Australian citizen. I initially only came for 6 months and ended up staying over 60 years!

I still remember arriving at immigration in 1954. When I was asked how long I intended to stay for, I said I thought I'd stay for one year. The officer said he couldn't let me in for that long, so I asked how long I was allowed to come in for and he said 6 months. I just revised my answer and said I'd stay 6 months then. I suppose at some point I must have renewed my status in order to stay longer, but in those days, everything was much more relaxed and informal than it is now. Back then, everyone knew who you were and where you were, and it was relatively easy to get your status changed if you wanted to stay longer.

Eventually I got my permanent right to remain in the UK, which meant I didn't have to become a British citizen and didn't have to give up my Australian citizenship. By the time they changed the law so that you could become a dual citizen I didn't see the point in changing the status quo. That said, it is rather frustrating because every time I renew my Australian passport I have to resubmit all the relevant documents that prove I have right of abode in the UK, because your status is only guaranteed while you have a valid, in-date passport of your country of citizenship. The documents are getting rather tatty now. I'm surprised they don't have a computer system where they can keep your documents on file, as they do with your driver's licence.

When my passport was last renewed in 2009, I made a speech in the Lords urging for a change in the law that would allow the proof of these documents to be kept on file. It was the fourth time I was applying and I had to send in originals of everything again… including my husband's birth certificate, his parents' marriage certificate and his father's birth certificate. We also had to provide a phone number for my parents. Sarah quite happily entered the number of the cemetery where they are buried in Sydney!

It also used to be completely free to renew your right of abode. The last time we applied it was £135 and shortly after went up to £140.

As my right of abode has to be reapplied for every time I renew my passport, my daughters tease me when renewal time is approaching (as it is again in 2019), saying that, if I don't behave they will have me deported. Sarah loves saying, "It's not too late!"

I am forever grateful that I was allowed to keep my Australian citizenship. It means the world to me. Australia is where I am from, and Australian is what I feel I am in my bones, even though the UK is my home and my work. You can take the girl out of Australia but you can never take Australia out of the girl.

My heart will always be Australian.

Portrait taken for my political campaign, 1970

Front page of The Sun, 19th February 1970

Canvassing in Blackburn, June 1970

Painting the front door blue in Blackburn, June 1970

On the hustings in North Cornwall, 1973

*On the Terrace at the
Palace of Westminster
after my Introduction,
23rd June 1981*

The Chamber in session, 1982

UN Commission on the Status of Women, 1984

Conservative Women's lunch with Margaret Thatcher, 1980

*Conservative Women's
Conference, 1980*

*Lord Mayor and Lady
Mayoress of Westminster
1987-88*

With HM the Queen at the opening of the Queen's Park Medical Centre, 1985

Plan International Trip to Peru, c. 1993

Kevin and the old bells of St Martin in the Field, 1987

The Longest Sitting
11.0am Thursday 10th March 2005
to 7.31pm Friday 11th March
Prevention of Terrorism Bill

5-6am Votes

CHIEF WHIP'S MEDAL OF THANKS

The "Longest Sitting" medal, March 2005

Opposition Chief Whip
House of Lords

Trixie

Many Thanks

John

THE RT HON THE LORD COPE OF BERKELEY

Thanks from the Chief Whip for the Longest Sitting, March 2005

PART FOUR

Family and Future

27

Kevin Gardner
1930–2007

On hearing the news, in 1956, that I had become engaged to Kevin Gardner, my eldest brother, Jack, was unimpressed. He told my mother that I'd made a "bad choice" because he (himself a heavy gambler) had seen Kevin several times at the horse racing and had recognised him as one of my fellow dental students. He said Kevin was obviously a no-good gambler and I'd be wise to break off the engagement.

Jack had been too quick to judge.

The real reason Kevin was at the racetrack every weekend was because he had a Saturday job helping him pay his way through university. He was one of the stewards who raised the flag at the start of the race.

"Bad choice" indeed! Jack could not have been more wrong. Kevin was one of the most decent, dependable, hard-working, kind, people you could ever meet and I owe so much of my success and happiness in life to him.

Kevin Gardner was born in Bondi, a suburb of Sydney, in 1930. His father, George, was from Jersey in the UK, and his mother, Rita, was Australian born. She was descended from one of the earliest settlers, possibly even a "First-Fleeter" (the people who came from England on the first fleet of ships; it's considered to be quite something to be related to a "First Fleeter".) He only had one sibling, his younger sister, Anne-Marie, who also ended up living in the UK.

When Kevin was just 21 months old, in 1932, he was carried across the Sydney Harbour Bridge by his father, who claimed that Kevin was the first baby to be carried across the bridge upon its opening.

I don't think I'd met Kevin's parents before we were married, or if I had it would have been only briefly, and with the parents of other students in our dentistry year. I'm sure they were very proud when he won Sydney University's Arnott Prize for Oral Surgery, the one that came with a one-year position on the teaching staff. It was very well deserved.

Kevin stood out for being the most skilled amongst us. He was particularly known for his beautiful bridge work, that he did with his steady hands. Throughout his career, patients would ask Kevin if they could pay more for a "better" crown. Kevin always said, "No, every crown I do is the best."

Despite how grounded and practical he was, I always thought of Kevin as being rather bohemian because he had such an artistic flair. He was always up on the latest trends in fashion, and he loved art and music. I was delighted when he took up designing and making beautiful jewellery, extending his fine craftsmanship.

As a dentist Kevin had excelled at manual dexterity and he was a real natural at jewellery making. He took up a course at night school, at the Sir John Cass College, to learn silversmithing. He went on to become a Liveryman of the Worshipful Company of Goldsmiths and had his own hallmark. It made him smile to think that people would be able to look at his work in the future and refer to him as a "little known silversmith." For a number of years he learnt all about casting precious metals and made some exquisite pieces of jewellery.

He made me some pieces I treasure, including a pair of earrings that are castings of a Georgian shilling. When Nonna first saw them she said he could have sold dozens of them. The necklace he made for me that comprises gold beads interspersed with cornelians is much admired whenever I wear it; it's one of my favourite pieces. People have always said he could have gone into business making jewellery, but I think he enjoyed it too much as a hobby and wouldn't have wanted the pressure of making it into an enterprise.

To Kevin, nothing was ever impossible. If you had ability, he felt it was your duty to keep pushing forward and eventually you would succeed.

He came from a very working-class background and had earned a scholarship to go to Waverley College, a very good Catholic school in Sydney. Kevin's father's idea of progress was that folks only got ahead because of the influential people they knew, and so it was luck of the draw; he believed that influence was everything because he worked in a factory and people got promoted by currying favour with their superiors. But Kevin believed in the opposite of this. He believed that you only got by – and you only *should* get by – on the strength of your own merits, on skill and hard work.

When he was at school, Kevin would go home at lunchtime every day to eat a meal his mother had prepared for him. However, she never ate with him. She would always use the time to go shopping. Going to the local shops at that time in Australia was the height of your social life. You really went to meet people and gossip!

Maybe because we'd been friends for a long time before we were married, or perhaps because, with all my uncertainty about marrying him, ours had been anything but a "whirlwind romance", Kevin and I were a strong partnership right from the start of our marriage. We were both very practical people, and we always had so much fun; we found the same things amusing and loved a good conversation. Some of the things he would say can still make me laugh today. For example, when we lived in Knightsbridge and he referred to our "corner store"… he meant Harrods!

The children tell me Kevin said he knew he was going to marry me the moment he laid eyes on me, which I suppose *is* rather romantic. If it's true then my fate was certainly sealed at that moment (unbeknownst to me) because once Kevin Gardner set his mind on something, he never wavered from it! If Kevin made a plan, he carried it through. If he ever made an arrangement – for example when he was organising some building work we were having done on our house in Cornwall – he expected everyone to abide by it. Builders are not known for their reliability, but they always abided by Kevin's scheduling!

People often ask me if Kevin supported my political career. Well, absolutely! I couldn't have done it without his support. Kevin supported me both practically, by helping with the children, and mentally, by helping me believe I could succeed. He was all for me becoming an MP when I was asked, helped me get over the disappointments when I didn't get elected, and was absolutely thrilled for me when I was offered the peerage.

I certainly don't believe Kevin's male ego was ever threatened by having a wife with a political career. He didn't have a fragile ego, like many men do. Kevin had unshakeable inner self-confidence so he was always pleased to see others succeed without feeling any jealousy or insecurity. He was very proud of all my achievements. Maybe a less talented man would have felt threatened, but Kevin was always so superior to me in dentistry; we both knew he was ahead in the overall race!

I was delighted when Kevin got his moment in the spotlight, too.

After we had several discussions about the idea of him doing something while I was stuck in the Lords late into the evening, Kevin decided to stand as a Councillor for Westminster City Council in 1982. He was elected to represent the ward that encompassed Lord's Cricket Ground, which delighted him as he loved his cricket! He made a fantastic Councillor and was very popular in the area. This led to him being made Lord Mayor of Westminster in 1987, a job I'd once believed was in my sights. I felt great pride that Kevin had become the first Australian-born Lord Mayor of Westminster. And it was perfect timing as 1988 was the bicentenary year, when Australia celebrated 200 years since the first fleet arrived in Sydney Harbour.

We were very excited to be invited to Australia for the Bicentenary celebrations in January 1988.

The Lord and Lady Mayor of Portsmouth were also invited because Portsmouth was the location from which the first ship had sailed to Sydney (consequently Sydney and Portsmouth have a "sister city" arrangement) and they were presenting the city with a replica ship in honour of this.

I did feel we got a *slightly* raw deal, though. Westminster City Council said we could go if we paid for the trip ourselves. Portsmouth Council not only paid for their Lord Mayor and Lady Mayoress to go, but also gave them a budget of £25,000 and a personal butler!

*

The star guests for the Bicentenary celebrations, however, were the Prince and Princess of Wales, and all eyes were on Diana's outfits, with everyone trying to work out how she kept looking so cool in that blazing hot sun!

There were so many boats on the water that day; you could have walked across Sydney Harbour on them. When the replica First Fleet sailed in it really was a breath-taking moment. The fleet was made up of 11 ships that looked extremely small next to the modern boats. One could only marvel at the bravery of those who had travelled over 12,000 miles through unknown waters on those tiny ships, which had sailed under the command of Arthur Phillip and succeeded against all odds to bring their passengers to Australia.

Like me, Kevin was driven by a passion to help people improve their lives by having the best access to health care and being able to enjoy a decent quality of life in their own homes. He was on the Westminster City Council Planning Committee and visited every single planning application personally; he was perfectly happy to walk from one end of the constituency to the other. Kevin loved to walk! He was also fascinated, when he visited Berlin in his role as Lord Mayor, to discover that many more people rented the properties they lived in than owned them in Berlin, compared to London.

Kevin had never been hugely into party politics because he felt like the focus was forever changing depending on whoever was the leader; he was much more into local politics, although he was thoroughly supportive in all my campaigns. Kevin always formed his own opinions and ideas after careful consideration, and had a strong sense of what, for him, was right and wrong. He was an extremely diligent local Councillor.

Another of Kevin's Australia-related duties as Lord Mayor was to present the church bells of St Martin-in-the-Fields to the University of Western Australia in Perth as part of their Bicentenary celebrations. There was a connection to Australia because the bells had been rung on the occasion of Captain James Cook's homecoming, when he arrived back in London. However, the bells had deteriorated quite badly over the years and there were plans to recast them. Keen to bring the original bells to Australia for the Bicentenary celebrations, Perth made St Martin-in-the-Fields a generous offer. They would supply the 12 tonnes of tin and copper required to recast the bells in exchange for the old ones.

And so the 12 Bells of St Martin's (that are also mentioned in the famous nursery rhyme, "Oranges and Lemons") arrived in Perth in April 1988 and were presented, along with 5 newly cast bells, to the University, the City of Perth and the people of Western Australia, by the Cities of London and Westminster. There's a plaque in the bell tower in Perth all about the exchange and Kevin presenting them in London. Sarah went to see them in position there when she visited Australia in 2016 and stayed with the Western Australia Governor, Kerry Sanderson (the first female Governor of Western Australia).

Kevin's attitude to life was a breath of fresh air after growing up in my family. I had never viewed them in any particular way before, but as I adjusted to Kevin's down-to-earth attitude and practical approach to life, I saw how exuberant and eccentric my family could be. There was always some drama going on in my family, but Kevin took it all with a pinch of salt and was expert at quelling the flames.

He just spoke his mind and stuck to what he said.

For example, my brother, Raymond, came over to visit us in London and rather overstayed his welcome. We were living in a tiny flat, Sarah was a baby and I was pregnant with Rachel. Raymond more or less took up occupancy in our living room and seemed to think he could stay indefinitely. Kevin explained that there wasn't room and we were too overcrowded, especially with a baby on the way.

When Raymond did nothing to find alternative lodgings, Kevin found and paid for a room in a flat around the corner, and took Raymond's possessions over there. There was quite a heated discussion when Raymond got home and started accusing Kevin of throwing him out, but Kevin quite calmly explained, "I can't have you back here. I've taken your bag over to the flat and paid the rent."

Raymond got quite hysterical: behaviour that would usually have got him his own way in our family. "You never know what I might do; I might throw myself under a train. I'll blame you for anything that happens to me," he threatened.

But Kevin was unmoved by Raymond's attempt at emotional blackmail! He simply said, "Well, that's your choice, of course, but we really hope you don't."

Kevin stood up to Raymond in a way that my family never would have done. My family had always coddled Raymond, but Kevin was having none of it.

Of course, I wasn't so brave; I was quite concerned. I genuinely thought there was a chance I might not see my brother again because he was going to throw himself under a train. However, a few months after Raymond was ejected from our flat, he showed up to Christmas lunch. I was delighted to see he was still alive and well. After Raymond left, I innocently said to Kevin, "Wasn't it marvellous that Raymond came!"

Kevin then admitted to me that, seeing how upset I was getting at not having heard from Raymond, he'd gone round to see him and said, "You turn up for Christmas lunch or never darken our door with your presence again."

Kevin was always very protective of me.

The McGirr brothers really were no match for Kevin, who also left my brother Gregory feeling rather sheepish during our visit to Sydney in 1962.

For years there had been a hole in a floorboard in one of the rooms in our house, *Sunray*. This was a small room off the big breakfast room, which was the most used room in that house. We had a formal dining room for Christmas and special occasions, but most of our meals were around the big table in the breakfast room. Everyone would congregate there. There was a big fire (it was terribly hard to heat that big house in the winter) and it was the heart of the house.

Just off the breakfast room was a smaller room where we stored the good china and my mother's collection of Lalique glassware. This room was also where we kept the radio, on which George had pencilled a mark for where the dial had to be for the horseracing results, in case anyone changed the station between results.

And in this room there was a small hole in the floorboard that the entire McGirr family had been stepping over for years.

When Kevin first came to stay he saw it and said he'd repair it. My brother, Gregory had a "ute" and took Kevin to get some wood and tools before going off to do something else. He came back a little later to find Kevin in the breakfast room with everyone enjoying a cup of tea.

"I would have thought you'd be getting on with the job," Gregory teased him, "instead of lazing around drinking tea." To which Kevin replied that he'd already finished the repair. Gregory didn't believe it until he saw it. Nothing had ever been done so fast in our house.

"Well, spare me days," was Gregory's response when he saw the new floorboard.

It was very typical in *Sunray* that things went unrepaired because there was no one around competent enough to fix them… until Kevin came along.

Kevin was probably best known and loved for his wicked sense of humour. There were many special family jokes. He loved to tell people that he'd met the man who carved the raspberry pips out of wood during the war. He earnestly explained that, as they couldn't afford to make jam out of real raspberries during rationing, they carved the pips out of wood. As a result, it became a family tradition to say, if we suspected someone of telling a lie, "Oh, that's a raspberry pip."

During the 1960s and 1970s, watching something on TV together was a favourite family pastime. Whenever there was an outdoor scene, Kevin would announce, "That's filmed in Dorset." According to Kevin, everything was filmed in Dorset! Over the Christmas or Easter holidays, when the BBC was showing a classic film that we all knew and loved – something like *Ben Hur* or *The Robe* – Kevin would say, as the film was starting, "The Beeb are showing the version with the different ending today." The children would fall for it, watching anxiously as the film was coming to its conclusion and then, realising that they'd been duped by Kevin, they'd shout, "No they didn't!"

Kevin really knew how to pull a leg. We once returned from a jumble sale where we'd bought a big leather suitcase. We'd probably been out of the house for a couple of hours. As we were approaching the front door, our dog was jumping up and down, barking excitedly. Kevin was talking to him through the letterbox (teasing him, actually!) Two women walked by, eyed the suitcase suspiciously and commented on how desperate the barking sounded. Kevin said, "Oh, he's just thrilled to see us as we've been away and he's been in there on his own for a week." The women looked horrified and scurried away! We knew it was a bit wicked of Kevin but they had been rather nosy. We couldn't stop laughing.

We almost always had a dog in the family while the girls were growing up. One was a pedigree Pug. We called him Tsuba, which is the name for the hilt of a Chinese sword. You could describe him, in Australian slang, as a "gutzer" because he loved his food. When we walked him we had to be very careful not to let him eat anything off the ground because he'd go after whatever he could get into his mouth! Pugs have limited ability to breathe because of the way their skin falls around their face and neck, and he was sometimes so keen to eat he'd choke. Kevin would have to pick him up by his hind legs and hang him upside down until the food dropped out.

The best dog story happened while we were living in St John's Wood. The incident went down in family history.

It was in the late 1980s and President Reagan was due to visit the American School in London that was literally just behind our house. Obviously all the roads had to be closed off for security, and we had several security guards patrolling up and down outside our house. Our family dog at that time was a brindle-coloured Staffordshire Bull Terrier called "Horrie". Kevin took him out for a walk and one of Reagan's security guards walked past them with a German Shepherd. Despite being on a lead, the huge dog just went for Horrie for some reason, barking loudly. Horrie defended himself and in the process the leads got tangled up. The two men eventually got the dogs untangled and Kevin returned home with Horrie (shaken up but unscathed), thinking nothing more of it.

The next morning a policeman arrived at our front door and asked to come in to discuss the previous night's events. Horrie sat quietly beside

Kevin whilst we listened to the officer explain that the US security guard had reported us for owning a dangerous dog and that he had come to remove said dog from our care. There was a complete hush in the room and Horrie, having understood every word we assume, got up, walked over to the policeman, sat down beside him and rested his head on the policeman's knees. No one said a word. After a while, the policeman stroked Horrie's head, looked up at us and said, "We can leave it there, I think."

After the policeman left, we all fell about laughing in relief after keeping straight faces for so long, and with the reassurance that Horrie was not going to be carted off to the pound!

Horrie had always been beautifully behaved and extremely friendly... except for one occasion when Alvan, Rachel's boyfriend (and future husband), came for lunch wearing a pair of very pale grey slip-on shoes. Horrie rushed over to these shoes and sunk his teeth into them angrily, completely ruining them. We had never seen him act like that before. We had no idea what caused this sudden outburst. We could only assume he took offence to Alvan's shoes. Kevin, ever the big follower of fashion, looked at Alvan's pale grey shoes and said, "I think Horrie speaks for us all."

We knew it was wrong, but we couldn't help but laugh. Once he recovered from the unprovoked attack, Alvan managed to see the funny side.

The girls were huge animal lovers. I remember the big campaign they waged to get gerbils. The school biology class had bred some and was selling the babies. Kevin said the girls could get one if they saved up their pocket money and bought it themselves. He was fairly sure there would be no gerbil babies left by the time the girls had enough money.

Kevin was wrong; in fact they saved up enough for three (having firmly reserved them)!

Thankfully we had a playroom at the top of the house, or we would have been kept awake all night. You'd think the cavalry was coming in from the sound of those animals on their wheel.

Sadly the experience of keeping pets also taught the girls about the natural order of the animal kingdom. They were playing with the little gerbils one day and the cat got hold of one of them. The girls rescued it but the poor thing lost a paw in the fight. I was able to tape up his stump, and he recovered and went on to live a few more years, managing admirably on three paws.

They didn't learn their lesson, however, because on another occasion they let a gerbil out of the cage and the last they saw of that poor mite was its tail disappearing into the cat's mouth.

We didn't get any more gerbils!

―

When Kevin was approaching retirement, we decided to move out of our St John's Wood house. We bought a lovely property across from Harrods (it had actually been built as the house for the store's then general manager in the 1950s) and spent a good deal of time re-designing the house and garden. We originally had a conservatory built off the lounge. I soon realised that there was a much better place for it off the kitchen. Kevin disagreed at first, saying he'd never use it. Of course, once it was built he was never out of there!

I also realised that we were never getting any frogs in the pond because it was in direct sunlight and got covered in algae. I grumbled about it so much, Kevin eventually asked me why I didn't do something about it. The whole family were astonished when I dug out a new hole, lined it, transferred all the stones and created a new pond that was soon home to a huge family of frogs!

We also bought a little house in an Oxfordshire village for long weekends, and to have as a place the children and grandchildren could go to for holidays and enjoy the countryside. It took forever to find exactly the right house in just the right area, with the walled garden we wanted, but once we did, it was perfect. It became the only place where Kevin felt able to completely relax.

Like me, Kevin loved to garden (we were Gardners by name and by nature!)

The Oxfordshire house was a huge hit with all the Australian visitors over the years, too. It was lovely to have enough rooms – between Oxfordshire and London – to accommodate my sizeable extended family whenever they wanted to come over!

Kevin's sister Anne-Marie also lived in London for most of her life, so she was always a big part of our lives. She originally lived in London for a few years in the mid-1950s, but had then gone to live in the US with her husband for some years. But they relocated back to London in the 1960s.

When Kevin and Anne-Marie's parents retired, we thought it would be nice for them to come and spend long periods in the UK. We even bought a house for them a few doors down from us in Knightsbridge. But in the end they just missed Australia too much. They had also found it hard to accept the gift of accommodation from us, so they eventually went back to Australia and we sold the house.

Kevin and I were both pretty healthy. Neither of us smoked, for example. I had tried a cigarette at university when it was the height of fashion to smoke – in fact women were not considered to be remotely sophisticated unless they smoked, but I'd had such a horrible reaction, coughing and spluttering for hours, that I'd never tried it again. I was rather envious of the people who managed to smoke without it provoking such an adverse reaction. Kevin had never chosen to smoke.

Neither of us had ever had anything go very wrong, health wise; we were very fortunate in that respect. So when Kevin's health started to fail it was a real shock.

The first time that Kevin had a serious health scare was in the late 1990s. He had been feeling particularly unwell and eventually went to the doctor, which he hardly ever did. The doctor told him to go to A&E. They did a scan and found nothing but kept him in for observation. But as they were transferring him into a wheelchair to take him to another ward, he collapsed. They rushed him into the operating theatre and discovered that he had a massive internal bleed due to an ulcer. Rachel's husband, Alvan, who is a consultant urologist, monitored Kevin's progress as he recovered. They found out that the scan he had been given had stopped just short of revealing the ulcer. It was very lucky that Kevin collapsed while he was still in the hospital; had he been at home he would have died from such a huge loss of blood.

I felt terrible that I didn't find out until later what was happening. I was unfortunately very preoccupied with what was going on in Parliament at that time. I was working on my High Hedges Bill.

In 2003, Kevin wasn't quite so lucky. I got home to find him in a very bad way, and he'd evidently been like that for some time. As soon as I saw him I knew I had to get him to the hospital. Because he was generally so healthy and hated to be unwell, he kept saying, "I don't need to go to the hospital," but I ignored him and told him we were going whether he liked it or not. I could tell it was serious.

We discovered that Kevin had suffered a stroke as the result of a clot. You can either have a clot or a bleed causing a stroke. For clots, if they are discovered early enough they can be dispersed using "clot busters". But at that time, clot busters were only available in Newcastle. They didn't become available in London for another three years after that time. If we'd had clot busters in London and Kevin had been taken to the hospital as soon as he started showing symptoms, there's a good chance his resultant symptoms would have been significantly reduced.

Unfortunately, Kevin suffered part paralysis in his left arm, limiting the use of his hand. It was terribly sad because it limited his superb manual dexterity. He also ended up with a slight limp and couldn't drive any more. But he was very good at doing all his exercises and he minimised the damaging effects that strokes can have on the body. He was particularly determined to be up and walking in time to come with the rest of the family to Buckingham Palace when I was to be awarded with the Order of Australia in November 2003.

Kevin was always such a positive person. He never complained. He was always looking at what he *could* do rather than what he couldn't do.

I later asked our cleaner, who was in our home at the time Kevin had the stroke, why she hadn't called an ambulance or contacted me immediately when she'd seen he was not okay. She said she thought he was drunk. She had seen he was moving in a strange way and slurring his speech, and that's what she assumed, that he was drunk! I don't think Kevin was ever drunk a day in his life; he just wasn't a drinker. I tried not to be cross with her for making that assumption. If you have no understanding of what a stroke is, if you've never been taught anything about strokes, when you see someone having a stroke, your only conclusion might be that they are drunk.

Several years later I put a lot of time into campaigning for better awareness of the signs that someone is having a stroke. Raising awareness is critical. I hate to think of anyone else making the potentially life-threatening assumption that our cleaner did.

I was very pleased when, in 2009, the Department of Health rolled out their campaign called "FAST" to raise awareness for spotting early signs that someone is having a stroke. It encourages people to look "FAST" for signs of stroke and uses the word as an acronym.

F: look to see if the **F**ace has **F**allen;
A: check if they can move their **A**rms;
S: look for signs of **S**lurred **S**peech; and
T: if you notice all three it is "**T**ime" to dial 999 immediately.

The campaign gained additional momentum recently following the death of the hugely popular crime writer, Ruth Rendell (who I knew and liked enormously). Ruth suffered a major stroke in January 2015 and died four months later.

I'm happy to say that, in the past 20 years, there have been huge improvements in awareness and treatment for stroke victims. Most people know that, if there is any chance someone is having a stroke you mustn't hesitate to get them to hospital. The statistics for people being treated successfully, and as soon as possible, are very good now. The clot busters are even more satisfactory and effective these days and it is rare for people suffering a stroke caused by a clot to suffer brain damage, as they often would in the old days. Of course, the clot busters are only effective when a clot has caused the stroke; a bleed is a totally different situation.

At the end of 2006, after Christmas, Kevin and I went on holiday to Bermuda. We saw in the New Year there. It was a lovely, peaceful holiday. He seemed in fine health to me. We spent hours wandering around. He insisted on walking for miles; it was one of his favourite things to do. It really was a lovely holiday.

When we got back to London, Kevin started to feel very unwell and was eventually admitted to hospital. He was diagnosed with a severe form of lymphoma, a blood cancer that affects most of the body. He was too ill to have chemotherapy, and died not long after going into hospital. By bizarre chance, some of his final days were spent in the intensive care bed at University Hospital where the poisoned former Russian secret service defector Litvinenko died; he would have been thrilled by that.

Kevin's death came as a huge shock to us all. It happened so suddenly it was hard to take it in. His becoming ill was totally out of the blue; I hadn't been aware that anything was wrong. Much later, when I was speaking to the receptionist at our local GP, she said she'd noticed that he wasn't quite looking himself the last few times she'd seen him, and Sarah tells me that she had noticed he hadn't been looking well since the October. She had told him to go to the doctor but he kept refusing.

Joanna was with me in the hospital when Kevin died in the early hours of Sunday 11 February 2007. She was a huge support to me. We were there when they took his body away, which is a rather surreal experience. Joanna was comforting me, but it must have been terribly hard for her, too, as she was so close to him. All the girls were close to their father, but in his later years, Joanna had a special bond with Kevin because they spent a lot of time together, just the two of them, after Sarah and Rachel had left home. Joanna stayed with me, in our house in Knightsbridge, that first night we were without him.

It was all very strange.

One of Joanna's friends pointed out what a shame it was that Kevin had only reached the age of 76 and hadn't made it to 100. "An Australian cricket fan always wants to score a century," he said.

I'm trying to score one for him. At time of writing, I am about to turn 92; I have just over 8 years to go. Here's hoping!

When the House resumed after Kevin's death, I returned to my routine as I felt this would help me in my grief. On Friday 23 February, Baroness Finlay of Llanduff, who is an Independent Crossbench peer and professor of palliative medicine, moved the Palliative Care Bill for a second time. I decided to speak, and the support from my fellow peers across the House was overwhelming. Sarah came to listen to the debate and I was grateful to know that she was there in the Chamber (she sat below Bar) for moral support.

I took my time, knowing that it would be hard to speak about Kevin, but it was important that I mentioned and thanked all the people at the hospital who had been so kind and caring towards Kevin and the whole family. When I briefly faltered, a doorkeeper rushed over to offer me a glass of water, which helped me continue.

Speaking in that crucial debate and receiving so much support, reminded me that all of us who work in the House of Lords form a kind of family, too. We always try to offer each other help and support.

Because it means so much to me, and is such a hugely important issue, I am reproducing here the entire text of my speech (as recorded by Hansard) in honour of Kevin. I have also included some of the kind responses by my fellow peers that followed.

PALLIATIVE CARE BILL,
HOUSE OF LORDS
23 FEBRUARY 2007

BARONESS GARDNER OF PARKES
My Lords, it is appropriate that such an expert on palliative care has introduced this Bill, and I thank the noble Baroness.

Until last month, palliative care was of academic interest to me; it was something of which I approved but really knew little about. All that changed when my husband became critically ill and was admitted to hospital on 24 January. On 2 February, he was moved to intensive care, where he remained for five days. Then, when it was decided, on expert medical advice, by all the family, including him, that his very aggressive lymphoma was untreatable, he was disconnected from all but the basic oxygen and nutrition tubes and transferred to an ordinary bed.

It was then that the family met the palliative care specialist, a capable and sympathetic young woman called Caroline Stirling, and heard about how my husband could be made more comfortable and what treatment she proposed to continue for him. Had his prospects been long term, it was intended that he move home or to a hospice, but within a day it was clear that time was very short, and none of us wanted him to face the added trauma of a move anywhere. Family were with him when he died peacefully in the early morning of 11 February, just 12 days ago.

I particularly wish to speak today not only to pay tribute to Kevin, who was a wonderful husband for over 50 years, and to my children, who have been so supportive throughout this difficult time, but also to speak out for palliative care. It was an enormous comfort to us all to see Kevin so calm, peaceful and well cared for and to see him as a human being rather than as an inert figure swamped by vast numbers of tubes and artificial supports. His end was peaceful, and we can all wish to go in that way when our time comes.

Noble Lords might wonder how I am able to speak on this so soon — and so badly, I might add. It is because it is so soon. I am still in that state of disbelief where I cannot really believe that a loved one has gone forever. My experience was of an acute and short-term situation. Not all conditions are so clearly defined, and many people with chronic illnesses live a very long time in suffering. Palliative care should be the right of all those in need of it, and I have no doubt that the Bill could help many people.

Cancer is considered to get the most supportive palliative care, and it is important that other terminal conditions should also be covered. Care at home means a great deal, and end-of-life care should become a mainstream service. We have all seen the figure that 64 per cent of people would prefer to die at home. That does not surprise me, as I am sure it is a natural feeling. However, I saw an interesting letter from a GP in a busy London practice, who wrote:

"Patients and relatives say that they want to die at home, but when it comes down to it dial 999 because as a society we have no experience of serious illness being looked after at home and relatives often have never seen anyone very ill and certainly have never seen anyone die (or even dead)... For stroke patients or heart failure patients who have bounced in and out of casualty for years, they simply cannot see them go blue and stop breathing without summoning the ambulance... Relatives/patients could not actually go through with it, even though very intensive doctor/nurse input at home was available. All of this has practical, clinical and ethical implications."

The GP also makes the important point that three-monthly meetings of palliative care teams are too infrequent for real care, but her calculation from other suggested schedules is that the local hospice team, which serves 50 practices, would need to attend 200 meetings a year, which would be equal to the loss of about 600 nurse practitioner hours of seeing patients. It is most important that this point be addressed.

The General Medical Council made some good points in making clear the need to ensure that, "All doctors — not just those involved in cancer care — are aware of the nature and value of palliative care and the importance of early identification and referral of patients who might benefit from such support."

It is good, too, that the GMC makes clear the need to involve a patient in decisions about the type of care provided for them and to take account of their wishes about the appropriate place for receiving care. I stress that this should not be just a medical point; everyone would benefit from discussing the priorities and wishes of those dear to them long before any decisions need to be made.

The only certainty in life is death. This Bill will help.

LORD CARLILE
My Lords, I am sure that the whole House would wish to join me in expressing our deepest sympathy to the noble Baroness at her sad and recent loss. I am sure also that the House would agree that she spoke with great fortitude in the circumstances. That she was able to make so cogent a speech in those circumstances is no surprise to those of us who have heard her speak on many occasions; nevertheless, it was a remarkable occasion.

BARONESS HOWE
My Lords, it is a privilege to follow my noble friend Lady Masham of Ilton and to take part in this remarkable and moving debate on the Bill of my noble friend Lady Finlay of Llandaff. I pay tribute to the many memorable speeches we have heard today, in particular that of the noble Baroness, Lady Gardner of Parkes.

LORD HUNT OF KINGS HEATH (Minister of State, Dept of Health)
All noble Lords are grateful to Trixie — the noble Baroness, Lady Gardner of Parkes — for her courageous speech, which we all found most moving. It is good that her daughter is sitting below Bar and listened to her wonderful speech. The noble Baroness spoke movingly about the wonderful contribution of palliative care and the need for all doctors and nurses to understand the role of and access to palliative care. I could not agree with her more.

One thing I was most grateful for was that Kevin and I had celebrated our Golden Wedding Anniversary the year before he died. We had a wonderful party on the Terrace at the House of Lords on 6th July 2006, which was the day before our actual anniversary.

Many members of my family and several friends flew in from overseas (mostly from Australia but also from the US and Europe) for the celebrations, and we had many friends and colleagues from London there. Sarah gave a speech and on display was a beautiful montage of photographs of us through the years that the girls had made. It was wonderful to look through a lifetime together: our days as a newly engaged couple, the wedding, the European honeymoon, the girls as babies, all the homes we'd loved, my introduction to the House of Lords, Kevin being made Lord Mayor, and many family parties and holidays.

The following weekend we had a big family lunch that we all helped to cater. It was lovely to have both the fancy party with colleagues and the more intimate celebration with family.

When we first got married, Kevin once mentioned he wasn't sure what we would have to say to each other in "twenty years' time" but in fifty years we never ran out of conversation. Our marriage never stopped feeling like an exciting new adventure to us. Only the previous Christmas Eve, we were walking home from mass, holding hands, and an elderly man we met in the street stopped us and said, "Do you mind me asking... are you newly weds?" It was very touching moment that made us both smile.

Losing the great love of your life leaves a massive hole. I was very lucky to have my children and grandchildren to help fill it.

We held a private funeral for Kevin in our local parish church in Oxfordshire on 15 February 2007. We just had family and a few friends. Sarah gave the address.

The letters had flooded in from friends, constituents, colleagues and patients, all saying such lovely things about Kevin, so we wanted to have a proper, formal commemoration service – that Sarah organised every detail of, beautifully – to celebrate his life and allow everyone to pay their respects and say goodbye.

We thought it would be fitting to hold the service at Westminster Cathedral, which we did later that year on 17 May (fittingly the first day of the Lord's Test Match). The location was perfect as the Cathedral is almost opposite Westminster City Hall and Kevin was still a Councillor when he died. The Council officers and Councillors held him in great regard and considered him a true friend. The Chief Executive of the Council allowed us to use the Civic Coat of Arms on the Order of Service. Lord Mayor of Westminster and the Westminster City Councillors attended in their civic robes as a mark of respect. I was very touched by their gesture.

The Cathedral was packed. Family from Australia flew over for it, friends from all walks of life attended, as well as politicians from every party, ambassadors and High Commissioners, and all of the people who felt Kevin had made a difference to their lives.

My niece, Clarinda, gave the most beautiful personal address, and both Rachel and Joanna gave readings from the Scriptures. The Tasmanian-born Soprano, Jassy Husk, sang "I am Australian," by the Australian band, The Seekers, which was a very special and moving moment for us all. Finally, the organist played "Waltzing Matilda" as the congregation departed.

I remained in our house for a number of years after Kevin's death. I hadn't intended to sell it, but when I was made an offer I couldn't refuse, out of the blue, I thought it was time to let go. The house really was too big for me; I was rattling around in it. And it wasn't easy for the girls just to pop in so I thought I should move closer to them. I decided to move back to Bayswater to be on the same side of Hyde Park as Sarah and Joanna (who lives in Notting Hill).

The family that bought the house were planning extensive renovations, including the creation of a two-level basement with underground garage space for 12 cars! They already owned London properties in Montpelier Square but had been frustrated that they couldn't do the renovations they wanted because the properties were listed so (I was told by the estate agent) they were "not much use for anything but keeping your Picassos in."

Kevin would have laughed at that!

The move was a huge undertaking and the girls spent months sorting through everything and deciding what to keep. But it was also cathartic and we had some laughs over some of the "treasures" I'd kept before being persuaded to bin them. They each picked a piece of furniture that they particularly liked, and it's lovely to see the pieces that Kevin and I chose together when I visit their homes now.

My family might tease me for being a hoarder but I'm all for keeping hold of things in case you need them again. I always bring up the following example to prove it!

When I was involved in overseeing the transferring of the National Heart Hospital's operations to the Royal Brompton, as Chairman of Health and Social Services for Westminster City Council, we had a huge number of records from the days when TB was rife. Everyone thought we should destroy them, arguing that they weren't worth keeping because we had "eradicated TB in Britain forever". But I'm jolly glad I fought to keep them and we never destroyed them because TB unfortunately came back! People started contracting TB overseas and then coming into the country. They had to be picked up at the airport and taken to a special TB treatment centre so that they didn't come into contact with the public. Those old records became extremely valuable. So hoarding can be a good thing sometimes!

―

I do believe that if there is any "secret" to my success it's my great fortune in having a wonderful, supportive family. You have to have people who have got your back when you take on challenges that will undoubtedly pile on the pressure, people who will stand by you no matter what. If you feel protected on such a personal level, you almost feel invincible. I came from such a close, loving and supportive family. And inspired by this, I went on to build my own solid family unit with Kevin, who was our backbone.

You can get very far in life if you believe someone truly cares about you, unconditionally… especially someone with very good character who you hold in high esteem.

There were numerous incidents when I saw Kevin's character tested and I always marvelled at the strength of his integrity and conviction. Even when I look back on that incident in Sydney when he didn't come to the big fundraiser I organised, I realise now that he was only being true to himself. He kept to his word and helped me set things up, but when it came to the party, that really wasn't his thing. I think his father was pushing him to come simply on the grounds that it was an important social occasion and it would be good for Kevin's "social standing". Well, the last thing Kevin would ever have given a damn about was his "social standing"; he only cared about what he truly believed in.

Kevin was the best husband I could have ever wished for and I feel very lucky indeed to have been married to him. We didn't have a bean in the old days, when we were first married, but if he was buying anything for me, even if it was a pair of socks, it had to be the best. And I know the girls feel blessed to have had such a wonderful father. We were so proud of him, for all his achievements, and he was universally popular. He could sometimes come across as quite shy but this was just his way of staying out of the limelight. He had an unshakeable inner confidence. He was such a down-to-earth person. I was always quite a practical person but Kevin was even more so. His approach to life rubbed off on me and together we were a great team, in life and in business.

Everyone loved Kevin because he was absolutely genuine, had a wicked sense of humour and was so caring. He came into contact with so many people through his work, first as a dentist, and then as a Councillor and Lord Mayor of Westminster. There is a lovely story of how Kevin was once stepping out of a Rolls-Royce dressed in his ornate Mayoral robes when a patient spotted him and shouted out, "That's my dentist, that is!"

Kevin was always so able and willing to do more than you'd ever expect from a person. When he retired, and was still a Councillor, he got involved with a lot of youth clubs and was very inspirational to young people, giving talks and offering advice. For someone who once had a stammer he became a wonderful orator.

When we had the dental practice in Old Street, all the market stallholders were our patients and held us in high esteem. Whenever they spotted Kevin walking down Whitecross Street they would call out to him, asking him to recommend their goods (whether these were fruit, vegetables or saucepans) to other patients.

"Mr Gardner, give us a mention to your customers," they would call. And Kevin would join in the friendly banter.

If we sent someone out to get some apples from our local greengrocer near the surgery, as soon as he would hear they were for us, he'd take any substandard apples out of the bag and put his best ones in. We also had a fishmonger who came around regularly and gave us some excellent fish. They were even worth the smell you had to put up with until you could cook them.

We were part of a wonderful community, where everyone did their best for people.

And Kevin had even reached communities we didn't know about.

Shortly after he died, a clerk in the House of Lords told me there was a big write-up about Kevin and the Bells of St Martin's story in a bell ringers' magazine. Obviously it's a very well known story in the bell-ringing community!

Sarah, Rachel and Joanna are still adjusting to life without their beloved dad. You do it in fits and starts, but the feeling of loss never fully leaves you. You never really get over losing someone you love that much; you just learn to live with it. I know that because not a day has gone by when I haven't missed my own father and haven't wished I could just have a chat with him about this or that.

Kevin really was everything to the girls. He had to be both mum and dad for long periods when they were growing up, when I was so busy with my work. I think he treated them the same as he would have treated boys if we'd had sons. They were all taught really good, practical skills, such as how to do DIY. They all knew how to do painting and decorating, and how to wire a plug or change a fuse. He taught them to be creative, too, like how to mix and match screws if you didn't have a set of the same ones.

He was a brilliant father. He was broadminded, kind and fair, and I think he probably had more to do with how well the girls turned out than I did. They have all inherited his sense of fairness and compassion, as well as his calm, rational common sense. They are all a little bit more Gardner than McGirr, I think!

I mentioned earlier that, when we were at dental school in Sydney, Kevin had a "chosen few" that he would help with their work, but I was never one of them.

Well, except for one time.

I finally persuaded him to help me with something (and not throw it out of the window!) Afterwards I said, "Thank you very much, if there's anything I can do for you, let me know." Of course, this was just a pleasantry, something you say. No one ever takes you up on it. I'd said it loads of times in my life but no one had ever said yes… until Kevin.

"Yes, actually," he said. "You could knit me a sweater." He had obviously taken note of the knitting needles that were rarely out of my hands!

Kevin chose this unusually beautiful mustard-yellow cashmere wool and bought a complicated pattern with a v-neck. I knitted him the promised sweater and he wore it throughout the rest of his life. It still lives in the drawer where he always kept it.

I really owe everything I hold dear in my life to Kevin. We were a good team. I still love him dearly and miss him every day.

When it's quiet, I can still hear his voice in my head.

He called me "Ticko".

28

So Many McGirrs

After my sister, Gwen, died in September 2016, I became the last surviving member of my immediate family, which still feels slightly strange. Fortunately, my siblings were prolific procreators and I have a small army of nephews and nieces, most of whom have produced tribes of offspring themselves, so the McGirr dynasty lives on in Australia and around the globe.

Of my generation, I was the only one of my siblings who moved overseas. All the others remained in Australia.

My eldest brother, Jack, studied medicine and became a doctor in the army, which gave him the nickname, "Doc McGirr" or just "Doc". After the war, Jack worked with the boxer, Jimmy Carruthers, who defeated the South African, Vic Toweel, to become Australia's first official world champion boxer, fighting in the "bantamweight" class (a class below featherweight) in the early 1950s. Many boxers, especially in those days, would suffer real health problems from all the blows to the head. But Jack helped Jimmy keep his marbles and even establish a few successful businesses, including a couple of pubs, long after he retired from boxing.

Jack married Joyce in 1940 and they had five children. Their eldest son, Greg, lives in Dubbo and has a huge collection of family photos.

Jack was a complex character and medicine was only one of his interests. He loved his sports. He played rugby and cricket, and boxed at university. There was a famous story of when Dad went to the dissecting room at the university looking for Jack, who was nowhere to be seen. One of the students told him, "Oh, he never comes in here, you'll find him in the gym."

After the war, Jack swam competitively for a time. He was a keen golfer and, as we know, he was mad keen on horseracing! Kevin and I were invited to the cricket at Lord's once, when he was Lord Mayor. I found myself sitting next to the Australian test cricketer, Keith Miller. It came up in conversation that Keith was very keen on horse racing and I mentioned my brother, Jack. Keith said, "Oh, yes, I used to see Doc there all the time."

Jack McGirr died in September 1987 at the age of 72.

My eldest sister, Beatrice (known to us as Muffie) became a barrister and was one of the first women in Australia admitted to the bar. She took on some high-profile cases, including the defence of a woman, Molly McGrath, who was charged with murder in the 1950s. Muffie turned up to court on that occasion carrying her youngest daughter, Therese, who was only a few months old, in a bassinet. She successfully got the NSW Attorney-General to terminate the case.

Muffie was tough as old boots and full of life, which is why the society pages loved her. She was definitely our father's favourite, although Gwen would have disputed this, claiming to be Dad's favourite herself. And some of the others thought I was Dad's favourite, which might have been true; he did make me feel that way. I believe that, deep down, parents love all their children equally, even if they *like* some better than others.

I worshipped Muffie as a child. I was always trying to gain the approval of my older siblings and Muffie was the most glamorous of all of them, in my eyes. I used to love washing Muffie's stockings for her, eager to hear her gratitude and praise for a good job done!

There was obviously plenty of speculation as to which suitor Muffie would choose to marry. I am sure she had plenty of offers. She eventually chose the handsome doctor, Tom Bateman. They made the most stunning couple and bought a two-seater car, a roadster, with a "dicky seat" or "rumble seat" which folded out of the back of the car. I'll never forget Nonna and I half freezing to death in that seat coming down from the Blue Mountains once, after visiting Grandma Hermes at Pomeroy. When it started to rain we were very jealous of Muffie and Tom sitting in the front with the roof over them!

Muffie had a huge run-in with the University because she was heavily pregnant and about to give birth when it was time to sit her law finals. The law department wouldn't let her sit the exams in case she went into labour. Tom went in to plead with them on Muffie's behalf and still they wouldn't let her, so she switched to a Master of Arts degree and finished her law degree later.

Muffie and Tom had seven children altogether and they were a lovely, happy family. It was such a tragedy that she died so young. She was only 43 when she had her fatal asthma attack in July 1960 and died in Tom's arms. Their youngest child, Therese, was only 2 at the time.

It is a huge credit to Tom and the children that they overcame this terrible trauma. Most of them became extremely successful. Their eldest daughter, Beatrice, became a lawyer and also joined the New South Wales bar. Their son, Edmund, became a very successful and wealthy doctor, who set up a huge private healthcare provider in Australia. He was a very generous man, giving millions to hospital foundations. And Therese is thriving, living in New York. Sadly, one of the girls, Rosamund, never fully recovered from her mother's untimely death (she was a teenager at the time) and took her own life by drinking rat poison when she was in her thirties.

Muffie's surviving children have become so successful, as have the grandchildren she never met, and I know she would have been extremely proud of them all.

Gwen followed in our eldest brother's footsteps and qualified as a doctor. We were generally a hardy lot in my family. Only Patty got faint at the sight of blood, the rest of us weren't bothered at all!

In 1945, Gwen married Michael Fitzpatrick, a doctor she'd met in Ireland. They got married in London at the London Oratory in Brompton Road. Tragically, Gwen lost her first babies, twin boys, during pregnancy, just around the time that our father died. But she and Michael went on to have two girls, Mary and Susan (who changed her name to Rachel) who were always adored by their parents.

Gwen was a law unto herself. She was very controlling. I remember she had a particular preference for the settings on their water system and wouldn't let another soul touch it. She was extremely dogmatic. If Gwen said something was so, then something was so, and there was no arguing with her. There was once a huge debate about the birth year of one of our late relatives. We all said it was "X" and Gwen said it was "Y". I took her to see the tombstone, which confirmed it was "X", and Gwen's response was, "And that's exactly how rumours get perpetuated!"

She absolutely believed that it had been written incorrectly on the tombstone and continued to insist it was "Y".

Michael was equally bombastic. They were both impossible creatures in their own ways. He had a way of needling you, which he called "humour". He knew exactly what to say to get you riled up. He could particularly upset the Bateman children with little jibes about relatively unimportant stuff, like the fact that they had a string of housekeepers helping out before Tom married again. I'm sure, in the years after Muffie's death, they were probably all a little extra sensitive. But outside of the family Michael Fitzpatrick couldn't put a foot wrong. He was a local GP, apparently adored by his patients, and was even once elected Mayor of North Sydney, getting more votes than everyone else put together.

As far as Gwen was concerned, she was always the cleverest person in the room. There was only ever one opinion that mattered, and that was Gwen's opinion. Michael had huge admiration for Gwen's mental ability and as Gwen shared this opinion, it was great common ground for them; in short, they were both in total agreement about how brilliant Gwen was!

Gwen lived to 98. The last time I saw her was in a nursing home in Australia. She had really lost the will to live but couldn't do anything about it because she had absolutely no control over her own physical functions. I felt terrible for her. I am particularly close to her younger daughter, Mary, who I know brought Gwen a great deal of comfort, visiting and caring for her mother in Gwen's final years. Mary has been over to stay with us many times over the years, and we love an occasional chat on the phone; our legendary phone calls have been known to go on into the wee hours!

Gwen died in September 2016.

*

Of course we never forgot our poor sister, Clarinda, who had died before I was born when she was just three. She is commemorated in Parkes (where her grave lies) with the Clarinda fountain and the plaque in the Catholic Church.

And Patty named one of her daughters after her.

Patty was rather overshadowed by her older sisters. She was just a quieter girl with a very sweet nature who was actually brilliant at organising things and running her home life. She married quite young, just before she turned 23. Her husband was a very tall and handsome man; Bing Molyneux was a real "matinee idol" type. He was born in Tasmania but his father had been a sea captain so the family had lived in many places all over the world. He had the kind of looks that give *some* men inflated egos and make them behave badly, but Bing was very humble and, like Patty, he had a lovely, gentle personality. He wasn't at all ruined by his looks.

In the 1950s, Bing was appointed the Australian Consul General to the Philippines. Although he was based in Australia for the most part, they made several extended visits to the Philippines. Patty excelled in her role of supportive spouse, organising the household beautifully and entertaining to perfection. She was gracious but also razor sharp. She understood all the nuances of the role she played. She obviously impressed Imelda Marcos with her love of shoes and they remained in touch. Mrs Marcos once sent over some beautiful embroidered pinafore dresses for Sarah and Rachel, which they adored.

Patty and Bing had six children; five boys and a girl (Clarinda). One of their sons, Marcus, was unfortunately born with spina bifida.

Patty, who hadn't gone to university after school like the rest of us McGirr girls, went to college later in life to study Occupational Therapy, which perfectly suited her caring character.

My sweet sister Patty died in October 2007 at the age of 87. We lost her the same year we lost Kevin, contributing to our *annus horribilis*.

Raymond was the most troubled of all my parents' children. He was my mother's sixth child and the one born a few months after Clarinda died. He was the first boy since Jack and although she was always very proud of Jack, she just doted on Raymond. As he got older, Jack placed himself firmly in a "man's world", and everything was about physical prowess in sports, whereas Raymond was very much an intellectual and more sensitive.

I remember a particular time when we were all sitting around the breakfast room table having lunch. We were in the middle of a group conversation. Suddenly our mother hushed us all up, saying, "Shh, shh, Raymond wants to say something." We all went quiet, waiting for Raymond to speak, assuming he had something interesting to add to the discussion. Finally Raymond spoke up to say, "I like stewed apple and custard" (the dish we were eating at the time for our pudding).

We really couldn't believe our mother had brought a whole conversation to a standstill in order for Raymond to say such a mundane thing, but this was what it was always like; she was endlessly fascinated by him and hung on his every word because he was exceptionally bright; probably a genius. He came top of everything and our mother liked that. He was a natural at languages. He studied both German and Japanese, which was significant since they were the countries we were at war with for several years. He was such a skilled linguist that, when he travelled through Europe and spoke German, no one could detect his accent; they assumed he was a native German speaker.

Later in life, Raymond introduced Japanese into the Australian educational programme. He discovered a way of having it taught through postal arrangements (with lessons being posted to students who could then post back their completed work) so that even people in remote places could learn it. That the teaching of Japanese existed at all in Australia at that time was really thanks to Raymond.

My nephew Peter Willis (Nonna's eldest son), who is a member of the Victoria Bar and an eminent QC in Melbourne, had a professor at law school who remembers Raymond's university days. He recalled that Raymond would get hold of an issue and simply would not stop talking about it. On one occasion he had to be physically removed from the lecture hall, still talking at the top of his voice. Moments later he reappeared through another door and carried on from where he had been so rudely interrupted!

Because our mother pandered to Raymond so much, he became quite the emotional manipulator. He always got his way (until he met Kevin!)

Raymond married Ellen ("Nell") in 1947 and for their honeymoon they decided to trek around Australia. They set off on horseback and no one heard another word from them for 18 months. When I heard that they were back in Sydney and living in quite a remote suburb on The Spit (between North Sydney and Manley), with a baby, I asked Michael Fitzpatrick to drive me there so we could check up on them. I rang the doorbell and the door opened. Raymond stood there and Michael said, "We've just come to see how you are."

Raymond said, "Well you've seen me now," and shut the door in our faces.

I did manage to see them a few times after that, though. I would help them by driving them where they needed to go as neither of them drove.

They eventually had seven children but Raymond just struggled too much with responsibility. I always wondered if Raymond's life would have been different if he'd found a stronger wife. I once suggested this to him but he was completely oblivious, telling me that his marriage was "perfect". But Nell wasn't strong enough to help him manage his problems and they separated at some point. He really had total mental paralysis later in life.

I don't think Raymond was helped by the fact that he inherited so much money from my father's estate. He didn't know how to manage it. Someone should have been appointed to help him; he could not deal with responsibility.

He died in July 1984 at the age of 60. He fell asleep in front of a heater, caught fire and died of the burns. After separating from his wife, he had lived like a recluse. Huge piles of unopened correspondence were discovered in his house after his death. They were mostly bills that hadn't been paid, despite the fact that he had inherited all that money. This shows you that money is not always the answer to people's problems.

When I think of how all my siblings fared, I really don't think money or lack of money has much to do with anything. If anything, lack of it helped me; I think the fact I had to start from scratch and make my own way was the making of me. Nonna and I could have been very resentful that we didn't get the inheritance that my brothers and sisters got. But I ended up feeling grateful. I think it was a blessing. If I'd inherited a great big sum of money, I would have spent it all and then said, "Where's the next lot coming from," and it wouldn't have been coming from anywhere (unlike the time I spent all my pocket money on the lizard-skin handbag on my trip to Melbourne and then called my father who sent more!) Then I would have been left with nothing, unable to manage. If I'd had money on tap I wouldn't have worked as hard as I did with Kevin to build our business and invest in property. It gave me the motivation I needed to succeed.

Gregory wasn't remotely as academic as his older brothers and he was a quiet, shy child compared with Raymond's big, dramatic personality. Raymond stole the limelight and tended to get the most attention. Gregory was more in the background.

Gregory spent some time at agricultural college learning how to be a farmer. He was impressionable, however, and at one point it looked like he might go down the wrong path. He got involved in a business with the wrong sort of blokes; they were highly irresponsible and would get boozed up every Friday night. They often left valuable pieces of equipment unlocked, resulting in them getting stolen.

They were out of hand because there was no woman amongst them to keep them in check!

The making of Gregory was Maureen, a girl who had been in the same class as me. Gregory and Maureen actually met because they had ended up, by coincidence, working as volunteers in the same canteen during the war, but they didn't marry until 1959.

Even though he married a strong woman, Gregory could sometimes display a very sexist attitude that was sadly very prevalent in Australian men when we were growing up (I believe it is getting marginally better now). There was an occasion when we were driving in his ute up to Maureen's parents' place as they were having a big party. I think Gregory was planning on proposing to Maureen that night (so I imagine this must have been on my visit back to Australia in 1958, after I got married and before I had Sarah).

During the journey, Gregory suddenly said to me, "Those who marry into our family are very fortunate." Just as I was about to agree (considering I was newly married myself and things were going rather well), he said, "Well, those who marry the boys."

All I could do was roll my eyes.

Gregory and Maureen had three children. One of them, Dr Joe McGirr, a highly successful medical professor, became a NSW Member of Parliament in a by-election in September 2018, winning the Wagga Wagga seat from the Liberals, who had held it for more than 60 years. He ran as an independent, which makes his success all the more impressive. His brother, Michael McGirr, became a Jesuit priest and is a published author. He wrote a travelogue of his experiences when he took his mother on a European trip, giving her the honeymoon that Gregory had been unable to give her because of his health problems. Michael has since left the priesthood and teaches English. He is married with three children. Gregory and Maureen's youngest child, Linda, is the same age as Joanna. She is a solicitor and lives in Sydney.

Unfortunately, Gregory struggled with kidney failure most of his life and, while he fought a long, hard battle, eventually succumbed to his illness and died in September 1979 at the age of just 54.

In stark contrast to Gregory's comments about how the women who married into the McGirr family were the lucky ones, I couldn't help thinking how the women two of my brothers chose to marry shaped those men's lives. Maureen was absolutely the making of Gregory. He had really faded a little into the background until he married her and hadn't made a success of himself. He blossomed when he met Maureen. Whereas I don't think Nell was the right wife for Raymond. He needed a much stronger person, who could help him with his emotional instability and take care of the practical side of life for him.

*

My sister, Nonna, really could not have chosen a more perfect husband in Peter Willis. He was quite a bit older than her, and they married when Nonna was young, which worried my family to begin with, but they were a beautiful match. He was a wonderful man and they made such a lovely couple. They were devoted to one another.

Nonna was the sibling with whom I shared the greatest bond. After the tragedy of losing their first baby, Vicky, it was a joy to watch Nonna and Peter go on to have another six children. The first five of these were boys. Nonna adored them all but was desperate to have a girl. When Nonna finally gave birth to Catherine, and the doctor told her it was a girl, she said, "I don't believe it!"

"It's very easy to prove," the doctor said.

We all were devastated to lose another of Nonna's children, Matthew, who fell victim to AIDS in 1992. We have a wonderful picture of him taking Rachel to a formal dance when she was visiting in 1978. They both look stunning.

Matthew's death hit Nonna very hard. I don't think she ever recovered from it.

One of Nonna's great passions in life was English literature; she adored her book club that she attended for years, and she could write beautifully. She completed an MA in English Literature later in life, as a mature student.

Nonna died suddenly in March 2016 at the age of 84. It was a very, very sad day for me. Poor Peter just couldn't cope at all after Nonna's death; she was his whole world. Once Nonna was gone, he simply stopped eating and died only a month after she did. He literally died of a broken heart, unable to live without her. I can't imagine what a difficult time it was for the children, but they had each other for comfort. I feel I have a particularly strong bond with all of Nonna's children because I was so close to their mother.

Losing my precious little sister was absolutely heart breaking. We wrote to each other avidly throughout our lives. I miss her and her wonderful letters more than I can say.

*

I always loved having my nieces and nephews to stay with us in London. When we moved into Porchester Terrace, it was such a wonderful, large house, we had plenty of room for visitors. The front door was open from May to October for the "rellies" – as we call them in Australia – to visit while they were doing their overseas travels around Europe between school and university.

"Oh, god, not *another* rellie!" Kevin would exclaim when I announced our latest visitor. He was only joking, of course; he absolutely loved having the nieces and nephews to stay. He particularly adored Clarinda, Patty's daughter. We both did, she was like a fourth daughter to us, and the girls looked up to her like a big sister (she was nine years older than Sarah); they adored Clarinda's warm personality and dry wit. She always had them howling with laugher. Clarinda lived with us for a whole year in England before she went to university and was so helpful when the girls were little. Joanna and Clarinda were especially close.

I think being part of our family for a while was good for Clarinda, too. She grew up in a family of six children, but they were all boys but her, so she'd never had to stand her ground with big female personalities, of which there are many in the McGirr dynasty, but Patty was quieter than most of us. With my girls, Clarinda learnt what it was like to fight to be heard.

Being the only girl may have been one of the reasons Clarinda wasn't taken seriously as an academic at first. I remember Gwen in particular would dismiss Clarinda, academically (secretly I suspect this was also because neither of Gwen's children were that academic.) Because everyone had treated Clarinda like she was just some trophy doll, they were all surprised when she got a law degree from the University of Melbourne, after which she became a solicitor and eventually joined the Victoria Bar (later becoming a QC); everyone, that is, but Kevin and me. She was as successful as we had always known she would be.

As a barrister, Clarinda specialised in Family Law. I once went to watch her in court and she was very impressive. She was always so courteous and would get her point across calmly and eloquently.

When Kevin died I was so glad that Clarinda was able to fly over and give the most beautiful eulogy. Kevin would have loved it.

We were all shattered when Clarinda died after a long battle with pancreatic cancer in March 2014. Joanna had visited her not long before this and knew Clarinda was very unwell. Joanna was terribly upset at having to leave Australia on that trip; she didn't want to get on the plane to come home, convinced she would never see Clarinda again, which – sadly – turned out to be the case.

I was devastated not to have been in Australia when my mother died in 1969, or to have been able to attend her funeral that July, but by then I had three children under the age of 10, a busy dental practice to help manage, and had just taken my seat on Westminster Council. So I had to say goodbye to my mother, privately, in my own way.

I am grateful to my mother for so much, not least for inspiring me. Although my father was the politician, in many ways I think my political career is a testament to my mother, who set such an example of strength. In all my darkest moments, when I really wanted to throw in the towel, when they were chanting "Go back to Australia" during my Blackburn campaign, or when they were turning their backs on me for being a Catholic during the North Cornwall campaign, or when I was snubbed after being appointed Chair of the EUW, or when Kevin and I were crawling along snow-covered roads trying to get to a pointless selection interview for an MEP seat in Norfolk, I thought of my mother. Nothing would have stopped her. I knew she would have soldiered on through anything, doing her duty. And so I did, too.

29

The Next Generation

Sarah, Rachel and Joanna are an absolute credit to Kevin and me. I couldn't be more proud of them. They are such interesting individuals and have all achieved their own personal and professional successes in life. I know Kevin would have continued to feel very proud of what they, and our grandchildren, have achieved.

Joanna is hugely sentimental and nostalgic. She always got the most upset whenever we moved house. She has always been sensitive and never liked change. When we sold Porchester Terrace and moved into the little mews house in the back for a year while we were doing up the house in St John's Wood, Joanna was forever disappearing. We'd always find her up at the top of the garden looking longingly at "the big house", or in the summerhouse that the children had always used as a playhouse, upset because she wouldn't be seeing it again. She lived at home much longer than the other two and we really didn't move her out properly until 1991. Kevin and I may also have found it harder to let go because she was our last child to move out. And she certainly had a very special bond with Kevin as the two of them had quite a lot of time alone together while I was flying around the world on political business.

Rachel has always been completely focused. She always knew what she wanted to do in life; from a very early age she knew she wanted to be a doctor and she knew what she had to do to achieve that. Whereas Joanna was reluctant to pin herself down like that. She is a very good lawyer and has always been very interested in politics but she's involved in many activities.

Sarah is so like Kevin: endlessly practical, utterly reliable and fiercely independent. She has always been the one who makes all our plans; she is the social secretary of the family. She is just very down to earth and gets things done without any fuss; a born organiser. Having decided to start working after she left school rather than go to university, Sarah expressed a wish to have her own flat quite early on, so we helped her with that and she moved out quite promptly in 1980.

Once Rachel went to medical school she often lived in digs. But when she was based in London, for a while she shared a little mews house with two friends who were nurses. I'll never forget the day they had a break-in. It was awful for them of course, but when the policeman who attended the scene walked into Rachel's bedroom, which was a tiny room not much bigger than a cupboard, he said, "Yes, I can see they've ransacked in here." Rachel had to admit that the thieves hadn't been in her room… she was just that messy. She was terribly embarrassed. We couldn't help laughing and teased her about it for many years after that.

Sarah has numerous interests and has also inherited Kevin's ability to get along with anyone. When Kevin was Lord Mayor, Sarah often stepped in to accompany him when I was tied up with my parliamentary duties. On one occasion, she and Kevin were walking into a banquet and overheard a woman behind them comment, "Every time I see that Lord Mayor, he's with a different woman!"

Kevin and Sarah both roared with laughter and turned to explain to the woman that the different women were a rotation of his three daughters, not a string of dolly birds!

Sarah married (and later divorced) a man who also became Lord Mayor. While Sarah was Lady Mayoress in her own right, she went to Norway to cut down the famous Christmas tree for Trafalgar Square. She has two glass polar bears that were presented to her at that time by the Mayor of Oslo.

When Sarah was 21, she was diagnosed with multiple sclerosis (MS), a disease that affects the nervous system. The memory of how we discovered this is deeply and painfully etched on my brain.

We had all gone round to Sarah's flat for a meal to celebrate Shrove Tuesday and, at some point during the evening, she became quite weepy and said, "I can't see any of you properly. My eyes aren't working."

She had been having problems with walking and co-ordination for some time and was under the care of the National Hospital for Neurology and Neurosurgery at their annexe in Maida Vale, but she hadn't had any official diagnosis. The morning after our visit, she went to see her consultant and they admitted her for observation and tests. After a couple of days we still hadn't had an official diagnosis and we asked Sarah's GP to help. He got us an appointment with the Senior Registrar. I remember it was very late, after 9pm, when the doctor finally called us into his office to give us the official diagnosis. He told us it was MS.

Kevin and I were completely shell-shocked. We asked to see Sarah but were told she couldn't be disturbed. We were furious to find out, later, that the doctor had told Sarah that we'd been there but had decided to go home. He didn't explain that he'd refused to let us see her! I couldn't believe that he had given her the diagnosis an hour later, without any of her family with her! She spent the whole night sitting in the corridor fully clothed because she had become so upset at the severe condition of a patient next to her. It was unforgiveable the way that was handled.

Kevin was particularly shattered by the diagnosis. He and Sarah had always had such a strong connection; I think he felt it physically. He had supported her decision not to go to university but had high hopes for what she might achieve in her future career.

It is a huge credit to Sarah that she carried on as best she could with a very pragmatic approach to life, and we grew ever more proud of her as we watched how she managed life with MS. We are all inspired by Sarah's courage. She has always approached life with a positive, stoic attitude, just like her father.

Having worked for Saatchi & Saatchi for some time, she then went to work for the NHS, running the Chairman's Office at South London Regional Health Authority. Her boss, Sir William Wells, allowed her to organise her work in a way that also allowed her to manage the MS. She then moved to the Department of Health, to the Ministerial Corridor, before taking early retirement to pursue her charity interests. Sarah is currently the Deputy Chairman of the MS Trust and has an impressive list of voluntary activities she has been involved with. She also swims every day to keep her muscle tone and to maintain her strength and balance. Sarah has loved swimming since childhood. Being a lousy swimmer myself, I made sure all the girls took lessons and became strong swimmers.

Sarah has campaigned tirelessly for improved disabled access on public transport. Several years ago, Sarah discovered that there was only one place you could get on to the tube with full disabled access. Fortunately it was where I spent a large portion of my day: Westminster. Unfortunately it was also the only place you could get *off* the tube with full disabled access! Although there are several more tube stations with disabled access now, Sarah learned that one of the reasons London Underground can't construct more disabled access is because they don't own the land on which the stations sit. Even staircases often belong to the landlords.

Over the years, Sarah became involved in campaigning to get facilities on London buses for people using mobility scooters like the one she uses occasionally, which has given her so much independence. She would go out with TfL engineers to test dropped kerbs and ramps in various parts of London. They would hail buses and then once they pulled up, the engineers would check how efficiently the boarding and disembarking process was.

My favourite story of Sarah's transport trials and tribulations is the one about how she was waiting at the bus stop in Parliament Square in the summer of 2008 to get on the bus to go home. When the bus pulled up and the driver saw her mobility scooter, he started grumbling about not having enough room to lower the ramp to get her on board. Luckily, our formidable friend, Betty Boothroyd, was also waiting at the stop and had been chatting with Sarah. She prompted the driver, loudly, by saying, "The ramp, my good man!"

He lowered the ramp immediately and passengers who recognised Betty and had seen her in action as the Speaker of the House in the Commons were very excited to have witnessed her putting her famous voice to good use!

Whilst there have been great strides in disabled access over the past 30 years, Sarah, and the many other people with disabilities, have to deal with endless challenges every day that able-bodied people take for granted and wouldn't even think about.

As Sarah can still walk with a stick, she was eligible to trial Functional Electrical Stimulation technology, which helps people improve the quality of their walking. A pair of electrodes is positioned over the relevant nerve in the leg and then connected to a pressure pad under the heel of the foot (inside the shoe) and to a battery. The combination of all three provides a small electronic stimulus reminding Sarah's muscle to flex her ankle as she walks so that she improves her swing and lift.

I will never forget the day, in December 2015, when I got home to an answerphone message from Sarah telling me that she had just been for a walk in the park. Her first in 30 years! She had gone on her own without telling anyone as she has always been one to tackle a new challenge by herself, only sharing it after it has happened. I have never erased the message; I treasure it. In it, she is typically matter of fact. She simply announces the fact she's just been for a walk and then goes on to chat about various other social matters. But I felt quite emotional when I first heard it, and still do whenever I replay it.

Sarah still uses her mobility scooter for certain things. For example, she uses it to get to the swimming pool, which she still goes to every morning. But it is a real joy to see her out and about on her feet now. I really marvel at her spirit sometimes. She has always kept a positive attitude about her condition, doing everything she can to make the best of her life, and she is very disciplined with her fitness regime and diet. Of course there are testing times when she gets thoroughly frustrated with her situation, but for the most part she soldiers on, working hard to keep herself in the best possible shape. She has the most wonderfully dry sense of humour, which helps her deal with most things.

Rachel is probably the most like me in terms of personality. She is able to focus her attention on a lot of people and projects at one time. She is passionate about helping members of the general public. Being a GP is not dissimilar to being a politician; you have to be able to make sure everyone you come into contact with feels as though you are there just for them, and you have to reassure them that you are going to do everything possible to help them.

The irony of Rachel becoming a doctor has never escaped us. At school she was the most enthusiastic gymnast but rather accident-prone. She was at the A&E department at the hospital near her school so often that they just kept her file at the front desk!

Joanna really has a lot of both Kevin and me in her. She has Kevin's focus and hard work ethic, which enabled her to study to become a lawyer, but she also really loves helping people, like me, and followed the family tradition by getting into politics.

I used to joke with the girls that I wanted a doctor, a lawyer and an accountant because it would take care of all my needs and I'd save on bills! But in reality I wanted them to do whatever made them most happy. I think Sarah and Rachel were a little more focused on what they wanted to do with their lives from an earlier age. Joanna was always a little less certain. After she read politics at the University of Essex, she went through a time of indecision and I encouraged her to consider law, which she did, later qualifying as a solicitor. Kevin and I were also very proud when she decided to run for political office. She stood as the Conservative Parliamentary Candidate in the South Shields seat, fighting David Miliband in the 2001 General Election. It was a tough election as it was the height of Tony Blair's "New Labour" fever when the Conservatives did very poorly. Traditionally, if Labour won a seat, the Tories would at least come second, but in that election the Lib Dems pushed virtually all the Tory candidates in the North East of England down to third place. Joanna did brilliantly to finish second to the Labour candidate in her constituency after fighting a hard campaign.

I remember that campaign well. Kevin and I spent a lot of time up in South Shields campaigning for Joanna, and the people were wonderful. Some local Conservative supporters gave us their house to stay in and we had a lot of help from local people with campaigning. I remember the night before the election, Kevin and I knocking on doors in the pouring rain. I'd learnt from my campaigning days in Cornwall that nothing pleases a prospective voter more than if they are inside, all dry and warm, but the prospective politician is outside soaking wet; it impresses them if they can see you've suffered for the cause! We were so cold when we got back to the car, Kevin could hardly open the car door.

In addition to her impressive 20-year legal career, which included working for Accenture for 10 years, Joanna has also had a successful career in local government for 18 years. She was elected a Councillor for the Royal Borough of Kensington and Chelsea in 1998 and served as Mayor of the borough in 2008–2009. She was also Chairman of the Western Riverside Waste Authority, a statutory body worth £54m, responsible for the waste disposal and recycling across four London boroughs under differing political majority control.

I know it was hard for the girls, growing up with a mother who was physically absent so much of the time. It was asking a lot of them, but they were endlessly supportive. They seemed to love helping with canvassing, which was always a family team effort, and they got very excited when we let them stay up to listen to results coming in. But they knew they were different. All their friends had mothers who were at home, while their mother was dashing out of the country every other week to a UN conference here and a parliamentary visit there.

While I know it was hard for them at the time, when I wasn't there for a birthday or a special occasion, as they got older (they tell me) they have come to appreciate the novelty of having a mother who has led such an interesting and prestigious life. I have always tried to involve them in my work; I took them campaigning and to watch important events when I could. They became quite the experts at handing round sandwiches and engaging with guests at receptions, sometimes with quite important dignitaries! Many of their friends have ended up with little to talk to their mothers about in adulthood, whereas I am told I have continued to be a source of real fascination to my daughters. I hope they would agree that, in the long run, they didn't get such a bad deal. It wasn't as if they were ever neglected in their childhood. They had the best hands-on father in the world in Kevin, and we always had wonderful helpers in nannies, au pairs and housekeepers.

I even set up and ran my own au pair agency for a while, back in the mid 1960s. As I'd found it difficult sourcing reliable and capable staff to help me with the family, I assumed other people would have the same problems. I placed some excellent girls with various families, but we did have the odd strange experience. One girl who came to help us at Porchester Terrace arrived with a suitcase so heavy that Kevin could barely lift. But she wanted it in her room on the top floor with the children, so up it went. We were all intrigued to know what was in it but didn't like to ask. A few weeks after arriving, she vanished without trace! After we failed to track her down – we tried everything we could – we decided to open the suitcase that she had left in her room. It was full of stainless steel cutlery!

Another au pair we had failed to pick the girls up from school one day. We had no idea where she was and got very worried. Then the police called to say that she had been arrested at an anti-Vietnam War protest outside the American Embassy in Grosvenor Square. Kevin had to go and bail her out. We were such a political family; even our au pairs were political!

Georgina was one of our favourites. She was a "mother's help" who was with us for many years. She started with us when she was only 16. She was lovely but had very little education and needed help with her numbers. Sarah, who was only around six or seven years old when Georgina came to us, used to help her do the housekeeping books, working out exactly how they were going to spend the £10 a week they had for groceries. As a result, Sarah excelled at mental arithmetic at school; in fact, she developed quite an entrepreneurial mind. When she was in the sixth form she and her friend were "energy monitors" because there was a government scheme going on, encouraging school children to save energy. They worked out that by lowering the temperature of the school swimming pool by one degree, the school could save thousands on their heating bills. They made the front page of the *Evening Standard* with their brainwave!

Georgina was terribly sweet and marvellous with the children, but she also had severe dyslexia. She couldn't read or write a thing, and would never be able to. If she had to be given directions to anywhere, you had to describe the route in terms of the landmarks that she would encounter along it, rather than give any road signs or ask her to look at a map. She couldn't recognise a single word. But she loved pop music, especially from the 1960s and 1970s, and had the radio on all day, which the girls loved. Georgina stayed with us until she left to get married.

My greatest joy, in recent years, has been watching my grandchildren grow up. Rachel has four children, Joanna has one, and Sarah has five nieces and nephews to dote on!

Joanna and her husband, Richard, have Lucy, who was born in 2005 and is growing up fast, into a lovely child. Lucy was still a baby when Kevin was in hospital. He had been devoted to her since she was born. He'd missed those early years with our older grandchildren because he was still so busy when they were small, so he really relished Lucy's company. He was fascinated with her.

Even though Kevin wasn't very aware of what was happening in his final days, having Lucy crawling around while we were in the waiting area always brought me a little joy at a very difficult time. I would think, fondly, about how much Kevin loved to watch her. She was such an adorable baby; and she's still adorable at 13. I love spending time with her and eagerly look forward to her visits. She often goes over to Sarah's for cooking lessons; Sarah is teaching her all the best-loved family recipes, including cheese soufflé, mince pies and marmalade!

Despite their demanding careers as doctors, Rachel and Alvan have found the energy to raise four children, one with special needs. Their eldest son, Christopher, was born with Down's syndrome (when she first got pregnant Rachel was just under the age limit to get the antenatal screen for Down's syndrome that the NHS offered) and much later he was diagnosed with autism. He was able to live at home until he was in his late teens, when he moved to a specialist boarding school. He has now moved into his own home, where there are always full-time carers present, although he still comes home for lunch on Saturdays.

Rachel and Alvan's next baby was a girl, Victoria, who was named after her birthplace because Alvan was on a one-year work placement at the Royal Melbourne Hospital (which is in the Australian state of Victoria). They were living in Carlton, a south-eastern suburb of Melbourne when they had her. Kevin and I went out to stay with them when they were there, to help look after Chris while they took a trip to Queensland shortly after Victoria was born.

Once they were back in the UK, Katie was born. She has recently finished her degree in medicine (the first of her generation to follow in this family tradition) at Bristol University. Philip is the youngest in the family. He is now studying medicine at Oxford University. Victoria read Politics at Warwick University and is currently on the Civil Service fast-track programme. I love having her in London as she visits me often.

When they retire, Rachel and Alvan plan to relocate to London. This might sound strange because you'd assume most people want to get away from the hustle and bustle of a big city in their retirement years, but I think they have always wanted to spend more time doing all the wonderful cultural activities London offers, things that they haven't been able to enjoy whilst being busy doctors and parents.

Once, when I was chairing a Social Services Committee for Westminster City Council, we had a doctor come in to give us some advice. I remember asking him if he thought it would be a good idea for some of our tenants to be moved to somewhere like Cornwall for their retirement and he said it actually wouldn't be good for them at all. He explained that people who have lived in a big, busy place all their lives could easily get bored and depressed if they moved somewhere quiet; it would be too much of an adjustment. I really saw his point. What you want in retirement is to be able to do all the things you never had time for while you were working. What could be better than retiring to a vibrant, fascinating city such as London where there is an endless list of interesting things to explore?

I love living in London, but our family house in Oxfordshire is a beautiful getaway for the holidays and weekends. We all love staying there, and it's a great place for Philip to use when he needs a quiet place to study for his exams during his time at Oxford. He also picks the apples for me, which is useful as our fruit trees are quite bountiful.

I always feel closer to Kevin when I'm in Oxford, as he is buried in our local churchyard. It's also the place where we had more time together without the hustle and bustle of our busy London lives. We could garden and read in peace; we loved eating *al fresco* in the summer when the weather allowed. We were both able to switch off as soon as we got to Oxford.

When I think about the next generation in the UK, I know that we are at a critical turning point for them, and it all hovers on the cliff edge of what has become known as "Brexit", the plan to withdraw the United Kingdom from the European Union.

In the past few years, Brexit debate – or should I say, brawl! – has swept the country like a fever. In homes and workplaces, *as well as* in Parliament, I have never known people so divided and set against each other. It has turned Parliament into the most antagonist place I have ever seen in all my time there. Debates are just a series of boxing matches, with people throwing verbal punches at each other. One person gets up to speak and the next person stands up and just shreds them, and it carries on like that back and forth.

I do hope I live to see an end to this rather spiteful atmosphere that the deep divisions over Brexit have caused in Parliament. It is as close to truly nasty as I have ever seen it. I got into politics at a time when I felt that we all, regardless of which party we belonged to, were united in our desire to ensure people's lives improved and the country prospered. No matter how much we disagreed on how to implement this, there was a sense that we were ultimately working together for the common good. The Lords, in particular, is traditionally a place where the debate is less heated. Insults are not appreciated in our Chamber. But I have watched both Houses become battlefields over Brexit. It is very disheartening indeed. With personal insults flying around, we have become divided, undecided and negative. I don't recognise it as the place I entered in 1981.

I decided only to include in this book whatever has happened up to the end of February 2019 and not to try and add last-minute updates as it is going to press, or I might be here adding updates forever! So as of the end of January, this is where we are…

In a huge mess!

In mid-January, my friend, Betty Boothroyd strongly urged the Government to allow another referendum to break what has become a parliamentary deadlock on the Withdrawal Agreement, to go back to the public and ask if they want this deal. She put it very succinctly: "In my book, if a democracy cannot be allowed to change its mind, it ceases to be a democracy." She quite rightly asked why the portion of the electorate who have turned 18 since the last referendum in 2016 should not be allowed a say in their future, asking, "What [is] the Government afraid of in refusing a people's vote? In answering that question, will [it] please explain to young people who have reached adulthood why they do not have the right to be heard on an issue that our generation has manifestly bodged? Brexit will shape these youngsters' futures for the next 50 years – not ours. I have no children or grandchildren; my quality of life will not be affected. I am all right, Jack. But what about the Jacks and Jills out there? Are they to be stripped of their rights on the whim of those who peddled rubbish in the referendum and are afraid to be challenged in another?"

Opinion polls have told us that young people overwhelmingly want to stay in the European Union, and those who were too young to vote in the last referendum are particularly insistent that they have a right to have their say. It seems wrong to deny them that right.

There is a lot of delusion over the practicality of Brexit. Regardless of what you may *want*, the simple truth is that you can't always have it. Many people use the past as an example of what "could be". But times have changed, the world has moved on, relationships are different, the structure of world order has shifted. I remember when we joined the European Union in 1973 and then when we had a referendum to stay in the European Union in 1975, and that was a very long time ago. We are not the country we were when we joined Europe; we have been irrevocably changed by the 45+ years of membership we have experienced. Some people want Brexit because they think we can be the country we were before we joined. But we can't. "Going back to the good old days" just seems like a pointless notion to hold onto. The biggest mistake I think people are making is to believe that we will simply "go back" to where we were before. The world has moved on and changed considerably since then.

At the time we were joining the EEC (the European Economic Community, as it was called before it became the European Union) in 1973, I was visiting Australia. I was in a hardware store and the shopkeeper mistook me for a British person. He said he was glad Britain was going to start trading with Europe more than Australia because in his opinion, "You Brits bled us white," suggesting the British had drained every drop of blood from Australia. He was referring to the fact that Britain had enjoyed highly favourable trading agreements with Oceania (which includes Australia and New Zealand). In Britain we were paying just 9p per pound (in weight) of Australian butter, whereas in Australia they were paying four shillings and sixpence (around 26p) for it! It was a 25-year contract so it was a poor deal for them for a long time.

It seems some people in the UK think we can just go back to these kinds of favourable deals with countries like Australia. But we don't have anything like the kind of bargaining power we once had to make these kinds of trade agreements. The world is far too competitive and complex now; it is a completely different place.

I really have no idea why seemingly sensible people are so fixed on this idea of being able to turn back the clock, thinking that we will suddenly have all this trading power. As strong as it once was, that ship has long-since sailed.

And when people suggest we could resurrect the Commonwealth as a trading block and it would be a match for the EU, I know that they are being implausibly idealist. I've participated in so many Commonwealth conferences and I know the general sentiment. The African countries, in particular, have become increasingly anti-Britain. In fact, I think they would really rather take over the power of the Commonwealth Parliamentary Association. I would be very sad to see Britain start to lose her role as the "mother" of the Commonwealth, I believe that the Commonwealth has a lot of positive value and I care deeply about it – particularly in the ways in which it can potentially help countries like Zimbabwe, which has struggled to maintain its membership during Mugabe's reign – but we have to respect what people feel they want in their countries. I know there are many people in Australia who want complete independence from the British monarchy. Equally, we still see an outpouring of support for the British monarchy in Australia when they visit, as was shown only recently when Harry and Meghan were there. Their 2018 tour, a few months after they were married, was made even more special by the fact they announced that Meghan was pregnant. And I was delighted to see them visit Dubbo where they were a good omen because they brought desperately overdue rain with them! This was highly appreciated as the region had been suffering from a serious drought.

I don't think that the 2016 referendum was put to the British people in a very helpful way or at the right time… *or* for the right reasons. It was really a desperate measure by David Cameron to appease the hard-right Eurosceptics who have long existed in the Conservative party. You couldn't blame anyone for voting to leave the EU given what the Leave campaign was promising them. But most of these promises were lies. We know that now. Yet when "remainers" point this out they are accused of "scaremongering". So I don't see why we shouldn't have a referendum to confirm what the electorate wants to do, especially now we know exactly what is on the table in the Withdrawal Agreement. Now we have an actual document and we know what the realities are, surely it is absolutely democratic to allow people to choose whether they want to go ahead with the agreement that has been negotiated. At time of writing, Parliament has voted this down and that has put an impossibly large spanner in the works. Parliament does not want to accept this agreement and yet won't put it back to the people. No one can decide what to do next and the whole issue is being used to push the agendas of the extremists in both parties. We are using people's lives and businesses like bargaining chips. That is very disappointing.

People can push this way and that as much as they want but in the end it all looks like the most unresolvable confusion. There's far too much of people *thinking* they know everything or claiming to know everything, when we can only know so much before events take place. I don't lose too much sleep over it because I trust it will all work out somehow. I feel that all things get resolved one way or another in the end, everything evolves in some way. People are always in a hurry to claim they know everything, but no one really knows everything. The screenwriter William Goldman said, of Hollywood, "Nobody knows anything… Not one person in the entire motion picture field knows for a certainty what's going to work. Every time out it's a guess and, if you're lucky, an educated one." He could have said exactly the same about politics!

I simply hold onto the faith that a reasonable solution will emerge in the end (whenever that may come!) I am keeping the faith. Sometimes, that's all you can do.

History has a way of repeating itself and I trust that, if Brexit does happen, and has the hugely adverse effect on the country that is being predicted from the most knowledgeable quarters, then the next generation will be so incensed that they will work together to clean up the mess and make things better than they have ever been before.

I do feel, going forward, that the public need to take more interest in what actually goes on in Parliament and do more than listen to highly unreliable hearsay or the latest squabble on social media. Ironically, in this digital age, the *real* facts are available to them any time they want. They trusted politicians to tell them facts and the Leave campaign for Brexit told a lot of lies. Many people feel angry with them for that, but we have no one to blame but ourselves. Maybe we all (politicians and people) should have done more research. We certainly should have had a more complex and realistic question in the 2016 referendum than a simple black and white choice: "Do you want to be IN or OUT?" Anyone could have figured out, with a bit of work, that this was *not* a useful question to put to the public…

because the execution is simply not that simple. No matter what the "no-deal" enthusiasts would have you believe!

In the end, it is all our own doing. We didn't do enough research. We didn't reach for the facts… that were right at our fingertips. We listened to the loudest voices on TV. It's been a harsh lesson.

As I write, at the end of February 2019, I obviously can't tell you what will happen next. I *can* tell you that Parliament is still in quite a state of disarray and absolutely dominated by Brexit. There is still no parliamentary consensus on the withdrawal deal, and it looks like the only way to break the deadlock is to take the decision back to the people and have an honest referendum, even though there is huge resistance to that from the Government. Obviously, by the time you read this you will know all the next twists and turns but, at this point, I can't even guess because British politics, like British weather, is changeable and wholly unpredictable… and, moreover, we are in uncharted territory with "Brexit".

A friend of mine recently recalled a conversation we had just before the 2016 referendum. Apparently I said, "If anyone is foolish enough to vote to leave the EU, they will soon discover that it is constitutionally impossible to achieve." Only time will tell if I am to be proved right.

30

Surviving!

Whenever people see me in the corridors of the House of Lords after not seeing me for some period of time (sometimes not disguising their surprise that I'm still alive!) and ask me how I am, I always say, "Surviving!"

And that is exactly what I feel I am doing every day: surviving!

At the time of writing I am 91 years old and I am often asked if I have any plans to retire. I can say with certainty that I do not. What would I do? There is no vision of "retirement" that I think of or long for. You need a really good reason to get up in the morning otherwise you'd never get out of bed. If the Queen, who is only a year older than me, can get up every day and go to work, then so can I!

My eldest daughter, Sarah, who does so much for me (all the girls do but she gets the short straw because she lives in the house opposite mine), shudders with horror at the idea of me retiring. She says at least she knows where I am and what I'm doing all day. She calls the House of Lords the "grandest day care centre in London".

I wouldn't actually know what to do with myself if I retired; I've always felt it's important in life to feel a sense of purpose and usefulness. Working gives me that.

I suppose I would garden more, and do more tapestry.

One of my very first presents from Kevin was a beautiful tapestry kit from Liberty's. I had noticed it once when we were window-shopping, and loved the pattern: a yellow and orange striped cat sitting in green grass surrounded by blackbirds. The design was very modern. However, it was rather expensive. Shortly before Christmas I went to look at it again but discovered, much to my disappointment, that it had been sold. I was absolutely thrilled when Kevin presented it to me for Christmas; he was always extremely thoughtful like that. I made it up into a cushion and it has lived on our sofas ever since, amongst a growing collection of other tapestries that have become cushions, each reminding me of the period of my life when I completed it.

I could also get back to crocheting. Inspired by a friend of my mother's who made such beautiful linen handkerchiefs with crocheted edges, I took a crocheting course at the Royal College of Embroidery in the 1960s. I was always a real whizz at knitting but crochet was a completely different skill I had to learn from scratch. I loved it. But then I got so caught up in my work I never got back to it.

However, I don't think a bit of crocheting or tapestry would be enough to fill my days.

I'm currently the oldest woman in Parliament; I'm the "grandmother" of both Houses. My great friend, Jean Trumpington (Baroness Trumpington) was five years older than me. She retired just after her 95th birthday in October 2017 and a year later, in November 2018, she died peacefully in her sleep. I'm not saying the two are related, but for the record, again, I have absolutely no intention of retiring! I intend to continue working in the House of Lords until they have to carry me out!

And there is no telling when that could be.

Not long ago, in October 2018, I was in the lift with Roger Bootle-Wilbraham (Baron Skelmersdale) who had been Secretary of State for Health at that time when I was trying to get the Government to keep free NHS dental check-ups for adults. (Incidentally, although we failed on that one, we did get the free glaucoma tests for people with family histories of the condition, which I was very pleased about. I was relieved that it was not reversed in the Commons, like the NHS dental examinations. This was all part of the same phase of adopting many changes in the NHS.) As we travelled up in the lift, Roger told me all about his business – he had started selling daffodil bulbs in Somerset.

Only a week later, I was shocked when the Lord Speaker announced Roger's death. Roger had gone back to his London flat one evening and had a fatal stroke. He had seemed so fit and healthy when we were speaking that day. I was very saddened by the news.

I was in awe of my fellow peers when I first joined the House of Lords, but I soon realised that talking to people in the House of Lords is just like talking to people anywhere. All the peers are normal people, with interesting lives and human feelings. Some are actually terribly lonely people because they have outlived a spouse or never had one, or because their family live in other parts of the country or the world. They're an interesting bunch, comprising people from all walks of life. I've seen peers arrive on bicycles and motorbikes, and in Mercedes and old bangers (like mine!) People say to me "I can't believe you're 91 years old and still driving to work every day." And I say, "I find it's the safest way to get there."

Ultimately, I do support the life peerage system. It has given me my job for life; and I think some of my colleagues would never have entered politics if they hadn't been made life peers through the appointment system; I don't think they would have put themselves up for election, or have had the personalities and thick skin you need to fight elections. Yet they make huge and vital contributions to British politics and the legislative process in the Lords.

I like feeling part of a community, especially one full of such diverse and fascinating people. You regularly cross paths with the same people over the years. On one of my visits to Australia, I met Helen Liddell who was the UK's High Commissioner for Australia from 2005–2009. Helen had been a Labour MP from 1994 to 2005 and when she returned from Australia, in 2010, she was made a life peer. Now we regularly bump into each other in the corridors of Westminster and have a quick chat to share our love of all things Australian.

Of course, you can't always agree on everything with your fellow peers, but you are a team and you need to get along. That is what I learnt in my family, when we all had to sit down together for meal times, around the big breakfast table, the long table, like the long table we have in the Lords' dining room, and the one we had in the GLC. It forces us to communicate properly, and thoroughly, when we all sit down together around the same table. You have to talk to each other, taking time to listen clearly and respond respectfully, to have any kind of relationship with someone. I think peers tend to get to know each other on a more personal level because we do make a real effort to communicate properly with each other.

To be someone's "peer" means to be their equal, no matter what side of the table or the House you sit on, and we should never forget that.

People always assume politicians from opposing parties must be in personal wars with each other. Not at all! Some of my dearest friends and some of the colleagues I hold in the highest regard are officially on the "other side". I couldn't respect them more, as people, even if we disagree on policies.

One of my biggest rivals in politics was Barbara Castle, who I unsuccessfully fought for the Blackburn seat in the 1970 General Election. I liked Barbara and got the impression that she liked me, too. Some years later, she was the guest of honour – in her role as Secretary of State for Health and Social Services within Harold Wilson's Cabinet – at a BDA (British Dental Association) event. Knowing that we had fought a seat in the 1970 General Election, my fellow dentists were expecting us to be clawing at each other, but as soon as she saw me she gave me a huge hug and said how pleased she was to see me. People were astonished to find out that some politicians could be extremely civilised with each other, despite being members of opposing parties.

Several more years later, when we were both peers, Barbara added my name to an amendment she was putting forward to stop people getting retrospective planning permission. She didn't even ask me (the usual protocol in the House of Lords) because she knew I would support her amendment. And I did. She knew me and understood me; she knew exactly what I believed in. That's friendship.

Ultimately, I wouldn't want to retire because I genuinely enjoy helping people, and that is what my job enables me to do to best effect. Of course my big crusade will always be public health. I have always done as much as I can, both in my role in Parliament and by serving on various health-related committees and boards of governors over the years. I was on the board of the Eastman Dental Hospital from 1971 to 1980, was Vice-

Chairman of NE Thames Regional Health Authority from 1990 to 1994, and sat on the board of the National Heart Hospital from 1974 to 1990. For a short time between 1994 and 1997, Kevin and I were each Chairman of a London NHS Trust: Kevin of the Royal National Throat Nose and Ear Hospital (RNTNE) and I was Chairman of the Royal Free Hospital. However, most of the Chairmanships changed under the new Labour government of 1997, including my own, which was very disappointing.

Another organisation I actively supported was the Suzy Lamplugh Trust. In 1986, Suzy Lamplugh, a 25-year-old estate agent, went missing after possibly attending a house viewing. She was officially declared dead, presumed murdered, in 1994. After Suzy's disappearance, her parents, Paul and Diana, set up a trust to help educate people about their personal safety, especially those who often have to work alone, like estate agents (this was especially important in the days before mobile phones).

Suzy's remains have never been found, even though the police have followed up many leads over the years. As recently as October 2018 they started digging up the garden in a house in Sutton Coldfield, following up a new lead. The Lamplughs were wonderful people. I had such a lot of time and respect for them. I can't imagine what they went through. Diana died in 2011 and Paul in July 2018. They had both been awarded OBEs and the work of the Suzy Lamplugh Trust continues today, with a National Stalking Helpline and an annual National Personal Safety Day.

People often write to me or tell me that they are retiring, and ask my advice about what to do because they have been offered various positions on boards of charities or as governors of institutions. I always advise them not to take the first offer they receive, to really think clearly and take their time over choosing what to give their time to. I know many people who accepted the first offer made to them and later found out it wasn't for them. But by that time, it's too late and they're stuck with it because they've made the commitment. It's important to give your time to something that you feel very strongly about or you won't give it your best.

You only have so much energy to give towards the end of your life; give it wisely!

As people age and fall ill, it can be so excruciatingly hard for them. They become desperate for some sense of security in the face of death. Every time we hear about a new "miracle drug" in the news – something hailed as being the new *real* miracle because the last one no longer works – people rejoice. They want hope that life can go on. But life can't go on forever. And at the end it can be a real struggle, especially if you lose control of your basic functions.

For at least the last five years of her life, my sister Gwen was in a care home (one with hospital-level facilities with qualified nurses and specialised equipment). The last time I went to see her she was very clear minded, but completely bed-ridden and unable to do anything for herself. She had all her mental faculties but was totally dependent on others for her physical wellbeing. She told me, "I don't really want to go on living but I'm still here." She said she'd felt that way for a couple of years. I don't think she was asking for help to die, I think she just wanted to state how she felt. She was very lucid but she couldn't move at all. She needed full-time around-the-clock total care. To bathe, she had to be lifted out of the bed in a sling and then lowered into the bath. I was very pleased to see her for that final time but I felt very sad for her.

I really don't think I would want to go on living in a vegetative state if I ever got to that point. But often the body goes before the mind. I don't like the thought of death, but what scares me more is the process of dying. The very thought of being in immense pain, or being completely incapacitated, fills me with horror. It was awful when Kevin died, but I'm glad he went peacefully and didn't have a long drawn-out and painful illness. Kevin was so independent; he would have absolutely hated to be utterly dependent on others and unable to move. So maybe it was a blessing he never had to experience the indignity of that. But we will never know if things could have been different. The lymphoma was quite severe when it was discovered; if it had been found earlier, it would have been treatable. That was the biggest blow.

But as long as you have the ability to function and you're in no pain, why shouldn't you keep going? We have several peers who are in their 90s and the odd one, over the years, has reached 100. One of Kevin's cousins is 101 now. She's in a home full time, with her granddaughter visiting and caring for her. She still plays bridge but she's got a reduced quality of life. The last email I received said she was still going but was extremely frail. But she's still there... surviving!

―

If I'd stayed in Australia, I honestly don't think I would have got involved in politics. I think I would have got married, had children and focused on my family. I just wasn't that interested in politics when I was young. I thoroughly enjoyed the process of debating, however. I got very wrapped up with debating teams at school and university, and was often chosen to make the closing comments for whichever side I was on. I'd learnt to argue my case well, growing up in my large family. With so many of us, every mealtime was a big debate about something or other. Maybe this was also partly why I took to politics so avidly once I found myself living in the UK. I just missed having a huge family to sit around arguing with! But in my wildest dreams, when I was that little girl growing up in Australia, I never could have imagined that I would end up a Baroness, living in London, having spent almost 20 years in local government and 38 (and counting!) as a member of the UK Parliament.

Kevin as a child in Sydney, 1936

Kevin on our wedding day, 7th July 1956

Kevin and me on our holidays, c.1958

The Gardner family, 1970

Sarah, Rachel and Joanna, c. 1968

Family outing to the park in Blackburn, 1970

The family at Trekenner in North Cornwall, 1973

Two dentists: a great partnership. London, 1981

Kevin as Lord Mayor of Westminster, 1987

*After the Order of
Australia Ceremony
in the Quadrangle
at Buckingham
Palace, 2003*

Kevin with Katie, 1995

*Rachel and Alvan's
children; my grandchildren
(L-R: Katie, Christopher,
Victoria, Philip), 2003*

*With my granddaughter,
Lucy (Joanna and
Richard's daughter), 2012*

*The last family
Christmas with
Kevin, 2006*

The Armorial Bearings of
BARONESS GARDNER OF PARKES

College of Arms
London

Lancaster Herald

My Armorial Bearings

EPILOGUE

Keep Going

When I was offered my peerage, as well as agreeing my title with the College of Arms, I had to design my official Coat of Arms. As a woman, you are given a diamond shape, called a "lozenge" (men get the traditional shield shape) with "standard bearers" either side. You have to pay quite a hefty sum for it and it obviously stays with you for life so it's worth spending some time over it to get it absolutely right. We had a lot of back and forth with the College of Arms over my design. I wanted to make sure it represented everything that was most important to me.

For my standard bearers, I decided upon the traditional lion to symbolise the UK on the left hand side, and the most obvious choice was to have a kangaroo on the right hand side, to symbolise my ties to Australia. The lion holds a spray of wattle blossom, and the kangaroo holds a red rose. I also wanted to acknowledge Parkes, so I needed a symbol with some local connection. I thought of displaying the famous Parkes radio telescope, but realised this might be difficult to portray in the design, so in the end we decided to include the star constellation of the Southern Cross (as depicted on the Australian flag); in other words, what you would *see* by using the telescope.

The negotiations to get all of this agreed took some time and even when we had the final picture agreed upon, there was one more element. I had to choose my motto. I assumed this had to be in Latin, which I had never studied, so I was rather pleased when they told me it could be in English. And this gave me a wonderful opportunity to include a nod to my father.

Dad had a great story he loved to tell you if he sensed you were ready to give up on some pursuit you'd been going after and you were a bit down about it.

The story goes that a commercial traveller set out from Sydney once, with various stops planned on his route. When he got to the first stop he discovered that another salesman had just been there and had made all the sales that were to be had at the time. The same thing happened at his next stop, and it kept happening to him every time he reached a new destination. Eventually he accepted he was always going to be pipped to the post by all the salesmen ahead of him, so he sent a telegram back to his head office saying,

"No point in going on, there's 50 ahead of me."

Immediately, the reply came back saying, "Go for your life! 50 more coming behind!"

So I made my motto: *Keep Going*.

And that's what I intend to do… for as long as I can.

But do we keep going forever? I think most people want to believe that death is not the end, that you don't finish your existence here on earth, that there is a better place to go to, where we will be reunited with our loved ones in some way. Of course, we have no way of knowing this for sure, we just have to believe that it's true, and that's why we call it "faith".

I remember when Kevin died, one of the girls said that they imagined him sitting "up there" with all the family around him, all the relatives who had died, looking after everyone and watching over us. It was a comforting thought. Religion is most welcome when it consoles you in your grief after losing a loved one.

Life is so uncertain and the death of a loved one comes as a terrible shock, especially if they are killed suddenly, or die too young, or when they go from diagnosis to death in a very short time. You are left with such a huge hole in your life. As we felt when we lost Kevin… and Nonna felt when she lost her children, Vicky and Matthew… and the Bateman children felt when they lost their mother, Muffie… and my parents felt when they lost their little girl, Clarinda… and we all feel when the unbearable happens, and someone we are deeply connected to is taken from us. The belief that, somehow and in some way, you'll see them again helps you get through the terrible days after you lose the person you love.

This is why religion has always been so important to us, as a family. It gives us that faith.

Joanna and I went to mass very early the morning after Kevin died. Of course we knew it couldn't bring him back, but it did give us some comfort.

We all need hope.

I have lived almost 100 years and one thing I have learned is that *almost* everything you can think of changes. Our methods of travel and communication change, we get better-designed dishwashers and sewing machines, we change how we build houses and roads, and how we grow food… but one thing doesn't change. People don't change. They will always have their loves and their fears. And that is what makes the world go round: people and their desires, for the good and the bad. For as long as the human race exists, we will continually mess it all up and then figure out how to make it all better again.

Onwards we will go, forever… unless we manage to wipe ourselves out in a nuclear holocaust or by causing some environmental catastrophe!

In the meantime, I intend to live by my motto and *keep going*, doing my duty in Parliament, enjoying my time with my family, and tending my garden at the weekends.

I am never happier than when I am in my garden… and my family are near by. My mother, Rachel Rittenburg Miller McGirr, loved her garden and would spend hours tending it. Most ladies of her social standing in those days would employ gardeners, but she considered gardening to be her work and only employed help with the heavier jobs that she couldn't physically manage. She particularly loved her camellias and would often invite Professor Waterhouse, who was Raymond's German professor at the University of Sydney, to walk with her around the garden and admire her collection.

Born in 1881, Professor Eben Gowrie Waterhouse was one of the leading breeders of camellias of his day and was trialling species in the garden of his home on Sydney's North Shore. He helped to found the

International Camellia Society in 1962. In July 1970, the E.G. Waterhouse National Camellia Gardens were opened in Sydney with over 450 individual cultivars and species.

As soon as we moved into Porchester Terrace and I had a proper garden for the first time, I asked Nonna to send me some camellia rootstocks. Sarah was very young but she remembers coming with me to the cargo area at Heathrow to collect the plants. The roots had been washed clean of all soil and pests, and were specially sealed. They thrived in the garden of Porchester Terrace and, over the years, we moved some of them from house to house (sometimes carefully excluding them in sales contracts to ensure we could keep them). All my daughters have camellias in their gardens as they have grown to love them, too. Sarah, who has inherited the family green fingers, has one of the original Australian plants in her garden.

These beautiful flowers have been so important to the McGirrs through the generations. All my sisters loved camellias; we thought of them as our "family flower" uniting us all. So even though, with the exception of me, the McGirr girls have all gone now, thanks to the magic of plants, when I look at my camellias I feel as though I have a little piece of my Australian family with me always.

Postscript

In May 2019, a couple of months before my 92nd birthday, our Chief Whip in the House of Lords, Lord Taylor of Holbeach, asked me to come and see him in his office. He greeted me warmly and asked, "Have you ever thought of retiring, Trixie?"

"Never given it a thought," I replied, promptly. Then added, with a smile, "I intend to keep going."

At my desk in the Lords, 2016

Appendix

Curriculum Vitae

1954 BDS (Bachelor of Dental Surgery), Sydney University
1955–1990: Dentist in general practice
1956: Diplome de Cuisine, Le Cordon Bleu, Paris

HOUSE OF COMMONS:

June 1970 General Election: contested Blackburn constituency for Conservative Party
February 1974 General Election: contested North Cornwall constituency for Conservative Party

HOUSE OF LORDS:

April 1981, raised to the peerage as Baroness Gardner of Parkes, of Southgate in Greater London and of Parkes in the State of New South Wales and Commonwealth of Australia
1999–2002: Deputy Chair of Committees
1999–2002: Deputy Speaker
2003–2005: Member, Information Committee
2005–2009: Member, Delegated Powers and Regulatory Reform Committee

LOCAL AUTHORITIES

1968–1978: Councillor, Westminster City Council
1970–1973: Councillor, Havering, Greater London Council (GLC)
1977–1986: Councillor, Enfield Southgate, GLC

PUBLIC BODIES AND OFFICIAL POSTS

1966–1971: Member, Inner London Executive Council of the NHS
1968–1978: Standing Dental Advisory Committee for England and Wales
1971–1997: Justice of the Peace for North Westminster
1971–1980: Governor, Eastman Dental Hospital
1974–1980: Governor, National Heart Hospital
1974–1981: Board Member, Westminster, Kensington & Chelsea Area Health Authority
1974–1997: Member, Industrial Tribunal Board for London
1980–1982: Member, North Thames Gas Consumer Council
1980–1989: Department of Employment's Advisory Committee on Women's Employment
1984–1986 and 1987–1991: Member, General Dental Council
1984–1990: Member, London Electricity Board
1987–1988: Lady Mayoress of Westminster
1990–1994: Vice-Chair, North East Thames Regional Health Authority
1992–1998: Trustee, Parliamentary Advisory Council on Transport Safety
1992–1999: Vice-President, National Housebuilding Council
1994–1997: Chair, Royal Free Hampstead NHS Trust

OTHER APPOINTMENTS AND AWARDS

2003: Awarded AM (Order of Australia)
1978–1982: British Chair, European Union of Women
1982–1988: UK Representative on the UN Status of Women Commission
1987–1988: Director, Gateway Building Society
1988–1993: Director, Woolwich Building Society
1997 and 2008–2011: Member, Executive Committee, Inter-Parliamentary Unions, British Group
1981–present: Member, Commonwealth Parliamentary Association (and Executive Committee)
2000–2002: UK Representative to Euro-Mediterranean Women's Forum
1984–1987: Honorary President, War Widows' Association of Great Britain
1990–2003: Chairman (UK), Plan International

1990–2012: President of Sydney University UK Alumni Association, then Patron from 2012
2010: University of Sydney Alumni Award for International Achievement
2018: Lifetime Achievement Award, Sydney University UK Alumni Association
1990–1993: President, British Fluoridation Society
1993–1996: Chair, Suzy Lamplugh Trust
1995–2011: President, Women's Guild of Friendship
1996: Chair, The Cook Society
1998–2010: President, Married Women's Association
2001–2006: Honorary Vice-President of British Legion, Women's Section
1992: Freeman of the City of London
1997: Honorary Doctorate, University of Middlesex
2007: Fellow of University of Sydney, Australia
2012: Award for Peer Contribution to Central Lobby, *PoliticsHome*

Born in Australia in 1927, Trixie Gardner retains her Australian citizenship but is a permanent UK resident. She moved to London in 1954 and worked for over 30 years as a dentist, owning a practice with her husband, Kevin Gardner. She was made a Conservative life peer in 1981, becoming Baroness Gardner of Parkes.

She has three daughters and five grandchildren.

Printed in Poland
by Amazon Fulfillment
Poland Sp. z o.o., Wrocław